MAKE AND LET DIE

MAKE AND LET DIE

UNTIMELY SOVEREIGNTIES

Kathleen Biddick

punctum books ⓟ earth, milky way

First published in 2016 by
punctum books
Earth, Milky Way
http://punctumbooks.com

punctum books is an independent, open-access publisher dedicated to radically creative modes of intellectual inquiry and writing across a whimsical parahumanities assemblage. We solicit and pimp quixotic, sagely mad engagements with textual thought-bodies, and provide shelters for intellectual vagabonds.

Cover Artwork: René Magritte, *Perspective: Madame Récamier by David* (1951), oil on canvas, National Gallery of Canada, © Estate of René Magritte.

Front Cover Design: Carol Gaines

ISBN-13: 978-0988234048
ISBN-10: 0988234041

Facing-page illustration by Heather Masciandaro.

To E, for her joy in bringing new things into the world. And to my students over the past decades—may you be fearless.

TABLE OF CONTENTS

ACKNOWLEDGMENTS

Twelve years have passed since the installation (October 2003) of *Cell* at Mountjoy Prison, Dublin. I remain grateful to the prisoner team, guards, and administrators for the initial inspiration for this collection of essays. The Fulbright Foundation supported my sabbatical in Dublin (2002-2003) and the Center for Creative Computing at the University of Notre Dame offered generous subvention. The warm hospitality of Dr. Carol Strohecker, Principal Investigator at Media Lab Europe, made the Mountjoy work possible.

Without my muses there would be no book. Among those many dear ones, I thank, in particular, Asma Abbas, Sergey Dolgopolski, Elena Glassberg, Graham Hammill, Geraldine Heng, Susannah Heschel, Eileen A. Joy, Michal Kobialka, Laura Levitt, Tomaž Mastnak, Michael O'Rourke, and Lisa Rofel. Production of the book also brought the delightful gift of a new muse, Paul Megna. When I moved to Temple University in Fall 2005, my new colleagues, especially Shannon Miller and Nichole Miller, collaborated to organize the Temple Premodern Studies Colloquium and to host two lively conferences on the question of sovereignty and political theology. A sabbatical granted by Temple University enabled me to attend the Dartmouth Humanities Center Symposium on Sovereignty (Spring 2008). The symposium professor, Eric Santner, and our Dartmouth hosts, Klaus Mladek and

George Edmondson, provided provocative commentary on my unfolding project. I was able to finish the draft of these collected essays as a Senior Fellow (Spring 2013) in the lively cross-disciplinary setting of the Baldy Center for Law and Social Policy, University at Buffalo, SUNY Law School. Errol Meidinger, Director and Laura Wirth (Assistant Director) were unstinting in putting my project into contact with legal thinkers and the Ecocritical Studies Research Group convened by Randy Schiff. The chance to sit in a wonderful café—the given time of conversation—with Graham Hammill, Sergey Dolgopolski, and collaboration with the superb editor, Jana Schmidt, of *Theory@Buffalo 17: Word, Flesh*, energized the last lap.

Preface

Diving into the Crypt
10 Theses on the Historical Materialism of Biddick

Eileen A. Joy

* The following Preface is indebted to and adapted from Adrienne Rich's poem "Diving into the Wreck," which sketches out the exploratory soundings of a sea-wreck of forgotten histories that bears uncanny resonances with Kathleen Biddick's own acedious and depth-charged historiography. Likewise, in also threading Walter Benjamin's "theses" (see footnote 2 below) into Rich's and Biddick's conjoined soundings, I hope to make more visible the relations between Rich's "drowned face always staring / toward the sun," Benjamin's "secret heliotropism" by "dint" of which "the past strives to turn toward that sun which is rising in the sky of history," and Biddick's desire to "quicken" the "dead zones" and "absent silences" of the premodern histories that contemporary theories of sovereignty and biopolitics pass over as "before" and "then" (and never "now"), and which histories, as Biddick well illustrates throughout this volume, always, uncannily and zombie-like, inhabit the present. See Adrienne Rich, *Diving into the Wreck: Poems 1971-1972* (New York: W.W. Norton, 1973), 22–24.

. . . how might *acedia*, with its rhythms and temporalities of performative slow love, in contrast to the urgent, explosive punctuality of Benjamin's *Jetztzeit*, the "now" of his "Theses," offer insights into the slow death of the "to make live" and the slow death (or not) of "to let die?

Kathleen Biddick, Make and Let Die

We have lingered in the chambers of the sea
By sea-girls wreathed with seaweed red and brown
Till human voices wake us, and we drown.

T.S. Eliot, "The Love Song of J. Alfred Prufrock"

The trees didn't volunteer to be cut into boards
nor the thorns for tearing flesh
Look around at all of it
and ask whose signature
is stamped on the orders, traced
in the corner of the building plans

Adrienne Rich, "For the Record"

FIRST, HAVING READ THE BOOK OF MODERN MYTHS

First having read the Book of Modern Myths,
and loaded the Turkish automaton,
and checked the cuts of the Real,
and knowing that
> *every image of the past*
> *that is not recognized by the present*
> *as one of its own concerns*
> *threatens to disappear irretrievably*[1]
she took with her into the trans/cryptum
the body-armor of the historical materialist
one indolent heart
the chronicles and the dead letters

---

[1] All italicized, indented portions of the text, unless otherwise noted, are direct or slightly altered quotations from Walter Benjamin, "Theses on the Philosophy of History," in Walter Benjamin, *Illuminations: Essays and Reflections*, ed. Hannah Arendt, trans. Harry Zohn (New York: Schocken Books, 1969), 253–264.

the spiraling of the becoming-spiral
the splicing of becoming-splice,
    that is to say, she was spiraling and splicing.
She was having to do this
not like Cousteau with his
assiduous team
aboard the sun-flooded schooner
but just there
and not alone.

SECOND, THERE IS AN OBELISK

There is an obelisk.
The obelisk is always there
rooted innocently
in the churchyard on a hillside,
or buried at sea.
We know what it is for,
the typology it measures.
Otherwise
it is a piece of messianic time
some sundry technology.

THIRD, SHE GOES DOWN

She goes down.
Aerial after aerial[2] and still

---

[2] "Aerial" here signals to something Biddick has written about Bracha Ettinger's work, but which could equally apply to Biddick's own thought and writing, which is indebted to Ettinger's psychoanalytic aesthetics: "Reading Ettinger is like diving into a coral reef and carefully observing the myriad creatures whose filtering of sustenance secretes the reef. Her text blossoms with what she calls 'eroticized aerials,' receiving and transmitting the incipiencies of a co-poesis. Habits of explication falter at such incipiencies": Kathleen Biddick,

the tears of the sovereigns immerse her
the blue lanterns of the Patriarchs
the shards of the mirrors of princes
the clear molecules
of our undeadly, thingly, arboreal air.
Yet
>   *nothing that has ever happened*
>   *should be regarded as lost for history*
>   *and the truth will not run away from us,*
so she dives into the spectral, untimely deep
and there is no one
to tell her where and when
the collateral damage will begin,
or where and when it will end.

FOURTH, THE AIR IS BLUE AND THEN

Fourth the air is blue and then
it is bluer and then green and then
black she is blacking out and yet
her body-armor is powerful
and she remembers
>   *that even the dead*
>   *will not be safe*
>   *from the enemy*
>   *if he wins*
but time is another story
messianic time is not a question of power
but of a spectral materialism
she has to learn to turn
the levers of the clock without force
in the deep of the dead beat.

"Daniel's Smile," in *On Style: An Atelier*, eds. Eileen A. Joy and Anna Kłosowska (Brooklyn: punctum books, 2013), 41 [37–46]. See also Bracha Ettinger, *The Matrixial Borderspace*, ed. Brian Massumi (Minneapolis: University of Minnesota Press, 2006).

FIFTH, AND NOW: IT IS EASY TO FORGET

And now: it is easy to forget
what she came for
among so many who have always
met their untimely ends here
and yet
 she regards it as her task
 to brush history against the grain
 and few will be able to guess how sad
 one has to be to resuscitate Carthage
among so many swaying their crenellated concordances
between the reefs
and besides
you breathe differently in the archive.

SIXTH, SHE CAME TO EXPLORE THE CRYPT

She came to explore the crypt.
The words of the medieval archive are alive.
The words of the medieval archive are maps.
She came to see the damage that was done,
 the *homines sacri*,
 the slaves of the sovereign,
 the Jew, the Saracen, the Illegitimate,
 the Untouchable, the Dispossessed, the Imprisoned,
 the ones *who have seen the face of the Gorgon*
 and did not return, or returned wordless.[3]
She came to explore the crypt,
and the revenants who lived there still.
She unrolled the scroll of the dead letters
slowly along the hull
of a disturbing sovereign violence.

---

[3] Italicized text cited from Primo Levi, *The Drowned and the Saved* (New York: Vintage International, 1989), 83–84.

SEVENTH, THE THING SHE CAME FOR

The thing she came for:
the archive and not the story of the archive
the kernel itself and not the modern myth
her face is turned toward the past
where we perceive a chain of events
she sees one single catastrophe
which keeps piling wreckage upon wreckage
and hurls it in front of her feet
she would like to stay, awaken the dead
and make whole what was smashed
but a storm is blowing in
from the furnaces of modernity
the drowned faces always staring
toward the horizon of history
the evidence of cuts and blood
the weeping stones, the lithic traces,
the ribs of the disaster
curving their assertions
toward the tentative cryptologist.

EIGHTH, THIS MUST BE THE PLACE

I guess that this must be the place

I can't tell one from the other
I find you, or you find me?
There was a time before we were born
If someone asks, this is where I'll be, where I'll be

We drift in and out
Sing into my mouth
Out of all those kinds of people
You got a face with a view

Talking Heads, "This Must Be the Place (Naïve Melody)"

This must be the place.
And she is there, Niobe whose marbled, stony hair
    is woven in ice
    her tongue frozen
    to the roof of her mouth
    her throat washed
    with snow-bright tears,[4]
and also the armor-wrapped historical materialist.
They circle silently
about the wreck
they dive into the crypt.
She is herself: She is her.

NINTH, SHE WHOSE FROZEN FACE SLEEPS WITH OPEN EYES

She is her whose frozen face sleeps with open eyes
whose stony body serves as the boundary-stone
    between living and dying
    between appearing and disappearing
    between being made to die and being allowed to live
    between being made to live and being allowed to die
    of being forced to live inside one's own death
    inside one's own murder
    inside one's own sacrifice
    inside one's own servitude
    to a victorious history
        and a triumphal procession
        in which the present rulers
        step over those
        who are lying prostrate.
She is her whose frozen body is also a mountain
whose silver, copper, vermeil cargo lies

---

[4] Italicized section adapted from Friedrich Hölderlin's translation of Sophocles's *Antigone*: see *Friedrich Hölderlin: Selected Poems*, trans. David Constantine (Newcastle upon Tyne: Bloodaxe Books, 1996), 97.

obscurely inside seahenges and porphyrions
half-wedged and left to radiate
entangled registers of historical light.[5]
She is the half-destroyed instrument,
the verge *and* the escapement,
that once held to a course
the broken speculum
the fouled horse's bit stuck in the mouth
a sovereign technology of the deadly kiss

TENTH, THEY ARE, SHE IS, WE ARE

They are, she is, we are
by cowardice or courage
the ones who find our way
back to this medieval archive
but there is something else too
that steadily regards everything
they, she, and we are going through

It sees
the violence

[5] Italicized section inspired by Biddick's thinking in this volume (in her Introduction) on medieval rabbinic commentary on the classical *porphyrion* as figures of messianic-futural time (in Greek mythology, *Porphyrion*, Greek Πορφυρίων, was one of the giants, who according to Hesiod, were the offspring of Gaia, born from the blood that fell when Uranus was castrated by their son Cronus): "Some historians regard this Ashkenazic version of the messianic as reductively vengeful, but that is not my point here. The *porphyrion* raises for me a more complicated question of the relationship of messianic and archival traces. The medieval Ashkenazi rabbis imagined the messianic, not so much as a radically different temporal register, but, like quantum physicists, more so as an entangled register of light. Their experience of 'to make die' criss-crossed on the *porphyrion* with 'to let live' in quantum patterns. In contemporary terms, we can think of their messianic *porphyrion* as an infrared apparatus whose spectrum would become visible in the light of justice."

embedded in silence
and its vision
must be unblurred
from weeping
though tears are on her face

its intent is clarity
it must forget
nothing[6]

---

[6] Italicized section adapted from Adrienne Rich, "From the Prison House," *Diving into the Wreck*, 17–18.

Chapter 1

Introduction: Untimely Sovereignties

THE BIOPOLITICS OF MESSIANIC MACHINES

This collection of essays, *To Make and Let Die: Untimely Sovereignties*, argues that the analysis and critique of biopower, as conventionally defined by Michel Foucault and then widely assumed in much contemporary theory of sovereignty, is a sovereign mode of temporalization caught up in the very time-machine it ostensibly seeks to expose and dismantle. For Michel Foucault biopower (epitomized in his maxim "to make live and to let die") is the defining sign of the modern and he famously argued that the task of political philosophy was to cut off the head of the classical (premodern) sovereign, the one "who made die and let live."[1] Entrapped by his

[1] Eric Santner has suggestively argued for sovereignty as a mode of temporality in *On Creaturely Life* (Chicago: University of Chicago Press, 2006), 66. I am inspired by his speculation to ask the question: do we also need to think of biopolitics as a mode of temporali-

supersessionary thinking on the question, Foucault argued that the maxim of "to make live and let die" of modern sovereignty superseded a premodern sovereignty characterized by the contrasting power "to make die and let live".

Foucault spoke too soon about the supposed "then" of the classical sovereign and the modern "now" and this became painfully apparent in his analysis of Nazism in his later lectures, *Society Must be Defended*. There Foucault groped to articulate an anguishing paradox: How could it be that the Nazis, as the ultimate biopolitical sovereign machine ('nor was there any other State in which the biological was so tightly, so insistently regulated"), would insist on an archaic (premodern) mode of sovereignty, "to make die," in their death camps?[2] Here is how he posed the question in that lecture: "How can the power of death [to make die], the function of death, be exercised in a political system centered upon biopower [to make live]?" [3] Foucault left this question hanging. He never further pursued the genealogical entanglements of biopower beyond the analysis he offered in the first volume (1976) of *La volonté de savoir* and his contempora-

zation? Foucault's call to "cut off the King's head" can be found in "Truth and Power," in Michel Foucault, *Power/Knowledge: Selected Interviews and other Writings (1972-77)*, ed. Colin Gordon, trans. Colin Gordon, Leo Marshall, John Melham, and Kate Soper (New York: Pantheon Books, 1980), 121. For critiques of Foucault's periodization, see Louise Fradenburg and Carla Freccero, "Introduction: Caxton, Foucault, and the Pleasures of History," in *Premodern Sexualities*, eds. Louise Fradenburg and Carla Freccero (New York: Routledge, 1996), i–xxiv; Karma Lochrie, "Desiring Foucault," *Journal of Medieval and Early Modern Studies* 27.1 (1997): 3–16; Eve Kosofsky Sedgwick, *The Epistemology of the Closet* (Berkeley: University of California Press, 1990), 44–48; and Santner, *On Creaturely Life*, 183–184. See also Paul Rabinow and Nikolas Rose, "Biopower Today," *Biosciences* 1 (2006): 195–217.

[2] Michel Foucault, *Society Must Be Defended: Lectures at the College de France 1975-76*, eds. Mauro Bertani and Alessandro Fontana, trans. David Macey (New York: Palgrave, 2003), 259.

[3] Foucault, *Society Must Be Defended*, 254.

neous lectures on the theme of "society must be defended" (1975-76).

What Foucault did not ask, and what this collection of essays will pose is: how are "to make die" and "to let die" entangled by time, space, matter, and the archival traces of such interactions? I contend that these modes of deathly biopower do not supersede each other as Foucault argued. *Make and Let Die: Untimely Sovereignties* claims the following: that there is a living death in the "make die" of the so-called classical sovereign and also in the "make live" of the modern biopolitical sovereign. These living deaths are untimely. Only the refusal among contemporary theorists to read the archives of medieval Christendom's sovereignty has foreclosed even mention of such entanglements. This collection of essays decrypts the medieval traces of "make live" in "make die," and also in "let die." When these dynamic temporal modes of death inhabiting "to make die" and "to let die" are better understood, the static, a-historical aspects of contemporary biopolitical discourse fall away. Further, this collection of essays, individually and collectively, argues that in view of the ever intensifying global mobilization of "to make die" *and* "to let die," there is something ob/scene, and in need of more critical attention, in the contemporary theoretical embrace of the messianic (see, for example, the work of Walter Benjamin, Giorgio Agamben, Roberto Esposito, and Jacques Derrida). [4]

My questions about the historical entanglements between "to make die" and "to let die" become even more pertinent as Foucault's work on biopower has re-emerged with force in the writings of Giorgio Agamben. Agamben has argued for a different temporal form: biopower as a kernel of power from the classical world to the present. The classical curse "esto sacer" produced *homo sacer*, a person who could

---

[4] Here I mean ob/scene in the sense of off-stage: scenes that do not belong to the light of day. See, for example, Carolyn McKay, "Murder Ob/scene: The Seen, the Unseen, and Ob/scene in Murder Trials," *Law, Text, Culture* 14.1 (2010): 79–93.

be killed without accusation of homicide, but who could not be sacrificed. Given such an atemporal concept, it is not surprising to find Agamben feverishly engaged in grafting onto contemporary biopower a temporal supplement in the form of messianic time. Agamben, in his much-cited reading of Paul's *Epistle to the Romans*, in which he investigates the relation of sovereign law to temporality, championed messianic time (a time when justice performs without the law, yet, paradoxically without abolishing it) as an unsovereign temporal paradigm. Agamben proposed the typological relation (the relation of letter (*littera*) to figure (*figura*) as the temporal lever capable of switching from *chronos* (empty chronological, sovereign time) into *kairos* (messianic time). Yet, when Agamben elaborated on the typological toggle, he decisively bracketed off *his* typological relation from "medieval" modes of typology. [5] At stake here is a hermeneutical decision: Agamben makes a sovereign temporal cut and excises the medieval. Thus, his messianic time becomes haunted by a temporal amputation of the medieval.

Make and Let Die: Untimely Sovereignties investigates how Agamben's messianic time machine of sovereignty and justice renders it impossible to understand the important entanglements of "to make die" and "to let die." It further questions how Agamben, in his Pauline system of sign and fulfillment, refuses to address what is at stake in medieval Western Christendom when "to make die" is also conceived as a typological relation in which medieval Jews become the "make

[5] Giorgio Agamben, *The Time that Remains: A Commentary on the Letter to the Romans*, trans. Patricia Dailey (Stanford: Stanford University Press, 2005). Agamben brackets off the medieval on pp. 74, 98, and 107. For an attempt to deal with the traumatic medieval kernel that Agamben brackets off, see my chapter, "Dead Neighbor Archives: Jews, Muslims, and the Enemy's Two Bodies," in this volume. For the vitality of considering temporality as a cross-disciplinary concern see, Michael Uebel, "Opening Time: Psychoanalysis and Medieval Culture," in *Cultural Studies of the Modern Middle Ages*, eds. Eileen A. Joy, Myra J. Seaman, Kimberley K. Bell and Mary K. Ramsey (New York: Palgrave, 2007), 269–274.

die" of the letter and the "make die" of the law: They become the dead letters that enable the "make live" of typological, messianic relations. Further, as discussed in the ensuing chapters, Muslims were declared the enemy of Western Christendom and as *homines sacri* (those that could be killed without taint of blood pollution or sin of homicide); they were "to let die." Even Freud entangled himself in the medieval "let die" of Muslims, when he articulated his theory of trauma in the wake of World War I.[6] The following chapters trace the deep roots of biopolitics in medieval Western Christendom, and yet these Christian political theological roots are foreclosed (and thus covered over) by the messianic time machines proposed by contemporary theorists such as Agamben, and he is not alone.

Just before his death, Jacques Derrida began to explore how bestiality and sovereignty were closely bound. In doing so he engaged in a lively critique of the biopolitical theories espoused by Foucault and Agamben. He attributed to them a violent temporal drive to ground sovereignty as a founding moment of modernity that supersedes premodernity.[7] For Derrida, biopolitics is "an arch-ancient thing and bound up with the very idea of sovereignty." The temporality he envisions for biopolitics is that of the *arkhē*, "at the commence-

---

[6] In a recent essay, I trace how Freud's theory of trauma is uncannily imbricated in the ongoing project of the "let die" of Islam in Western discourses: see my entry on "Trauma" in *Medievalism: Key Critical Terms*, eds. Elizabeth Emery and Richard Utz (Cambridge: D.S. Brewer, 2014), 247–253.

[7] The core of Derrida's critique of the violence of periodization in arguments about biopolitics advanced by Foucault and Agamben can be found in the Twelfth Session (March 20, 2002) of his published lectures on the beast and the sovereign. See Jacques Derrida, *The Beast and the Sovereign, Vol. 1*, trans. Geoffrey Bennington (Chicago: University of Chicago Press, 2009), 408–443. Derrida's statement that, "One has simply changed sovereigns" (379), exemplifies this temporal aporia. He ventures further that, "Aristotle might already have apprehended or formalized, in his own way, what Foucault and Agamben attribute to modern specificity" (435).

ment [also command for Derrida], at the sovereign principle of everything."[8] Yet, paradoxically, it is precisely from the *arkhē* of the archive that Derrida appropriates his own brand of the messianic: "the question of the archive is not, we repeat, a question of the past. It is not the question of a concept that we can dispose or not dispose of *already*, a subject *of the past*, an *archivable concept of the archive*. It is a question of the future, the question of the future itself, the question of a response, of a promise and responsibility for tomorrow."[9]

Derrida imagined the archive of the past as a dead letter only to be fulfilled in the messianic—the future to come. His messianic concept of the archive seems to me to be all too close to Agamben's Christian typology.[10] Just as medieval Christian typologists had named the Jewish law and the Hebrew Scriptures to be a "dead letter" that could only be re-animat-

[8] Derrida, *The Beast and the Sovereign*, 439, 419.

[9] Jacques Derrida, *Archive Fever*, trans. Eric Prenowitz (Chicago: University of Chicago Press, 1996), 36, his emphases.

[10] The more I read contemporary theoretical literature on sovereignty and biopolitics, the more I realize that its key debates also play the troubling typological game of sign and fulfillment. I am not alone in such a reading. Noted scholars such as Tracy McNulty and Jeffrey Librett also found the evidence for the game of typology too overwhelming to ignore. They analyzed typological drive in the work of Walter Benjamin, Jacques Derrida, and Giorgio Agamben. In my chapter in this volume, "Dead Neighbor Archives: Jews, Muslims, and the Enemy's Two Bodies," I offer my own blueprint of the typological-machine in these theoretical works (and also that of Jacob Taubes). The typological imaginary (or, in philosophical terms, presentation-representation) never lets go. For a brilliant analysis of how persistently shaping is the Pauline typological concept of the dead letter of the law (Judaism) and its vibrant fulfillment in the Christian spirit see, Jeffrey Librett, "From the Sacrifice of the Letter to the Voice of Testimony: Giorgio Agamben's Fulfillment of Metaphysics," *Diacritics* 37 (2007): 11–33; Tracy McNulty, "The Commandment Against the Law: Writing and Divine Justice in Walter Benjamin's 'Critique of Violence'," *Diacritics* 37 (2007): 34–60; and my study, *The Typological Imaginary: Circumcision, Technology, and History* (Philadelphia: University of Pennsylvania Press, 2003).

ed by Jesus Christ and the New Testament, Derrida, not un-like such Christian typologists, constituted an archive of the past as a dead letter in order to fabricate a messianic future to-come. No matter how much Derrida insisted that his mes-sianic was without a messiah (Christ) or a Scripture (indeed, without any religion whatsoever), nevertheless, the messianic structure of his thinking, I argue, partakes of the Christian epistemology of typology. A dead letter archive of the past works as a sign of the fulfillment to come: "it is necessary [that there be] the future," a promise.[11] And such a typologi-cal relation was historically violent, which is the purpose of the following essays to trace out.

More recently, Roberto Esposito has also grappled with the temporal relations of sovereignty and biopower. He, like Foucault, sides for biopower as one of the penultimate signs of the modern. The purpose of his work is to think through an affirmative biopolitics capable of suspending the processes of immunity that he regards as intrinsic to biopolitics. Such a suspension would enable the transformation from immunity to community. He defines immunity according to the classi-cal Roman usage of *munus*, implying both *onus* and *officium*: "Immunity connotes the means by which the individual is defended from the 'expropriating effects' of the community, protecting the one who carries it from the risk of contact with those who do not (the risk being precisely the loss of in-dividual identity)."[12] Immunity matters to Esposito because,

---

[11] For an excellent discussion of Derrida's notions of time and the messianic, see Martin Hägglund, *Radical Atheism: Derrida and the Time of Life* (Stanford: Stanford University Press, 2008), 132–139 (citation at 133).

[12] Roberto Esposito, *Bíos: Biopolitics and Philosophy*, trans. Timothy Campbell (Minneapolis: University of Minnesota Press, 2008), 11. For an important study of medieval *immunitas* that challenges Es-posito's normalizing understanding of immunity and exemption, see Barbara H. Rosenwein, *Negotiating Space: Power, Restraint and Privileges of Immunity in Early Medieval Europe* (Ithaca: Cornell University Press, 1999).

he argues, it is the immunity mechanism that links community to biopolitics; but immunity seems to elude his quest for periodization: How can "modern man (sic)," he asks, "tear himself from the theological matrix?"[13] This violent periodizing image, with its incisive overtones of caesarean section (*Kaiserschnitt* in German), alerts the reader that sovereignty might be lurking even in his supposed affirmative deconstruction.[14] In the course of his exposition, Esposito anxiously returns again and again to speculating on the temporal relation of sovereignty to biopower. Early on in his argument he wonders, "Once again, how do we wish to think the sovereign paradigm within the biopolitical order, and then what does it represent? Is it a residue that is delayed in consuming itself, a spark that doesn't go out, a compensatory ideology or the ultimate truth … ?"[15] And so Esposito poses the question upon which he decides as the sovereign: biopolitics is a sign of the modern.

Foucault, Agamben, Derrida, Esposito, and as this Introduction shall subsequently unfold, also Walter Benjamin, all, I argue, immunize biopolitics from the "medieval" (whatever their fantasy of the medieval might be) and in so doing they relegate the "medieval" to the historical unconscious of their theory.[16] *They make die the medieval archive.*

---

[13] Esposito, *Bíos*, 55.

[14] For insight into this uncanny persistence of sovereignty in these purported acts of deconstruction, see Kathleen Davis, *Periodization and Sovereignty: How Ideas of Feudalism and Secularization Govern the Politics of Time* (Philadelphia: University of Pennsylvania Press, 2008). For my review of her book in *The Medieval Review*, see here: https://scholarworks.iu.edu/dspace/bitstream/handle/2022/6531/09.04.06.html.

[15] Esposito, *Bíos*, 42.

[16] The question of the medieval as the unconscious of contemporary theory grows more pressing. See, for example, Bruce Holsinger, *The Premodern Condition: Medievalism and the Making of Theory* (Chicago: University of Chicago Press, 2005), and Andrew Cole and D. Vance Smith, eds., *The Legitimacy of the Middle Ages: On the Unwritten History of Theory* (Durham: Duke University Press, 2010). For my review of Cole and Smith's volume in *The Medieval Review*,

The chapters that follow track the effects of such archival expunctions in contemporary debates on sovereignty.[17] In these unconscious blanks, I show how medieval Christian sovereignty had fabricated itself by naming the enemy (Muslims) and concomitantly declaring the state of exception (naming Jews as the *servi*, 'slaves,' of the sovereign).[18] Medieval theologians then sutured sovereignty once and for all to the Real Presence (the orthodoxy that the flesh and blood of Christ become real, material presences in the consecrated bread and wine of the Eucharist) by declaring it an act of treason (the gravest crime against sovereignty) to deny the Real Presence. Medieval Christian typological relations were thus biopolitical relations. Jews and Muslims become the collateral damage of Christendom's sovereign violence. That is why *Make and Let Die* stakes out these problems of the immunizing medievalisms of contemporary theory, in order to foreground the repetitious trauma of the contemporary theory of sovereignty in hegemonic Western discourse which leaves unmarked its ongoing Christian political theology.[19]

see here: https://scholarworks.iu.edu/dspace/bitstream/handle/2022/9063/10.09.12.html. I am aware that Agamben has written extensively on medieval subjects. Indeed, his short essay on *acedia* is a major inspiration of my methodological practice for reading archives. However, and this must be underscored, when it comes to his Pauline messianism, he emphatically forecloses the medieval typological relation which is, as this book argues, a biopolitical machine. It cannot be foreclosed; it demands a deconstruction.

[17] Davis, *Periodization and Sovereignty*, also points to the traumatic medievalisms among early modern theorists of sovereignty—notably, Jean Bodin (1530-1596)—who paradoxically sealed over the history of medieval European sovereignty because they regarded the European Middle Ages as a time of slavery in contrast to a "slave-free" early modern Europe.

[18] Indispensable to my project is the work of Gil Anidjar, *The Jew, The Arab: A History of the Enemy* (Stanford: Stanford University Press, 2003).

[19] In a recent essay I trace how Freud's theory of trauma is uncannily imbricated in the ongoing project of the "let die" of Islam in

We have never been secular.

"A MASSIVE HAUNTED HOUSE IN A REAL PRISON"

To be clear at the outset, this project did not begin in a medieval archive. Instead, it began over a decade ago in Mountjoy Prison, Dublin, a panopticon-style superstructure built in 1850 by the English for their colony. Having just finished my book *The Typological Imaginary*, I had the chance to be a Fulbright scholar in residence at the recently founded Dublin Media Lab Europe (MLE). I had proposed to think about digital memory and technology. The MLE graduate students, with their expertise in computer engineering and digital design, were eager to read Michel Foucault because of his work on panoptical technologies and biopolitics—defined by Foucault as the power "to make live and let die." As I reread *Discipline and Punish* with the MLE students, it struck me that Foucault ended his intense optical analysis with an abrupt auditory displacement relative to the "the distant roar of battle" at the edge of the carceral city. [20]

Was this some kind of biopolitical synesthesia in need of more thought? Could such clamor, I asked, be heard in the stony hulk of Mountjoy Prison, which loomed over the edge of my Dublin neighborhood? After all, Mountjoy was an early panoptical example of Foucault's biopolitical laboratory for producing docile bodies, a colonized subject population. I thus began to work with a "volunteer" team of Mountjoy prisoners (what counts as volunteer in a prison?). The inmates had responded to my circulated invitation for prisoners to join a MLE media project on memory, discipline and punishment. The opportunity to work with prison archives and training in video provided the lure. Prison guards also became part of the team, too, since they had to supervise me

Western discourses (see footnote 6 above).
[20]Michel Foucault, *Discipline and Punish: The Birth of the Prison*, trans. Allen Lane (New York: Penguin Books, 1977), 308. See also Steven Miller, *War After Death: On Violence and Its Limits* (New York: Fordham University Press, 2014), 170.

when I worked with the prison team. Painstakingly, this odd-couple "we" of prison guards, prisoners, and historian developed a plan for a performance project called *Cell* to be presented to the public in an abandoned wing of the prison during lock-down, when each prisoner inhabited his isolated cell from 7:00 pm to 7:00 am.[21]

As the work with the prisoners unfolded and as I delved more closely into the writings of Jeremy Bentham (promoter of the architectural panopticon for all manner of institutions), I learned that he intended the panopticon, not only as a silent optical machine (the focus of Foucault), but also as a noisy writing machine. As I show in detail in the last chapter of this volume, Bentham imagined a panopticon with two bodies, that of the inspector and the inscriptor. Suffice it to say that Bentham had to solve the problem of how the inspector of the panopticon, sitting in his surveillance lodge, could continue to write when darkness fell. Bentham imagined a contraption, a life-sized, hour-glass shaped lampshade, inside of which the inspector would sit on a stool set close to a light source.[22] A series of small pinpricks in the shade, set at eye level, enabled the inspector to look out from the lodge at the galleries of convict cells at the same time he kept his books by candlelight. He could be present or absent as long as the candle burned (like a camera running on an empty set) and produced a shadow observable by the prisoners. When he did enter the lodge for bookkeeping, he could decide on when he wished to scan activity in the cells and through which vantage provided by the spacing of the pinpricks. Cut into the fabric of the writing lantern, the pinpricks enabled the inspector to survey strategically the dead time of evening lockdown. By "dead time," I mean a sovereign time in which it is decided that "nothing happens, time

[21] See the last chapter of this volume, "Doing Dead Time for the Sovereign: Archive Abandonment, Performance," for further analysis and bibliography.

[22] Miran Božovič, *Jeremy Bentham: The Panopticon Writings* (New York: Verso, 1995), 105–106.

which is in some sense 'wasted,' expended without prod-uct."[23] It is a time that is cut out from what counts as event-fulness. The dead time of evening lockdown and the archive thus sutured themselves in this panoptical lantern of the in-scriptor who, as its sovereign, could decide to be present or absent, and further, to decide on the eventful, or not, by choosing selected pinpricks as points of archival recording.

The Mountjoy prisoners, it turned out, were on to Ben-tham. They were all too aware of Mountjoy's two bodies (in-spector and inscriptor). From the outset, their projects for *Cell* experimented with ways of writing back to the panopti-cal archive, which they understood rendered them invisible. They foregrounded the dead time of prison life rather than cutting it out. The collateral archive of dead time produced by the prisoners prompted me to ask the following question: Did the distant roar of battle at the edge of the carceral city, overheard by Foucault, come from the roar of the writing machine that inscribed the dead time of *death* intimately cohabiting with the "make live" of biopolitics? Might histori-ans listen as carefully as the Mountjoy prisoners did as they were doing their "time"?

Now, just about a decade since the Mountjoy perfor-mance, I am drafting the Introduction to this volume of es-says in the shadow of yet another panoptical-style prison, the Eastern State Penitentiary, Philadelphia. On my daily trips to the shops and the bus stop I pass this massive heap. Opened in 1821, Eastern State Penitentiary embodied the most avant-garde panoptical architecture of prison reform at that time. Each prisoner sat solitary in his cell; panoptical supervision and solitude were imagined as the leaven of conversion to the norm. On his reform tour of prisons (1831), Alexis de Tocqueville raved about his visit there. The British Surveyor General of Prisons, Joshua Jebb, who would later build ver-sions of the panopticon at Pentonville Prison (1844) and

---

[23] Mary Anne Doane, *The Emergence of Cinematic Time: Modernity, Contingency, the Archive* (Cambridge: Harvard University Press, 2002), 160.

Mountjoy Prison (1850), took note. Closed in 1971, Eastern State Penitentiary just missed the French publication of *Surveiller et Punir* (1975). Now too costly to dismantle, it pays its way as a major tourist attraction—crowds peak around Halloween. Dedicated "Ghost Buses," painted gray and black, loop around Center City to pick up and drop off ticket holders for the nighttime show. A corps of security guards theatrically garbed in prison-guard uniforms from the nineteenth century, each carefully made-up with the cosmetic effects of rotting zombies, and occasionally accessorized with a festered limb, supervise the lines of ticketholders, who pay $35.00 for admission. Two huge gargoyles, stoutly chained to the entrance portal of the prison, offer a Gothic touch.

This Halloween liturgy, the spectacle of an empty panoptical prison (and populated panopticon prisons were, indeed, spectacles in their own day, regularly visited by zealots of prison reform, such as de Tocqueville) speaks to the urgency of finding fresh ways of talking about biopolitics, modes that do not reduce it simply to a grammar of optics, the logos of the archive, the identity of sovereign temporality of the now, or the future-to-come.[24] Zombies are what happen when biopolitics is so reduced and, as popular culture repetitively reminds us, they are everywhere. They have reterritorialized the spaces of Bentham's panoptical fantasy (the zombie security guards of Eastern State Penitentiary, the humans of the *Walking Dead,* the AMC television series, who paradoxically find refuge from the zombies in a prison; the zombies of *Warm Bodies* who occupy the airport); and such invasions, it is said, started in shopping malls. The Halloween mayhem at Eastern State Penitentiary enables us to catch a fresh glimpse

---

[24] For an important critique of Walter Benjamin's concept of the "now" (*Jeztzeit*), see Cesare Casarino, "Time Matters: Marx, Negri, Agamben, and the Corporeal," *Strategies* 16 (2003): 185–206, and also Asma Abbas, "In Terror, In Love, Out of Time," in *At the Limits of Justice: Women of Color Theorize Terror*, eds. Sherene Razack and Suvendrini Pereira (Toronto: University of Toronto Press, 2014), 501–525.

of the violent core of contemporary biopolitics—its afterlife in the "let die" of "make live." It raises important questions about the translation of dead time at Eastern State Penitentiary into its featured scary show billed today as follows: "Terror Behind the Walls: A Massive Haunted House in a Real Prison."

To Make and Let Die: Untimely Sovereignties addresses the "let live" in the "make die" and the "let die" in the "make live" in its multimodal manifestations—in medieval Christendom, in contemporary Philadelphia, and in its grip on the discourses of sovereignty clamoring in the academy today. More specifically, the essays collected here (some published previously, and some original to this volume) track how contemporary debates over sovereignty have consistently expunged the archives of medieval Christendom's sovereign violence against their Jewish and Muslim neighbors and their artifacts (synagogues, mosques, archives, personal property, as well as intangible traditions) for the drive of periodizing biopolitics as a sign of the modern and keeping it secular. This drive also renders a provocative historiography on medieval Christian-Jewish-Muslim relations untheorized in the contemporary discourses of sovereignty and biopolitics. The unconsciousness of such theory, and thus the elision of these earlier histories, produces troubling collateral damage.[25]

---

[25] Miller, in *War After Death*, puts this succinctly: "All violence, structurally speaking, proves to be collateral damage" (17). I deliberately invoke this anachronism, "collateral damage" (its usage harks back to strategic assessments involved in Allied decisions about carpet bombing of German and Japanese cities during World War II) in order to underscore that the historiographical assumptions about "kinder, gentler" wars in premodernity mask a history of the sovereign violence of medieval Christendom: see Charles S. Maier, "Targeting the City: Debates and Silence about the Aerial Bombing of World War II," *International Review of the Red Cross*, 87.859 (2005): 429–444; Kelly De Vries, "Medieval Warfare and the Value of Human Life," in *Noble Ideals and Bloody Realities: Warfare in the Middle Ages*, eds. Niall Christie and Maya Yazigi (Leiden: Brill 2000), 27–56. For a study of medieval collateral damage with specific reference to the mosque at Cordoba and its ongoing Christian

My project thus faces a methodological challenge: how might *Make and Let Die* investigate medieval sovereignty and biopolitics without embodying typologizing violence? I did not want to erase medieval archives of violence, as Ernst Kantorowicz had magisterially done in his 1957 study of medieval political theology, *The King's Two Bodies*.[26] Closer to home, as a medievalist, I remain troubled by the ways in which the traumatic archive of Kantorowicz, whose work is still regarded as the epitome of contemporary sovereignty studies for its profoundly secularizing argument about political theology, also underwent typologizing vicissitudes. Treat the painful and conflicted archive of the young Kantorowicz, I was admonished, as the dead letter of incidental biography: grandson of a renowned Orthodox rabbi, decorated WWI veteran, an overseer of the completion of the German leg of the Orient Express from Istanbul to Aleppo, author of a doctoral dissertation on Muslim craft guilds, right-wing member of the *Freikorps* (an anti-socialist paramilitary brigade fighting in the streets of Munich and Berlin), beloved acolyte of Stefan George and his anti-Semitic Kreis, impresario of a mystical nationalism in his study *Kaiser Friedrich der Zweite* (1927), and, for gossip's sake, the loathed acquaintance of Benjamin (could queer ambivalence be at play here between these two dandies?). Is not the very reduction of these traces of the young Kantorowicz to the dead letter of "mere" biography a troubling refusal to engage discursively with contested Weimar archives of traumatic German-Jewish symbiosis?[27] To continue to expunge, in the ways he and his con-

purification, see Kathleen Biddick, "Unbinding the Flesh in the Time that Remains: Crusader Martyrdom, Then and Now," *GLQ* 13.2-3 (2007): 197–225.

[26] Ernst Kantorowicz, *The King's Two Bodies: A Study in Medieval Political Theology* (Princeton: Princeton University Press, 1957). The digitized collected papers of Ernst Kantorowicz may be found at the Leo Baeck Institute, New York.

[27] See Martin A Ruehl, "'Imperium Transcendat Hominem': Reich and Rulership in Ernst Kantorowicz's *Kaiser Friedrich der Zweite*,"

temporary interpreters have done, would be to fail to grapple with the biopolitical relationships of the archive, its death drive and violence.[28] As will be detailed, I paradoxically found an answer to this methodological dilemma in the work of Walter Benjamin, who suggested to me that there might be surprising and powerful resources to offset typological thinking in the medieval vice of *acedia*.

ACEDIA AS AN ARCHIVAL PRACTICE

Theorists of sovereignty and biopolitics have not been subtle about silencing medieval archives. They have done so violently. Take, for example, Benjamin writing in one of his last fragments, "Theses on the Philosophy of History," composed in 1940, just months before his suicide. In Thesis 7, Benjamin insisted that historical materialists break with *acedia*, a complex medieval vice characterized by withdrawal from the good, indolence of the heart, or "slow love" (*lento amore*), as Dante dubbed it. *Acedia* epitomized for Benjamin the practice of Rankean historians: "It is a process of empathy whose origin is indolence of the heart, *acedia*, which despairs of grasping and holding the genuine historical image as it flares up briefly. Among medieval theologians it was regarded as the root cause of sadness."[29] Benjamin's spirited rejection of

in *A Poet's Reich: Politics and Culture in the Georg Circle*, eds. Melissa Slane and Martin Ruehl (Rochester: Boydell and Brewer, 2011), 204–248. For Benjamin's encounter with Kantorowicz, see Howard Eiland and Michael W. Jennings, *Walter Benjamin: A Critical Life* (Cambridge: Harvard University Press, 2014), 497–498, where they include this from one of Benjamin's letters: "Only the notorious corks float to the surface, as for example the unspeakably dull and subaltern Kantorowicz, who has promoted himself from theorist of the state party to a position of communist officiousness."

[28] In *Archive Fever*, Derrida linked the archive with the death drive: "Consequence: right on that which permits or conditions archivization, we will never find anything other than that which exposes to destruction, and in truth menaces with destruction" (11–12).

[29] Walter Benjamin, "Theses on the Philosophy of History," *in Illuminations: Walter Benjamin Essays and Reflections*, ed. Hannah

acedia, which Dante, in contrast, poetically related to mourning, strikes a strange note. I wondered if it constituted his homeopathic defense against and foreclosure of medieval archives of disturbing sovereign violence.[30] Are not his binary labels—"historicist," "historical materialist"—and his binary typological opposition of *acedia* to the flashing leap to *Jetztzeit*, "the time of the now" (Thesis 14), yet one more version of the dead letter versus the spirit?[31]

Arendt (New York: Schocken Books, 1968), 256. What is strange about this flash of *acedia* in the "Theses" is the fact that Benjamin understood so well the melancholic structure of philosophy. Ilit Ferber studies Benjamin's understanding of melancholia and his ambivalent distancing from pathologizing distinctions between melancholia and mourning advanced by his contemporary, Sigmund Freud, in her *Philosophy and Melancholy: Benjamin's Reflections on Theater and Language* (Stanford: Stanford University Press, 2013). Agamben spotted this clue several years ago in "The Noonday Demon," in Giorgio Agamben, *Stanzas: Word and Phantasm in Western Culture*, trans. Ronald L. Martinez (Minneapolis: University of Minnesota Press, 1993), 3–10. Agamben's insistence on the productivity of *acedia* inspired the important collection *Loss: The Politics of Mourning*, eds. David L. Eng and David Kazanjian (Berkeley: University of California Press, 2003). Ann Cvetkovich has elaborated on the temporal and political possibilities of *acedia* in her *Depression: A Public Feeling* (Durham: Duke University Press, 2012), especially 85–114.

[30] Dante encounters those guilty of the vice of *acedia* in the fourth cornice of Purgatory (*Purgatorio* XVII-XVIII). For a classical analysis, see Siegfried Wenzel, *The Sin of Sloth: Acedia in Medieval Thought and Literature* (Chapel Hill: University of North Carolina Press, 1967), 128–135, and Jeffrey Tambling, "Dreaming the Siren: Dante and Melancholy," *Forum for Modern Language Studies* 40 (2004): 56–69. Paradoxically, according to medieval Christians, Jews were essentially acedious: see Irven M. Resnick, *Marks of Distinction: Christian Perception of Jews in the High Middle Ages* (Washington, DC: Catholic University of America Press, 2012), 175–214.

[31] In his critical reading of Benjamin's "Critique of Violence," Derrida chided Benjamin for the "archeo-eschatological" quality of his concept of divine violence and the messianic (*Make and Let Die*

Rather than distance itself from *acedia*, this study embraces historical materialism along with *acedia* in its "ambiguous negative value." The collection as a whole stakes the claim that the infamous "noonday demon," as medieval writers fantastically embodied *acedia*, might have something important to teach us about reading the unconscious of expunged archives.[32] Put another way, how might *acedia*, with its rhythms and temporalities of performative slow love, in contrast to the urgent, explosive punctuality of Benjamin's *Jetztzeit*, the "now" of his "Theses," offer insights into the slow death of the "to make live" and the slow death (or not) of "to let die?[33]

To prepare the readers for the essays that follow, I want to offer an example of how an *acedious* reading of the archive works. I have taken as my text Walter Benjamin's inexhaustible essay, "Critique of Violence" (drafted in December 1920 and published in August 1921), because it has so profoundly shaped contemporary debates over sovereignty and biopolitics.[34] Archives of violence mattered to Benjamin. In that

seeks to provide an archaeology for Benjamin's cloven distinctions). See Jacques Derrida, "Force of Law: The Mystical Foundations of Authority," *Cardozo Law Review* 11 (1989-90): 921–1045. See page 1045 for Derrida's term "archeo-eschatological."

[32] "The ambiguous negative value of *acedia* becomes in this manner the dialectical leavening capable of reversing privation as possession. Since its desire remains fixed in that which has rendered itself inaccessible, *acedia* is not only a flight from, but a flight toward, which communicates with its object in the form of negation and lack" (Agamben, "The Noonday Demon," 7).

[33] See footnote 24 for references to important critiques of the temporality of Benjamin's "*Jetztzeit*."

[34] Benjamin's essay, "Kritik der Gewalt" appeared in August 1921 in the *Archiv für Sozialwissenschaft und Sozialpolitik*. I have used the translation, "Critique of Violence," published in Walter Benjamin, *Reflections: Essays, Aphorisms, Writings*, trans. Edmund Jephcott (New York: Schocken Books, 1978), 277–300 (all subsequent references to this text cited parenthetically in text, by page number). For an overview of its reception history in the writings of Derrida and Agamben, see Robert Sinnerbrink, "Violence, Destruction and Sov-

essay, he sought to distinguish law-making and law-pre-
serving mythic violence from divine violence, which destroys
the law. He further argued that an archive of blood—its presence or absence—is the trace that separates mythic violence
(law making, law preserving) from divine violence (law de-
stroying).

NIOBE'S TEARS

Benjamin exemplified mythic violence with the Greek myth
of Niobe and divine violence with the revolt of the band of
Korah, a story recounted in the Hebrew Scriptures (Numbers
16:1–40). What is common to both his readings is the way in
which he radically excluded what I call the collateral archives
of these narratives, because they had nothing to do with
blood. In what follows, I show how an *acedious* reading of
these stories puts disturbing collateral archives in the light of
the noonday (demon) sun.

Benjamin used the classical myth of Niobe to argue about
law-making mythic violence. Her story goes like this: Daughter of the Phrygian (read non-Greek) Tantalus, well-married
queen of Thebes, and mother of seven sons and seven daugh-
ters, Niobe boasted of her fertility to her girlfriend, the Greek
goddess Leto, who had borne only two children, Apollo and
Artemis. Outraged by such mockery, the jealous Leto commanded her son and daughter to punish the arrogant Niobe

ereignty: Derrida, Agamben on Benjamin's Critique of Violence," in
Walter Benjamin and the Architecture of Modernity, eds. Andrew
Benjamin and Charles Rice (Melbourne: re.press, 2009), 77–91. For
recent compelling readings of this essay, see Judith Butler, *Parting
Ways: Jewishness and the Critique of Zionism* (New York: Columbia
University Press, 2012), 69–98; Sigrid Weigel, *Walter Benjamin:
Images, the Creaturely, and the Holy*, trans. Chadwick Truscott
Smith (Stanford: Stanford University Press, 2013), 30–58. Beatrice
Hanssen's reflection on Benjamin's essay has also provoked my
thinking: *Walter Benjamin's Other History: Of Stones, Animals,
Human Beings, and Angels* (Berkeley: University of California Press,
1998), 127–136.

by shooting down with arrows all of her offspring. Overcome with grief amidst the carnage, Niobe turned into a weeping stone. A whirlwind carried this "slow stone" (*langsamen Fels*, as Friedrich Hölderlin weighed it) back home and deposited it on Mount Sipylus in Turkey, where tears trickle down, supposedly even today.

Why did Benjamin choose the story of Niobe, who stands as only one possible figure among a panoply of brutal mythical violence in Greek and Ovidian traditions? As a gymnasium student, Benjamin would have read about Niobe in Ovid's *Metamorphoses*.[35] Precociously (c. 1915), he also commented on the poetry of Friedrich Hölderlin, who embraced Niobe as a muse in his translations of Sophocles' *Antigone*. Here is how Hölderlin translates the scene in which Antigone likens herself to Niobe: "She [Niobe] is couched and struck to a slow stone [*langsamen Fels*]. They put her in a chain of ivy and winter is with her. Always people say, and it washes her throat with snow-bright tears, from under her lashes, like her exactly a ghost brings me to bed."[36] Ovid further embroidered her myth: "The picture of utter grief, and in the picture no sign of life at all: the tongue was frozen to the roof of the mouth; no pulse beat in the veins; neck could not bend, nor arms be moved, nor feet go back or forward; and the vitals hardened to rock, but still she weeps; and she is carried,

---

[35] On Ovidian pedagogy, see Theodore Ziolkowski, *Ovid and the Moderns* (Ithaca: Cornell University Press, 2004), where we learn that Kafka had read Ovid with a Catholic monk at the Altstäder Gymnasium in Prague (79). The emblematic character of Niobe's story ("her body is becoming stone, and her story is becoming an emblem") would have also drawn in Benjamin, given his interest in emblems, on which point see Leonard Barkan, *The Gods Made Flesh: Metamorphoses and the Pursuit of Paganism* (New Haven: Yale University Press, 1986), 69.

[36] The translations of Hölderlin are from David Constantine, *Friedrich Hölderlin: Selected Poems* (Newcastle upon Tyne: Bloodaxe Books, 1996), 97. See also David Farrell Krell, *Tragic Absolute: German Idealism and the Language of God* (Bloomington: Indiana University Press, 2005), 350.

caught up in a whirlwind, to her native mountains, where, on a summit, a queen deposed, she rests, still weeping: even to this day the marble trickles with tears."[37] Niobe would have also been on Benjamin's mind at the time of drafting his essay in 1920, since he mentions receiving a birthday gift that summer from his dear friend, Gershom Scholem: a text on the subject of Niobe.[38]

Benjamin starkly summarizes the figure of Niobe "both as an eternally mute bearer of guilt and as a boundary stone on the frontier between men and gods" (295). Later on in the essay, he observes that mythical law-making violence is, moreover, "bloody" (297), and the blood of Niobe's murdered children is thus its archival trace.[39] Strangely, in his account of Niobe, Benjamin overlooked what his cherished Hölderlin and Ovid poetically singled out as the archival pathos of her stony metamorphosis—her perpetual tears. It is the forgotten archive of her tears, a lithic trace, I argue, that can help to disclose a relationship between the biopolitical archive *within* messianic divine violence.[40] Are not her tears the gushing

---

[37] Ovid, *Metamorphoses*, trans. Rolfe Humphries (Bloomington: Indiana University Press, 1983), 139.

[38] I have not been able to identify the source of this text on Niobe; see Benjamin's letter to Gershom Scholem dated 23 July 1920 in *Correspondence of Walter Benjamin*, eds. Gershom Scholem and Theodor W. Adorno, trans. Manfred R Jacobson and Evelyn M. Jacobson (Chicago: University of Chicago Press, 1994): "Now let me get around to thanking you for your absolutely beautiful gifts. I do not know which of them gave me more pleasure and, above all, which will give more pleasure. For I have not been able to read *Niobe* yet. But any mythological work from you fills me with the greatest sense of expectation. The subject is significant too" (166).

[39] Gil Anidjar opens his important study of the circulation of blood and violence with a discussion of Benjamin and the blood of law-making violence: *Blood: A Critique of Christianity* (New York: Columbia University Press, 2014), 1–30.

[40] My reading is indebted to Judith Butler's reflections on Niobe in *Parting Ways*: "it may be that Niobe's tears provide a figure that allows us to understand the transition from mythic to divine vio-

aftermath of the make live in the make die? The lithic tracks of her tears question Benjamin's fantasy of pure divine violence and the messianic without archival trace.

As mentioned above, Benjamin uses the scriptural story of the revolt of the Korah brothers against Moses and Aaron (Numbers 16:1–40) to exemplify divine violence.[41] The brothers insisted that all the Israelites were holy and challenged the priestly hierarchy embodied by Moses and Aaron: "And they gathered themselves together against Moses and against Aaron, and said unto them, Ye take too much upon you, seeing all the congregation are holy, every one of them, and the LORD is among them: wherefore then lift ye up yourselves above the congregation of the LORD?" (Numbers 16:3) In response to this mutiny, God struck down the tents of the Korah brothers and all the family members, animals and household possessions sheltered therein. The earth swallowed up the tents, hook, line, and sinker. According to Benjamin, it is the absence of blood, the absence of any (surface) archival trace, that signs and seals divine violence—an invisible signature. But once again Benjamin overlooks other traces of archival violence mentioned in the Korah story. The scripture relates how God burnt to ash the entourage of two hundred and fifty princes, who, swinging their smoking incense censers, had accompanied the Korah brothers on their mission. God further commanded that the molten censers be refabricated as metal cladding for the altar: "The LORD said to Moses, 'Tell Eleazar son of Aaron, the priest, to remove the

lence" (89). And that transition, I argue, has to do with the question of the relationship between the archival trace and the messianic. Likewise, I have found helpful Stathis Gourgouris's brilliant critique of Benjamin's Romantic concept of myth and his own understanding of myth as "the profoundly ambiguous, indeed indestructible, performance of the allegorical as real": *Does Literature Think? Literature as Theory for an Antimythical Era* (Stanford: Stanford University Press, 2003), 81–83; 90–115 (citation at 354).

[41] Petar Bojanič discusses Benjamin's sources and influences for the Korah story: "God the Revolutionist: On Radical Violence for the First Ultra-Leftist," *Filozofski vestnik* XXIX.2 (2008): 191–207.

censers from the charred remains and scatter the coals some distance away, for the censers are holy—the censers of the men who sinned at the cost of their lives. Hammer the censers into sheets to overlay the altar, for they were presented before the LORD and have become holy. Let them be a sign to the Israelites'" (Numbers 16:37). Further, God struck down with plague the 14,700 bystanders who grumbled at the fate of the Korah brothers. Their dead and rotting bodies also litter the verses of *Numbers.*

Why did Benjamin overlook the collateral damage of both mythic violence (perpetual tears) and divine violence (the ashes of 250 burnt bodies of the Korah collaborators; the molten metal of their 250 censers; the rotting corpses of 14,700 Israelites)? Why is blood his absolute archival criterion between mythical and divine violence? In what ways does Benjamin miss the death drive of archival violence in such a simplistic distinction? I wondered if this early Benjamin of the "Critique of Violence" had unconsciously distanced himself from things medieval—in this case, the medieval archive of Ashkenazi Judaism? The 1892 Hebrew edition and German translations of the medieval manuscript of the *Hebrew Chronicle of 1096*, which offered several examples of a messianic archive, would have been available to Benjamin and Scholem. In the later Middle Ages, the Ashkenazic concept of a messianic archive would also be taken up in the Sephardic *Zohar* on which Scholem became an expert. Could Benjamin have known of this Ashkenazic tradition of divine violence—if not on his own, then from Scholem, who delved deeply into rabbinical mysticism?

I ask this because Benjamin's insistence on bloodless divine violence contradicts the medieval Ashkenazi vision of the messianic. Medieval Ashkenazi Jewry, collective targets of the violent marauding of Crusader bands in the Rhineland in 1096, believed that their martyred blood became the archival trace recorded on the Messiah's *porphyrion* (an imperial purple garment) and that each drop of this sanguinary archive would be justified by the divine violence of the messianic coming.[42] Here is just one poetic example among many written after the Christian persecutions of Jews in the Rhineland in 1096 and subsequent Christian persecutions of medieval Ashkenazi Jewry:

> Drops of my blood are counted one by one
> And spray their life-blood on your porphyrion
> He will execute judgment among nations
> Filling them with corpses.[43]

Some historians regard this Ashkenazic version of the messianic as reductively vengeful, but that is not my point here. The *porphyrion* raises for me a more complicated question of the relationship of messianic and archival traces.[44] The medieval Ashkenazi rabbis imagined the messianic, not so much as a radically different temporal register, but, like quantum physicists, more so as an entangled register of light. Their experience of "to make die" criss-crossed on the *porphyrion*

---

[42] A Hebrew-German edition of the *Hebrew Chronicle of 1096* appeared in 1892. It contained the edited Hebrew text with a German translation by Seligman Baer: *Hebraische Berichte über die Judenverfolgungen während der Kreuzzuge: Quellen zur Geschichten der Juden in Deutschland*, eds. Adolf Neubauer and Moritz Stern (Berlin: Leonhard Simion, 1892). Israel Jacob Yuval engages the figure of the *porphyrion* in his *Two Nations in Your Womb: Perceptions of Jews and Christians in Late Antiquity and the Middle Ages* (Berkeley: University of California Press, 2006), 91–114. For an important critique of Yuval and the historiographic discourse around the medieval blood libel see, Hannah Johnson, *Blood Libel: The Ritual Murder Accusation at the Limit of Jewish History* (Ann Arbor: University of Michigan Press, 2012), 101–128.

[43] This verse describing the messianic *porphyrion* is by Kalonymus ben Yehudah, who wrote in Speyer in the mid-twelfth century: see Yuval, *Two Nations*, 95.

[44] In the spirit of Butler, *Parting Ways*: "I continue to think about Benjamin in order to understand the right to wage public criticism against violence, but also to articulate the values of cohabitation and remembrance—the values of not effacing active traces of past destruction" (99).

with "to let live" in quantum patterns. In contemporary terms, we can think of their messianic *porphyrion* as an infrared apparatus whose spectrum would become visible in the light of justice. Benjamin, understandably reactive to strong nineteenth-century statist concepts of the archive, missed out on this rich medieval Ashkenazi quantum messianic entangled in light and justice.[45]

Benjamin's treasured watercolor, *Angelus Novus* (Paul Klee, 1920), the source of his interpretation of the angel of history in his "Theses" is intuitively closer, I think, to the quantum vision of the medieval Ashkenazi rabbis than to Benjamin's ekphrasis.[46] To fashion this watercolor (now in collection of the Israel Museum, Jerusalem), Klee had innovated an oil-transfer process that was archivally based. Here is how his process worked: He selected a pre-existing drawing of this angel, already registered in his archive, and laid it on top of black oil-coated paper. The black coating touched a sheet of fresh drawing paper. He then used a stylus to trace out the image of the original (something like Freud's mystic

---

[45] The concluding chapter of this volume, "Doing Dead Time for the Sovereign: Archive, Abandonment, Performance," elaborates on how the mid-nineteenth century used the concept of the panopticon to found "national archives" of the state. The concept of the archive in Benjamin, Foucault, and Derrida never deconstructs this nineteenth-century epistemology of the archive.

[46] My reading of Klee's *Angelus Novus* and its analogies to Ashkenazi concepts of a messianic archive of blood is inspired by Tama Trodd's beautiful essay that clarifies the method and implications of Klee's oil transfer technique and their relations to the contemporary mystic writing pad of Freud: "Drawing in the Archive: Paul Klee's Oil Transfers," *Oxford Art Journal* 31.1 (2008): 75–95. Klee's inspiration for the technique might have also been drawn from the new, popular experiments in rotoscoping around 1915. Filmmakers would trace over original footage to produce an animated copy for cartoon production. The drawing by Klee is now housed in the Israel Museum in Jerusalem, and you can see a digital reproduction here: http://www.english.imjnet.org.il/Popup.aspx?c0=13336.

writing pad). The stylus penetrated the black oil coating and registered the outline on the copy. Once the copy was dry, Klee would then splash watercolors on the copy. *Angelus Novus* was one such example of Klee's oil transfer process. His artistic practice embodied the disjuncture of inscriptional technologies, their disjointed temporalities, and the supplement of color washes, just as did the "blood transfer process" into the messianic envisioned by Ashkenazi rabbis. This volume, *Make and Let Die*, too, is intended to function as an oil transfer process of the medieval archive of violent sovereignty onto contemporary discourses of sovereignty and biopolitics.

With this notion of the archival *porphyrion* and oil-transfer process in mind, the question becomes not a study of the proper "periodization" of sovereignty (although temporalization hovers over each chapter), but rather, an investigation of medieval archival passages and what they might have to do with reimagining a quantum-biopolitical archive entangled in time, space, and matter. This volume argues that divine violence (a version of Benjamin's messianic concept) does not dissolve the archive (that was Benjamin's fantasy). Instead, readings of divine violence can illuminate the labyrinth of archival passages of medieval Christian sovereignty like an infra-red spectrum. Medieval Christian sovereignty constituted itself on collateral archives that, as this volume shows, declared Muslims the enemy of Western Christendom and designated Jewish neighbors as *servi* (that is, slaves) of the sovereign, subject to his declaration of the state of exception.[47] The archive of western Christendom was thus always

[47] Carl Schmitt, the German juridical theorist, writing in the 1920s, famously argued that the sovereign is the one who suspends the law and that such suspension was akin to the theological suspension of the natural law at stake in a miracle: "The exception in jurisprudence is analogous to the miracle in theology" (Carl Schmitt, *Political Theology: Four Chapters on the Concept of Sovereignty*, translation of *Politisches Theologie* [1922] by George Schwab [Chicago: University of Chicago Press, 1985], 36). Walter Benjamin, Schmitt's contemporary and erstwhile interlocutor, argued against Schmitt.

threatening, but also threatened by the very categories of the enemy (Muslim, Jews) that it constituted in order to fabricate its power.

TURN OF TIME (*WENDE DER ZEIT*)

The chapters of this collection are not organized chronologically. Instead, the configuration is inspired by a notion of time advanced by Benjamin in an early essay on the poetry of Hölderlin (c. 1915), where he analyzed the poet's expression, "turn of time" [*Wende der Zeit*].[48] He and Scholem, drawing upon the most sophisticated mathematics of their day (originally Scholem had matriculated for a PhD in mathematics before his turn to Kabbalah studies), surmised, as Benjamin scholar Peter Fenves has brilliantly observed, that the "curvature of historical time would be expressed by a continuous non-differential mathematical function [the Weirerstrass

Benjamin conceived of the miracle as the form for revolution, a suspension of the sovereign's suspension. Samuel Weber trenchantly summarized this Schmittian-Benjaminian conundrum as follows: "does the decision take place by determining the exception, or does the exception take exception to decision itself?" Agamben has famously argued for the state of exception, but his use of this term and its relation to Benjamin and Schmitt has come under much criticism. See Samuel Weber, "Taking Exception to Decision: Theatrical-Theological Politics: Walter Benjamin and Carl Schmitt," in *Walter Benjamin, 1892-1940*, ed. Uwe Steiner (New York: Peter Lang, 1992), 123–138 (citation at 136). Adam Kotsko makes an analogous critical point concerning Giorgio Agamben's reading of Walter Benjamin in his essay, "On Agamben's use of Benjamin's 'Critique of Violence'," *Telos* 145 (Winter 2008): 119–129.

[48] The essay by Peter Fenves inspires my image of "turn of time": "Renewed Question: Whether a Philosophy of History is Possible," *Modern Language Notes* 129.3 (2014): 514–524. A translation of Benjamin's essay on "Two Poems by Friedrich Hölderlin," where he discusses the turn of time and plastic temporality, can be found in *Walter Benjamin: Selected Writings, Volume 1: 1913-1926*, eds. Marcus Bullock and Michael William Jennings, trans. Edmund Jephcott (Cambridge: Harvard University Press, 1996), 18–36.

function of the 1870s] ... . In other words, 'historical time' is so severely turned at every 'moment' that its 'course' cannot be sketched, represented, or even imagined."[49]

So this collection opens with a "turned" account, "Transmedieval Mattering and the Untimeliness of the Real Presence," which is a critical review essay of an innovative study of the quantum physicist Neils Bohr (1885-1962) brought into contact with two other major texts on the cultural politics of mattering by Jane Bennett and Eric Santner. I read these contemporary narratives of mattering with a formative medieval treatise authored by Lanfranc (1005-89) (erstwhile Archbishop of Canterbury and royal justice to the English monarchy). Lanfranc championed as orthodoxy the physical mattering of the flesh and blood of Christ in the bread and wine of the sacrament of the Eucharist. The juxtapositions are not capricious. Instead, I argue that Lanfranc, by binding the orthodox doctrine of the physical mattering of the Eucharist (the flesh and blood of Christ) to the body of the sovereign, condemned those who denied such mattering to treason (the unique crime against sovereignty). This essay argues that it is precisely the medieval concept of the Real Presence that haunts the studies by Bennett and Santner. It further asks how a quantum notion of mattering might interrupt a biopolitics of the Real Presence entangled in contemporary theories of sovereignty. "Transmedieval Mattering" aims to argue for the untimeliness of the theological and sovereign concept of the Real Presence—a medieval apparatus of mattering and sovereignty—that continues to haunt the discourse of virtual and material objects and their biopolitics today—the death inhabiting to "make live."

With Chapter 2, the volume turns to a prototype of the larger project, "Arthur's Two Bodies and the Bare Life of the Archives," first drafted in 2006 and published in 2008. This study represents an early effort to question the modern and secularizing claims made in contemporary theoretical and historiographical debates over sovereignty, particularly over

[49] Fenves, "Renewed Question," 524.

the terms of "bare life" and the "king's two bodies"—terms typically regarded as signs of the early modern turn to the sovereign. What troubled me when I began this essay was the way in which fictions of the earlier twelfth century (notably, Geoffrey of Monmouth's *A History of the Kings of Britain*), with its intense interest in massacres mounted on new and devastating fictional scales, performed the convergence of three critical aspects of political theology: 1) the papal designation, in 1063, of Muslims as the "enemy" [*homines sacri*] of Christendom. Pope Alexander II (d. 1073) declared that Muslim blood could be shed by Christians without any taint or sin; 2) the precocious theological conceptualization of a twin body for the king [*gemma corpora*]; and 3) the inauguration of legislation in medieval Christendom declaring Jews to be the slaves [*servi*] subject to the regional leader (king, or bishop, duke, etc).

My exploration of the political theological fiction of the once and future body of Arthur foregrounded by Geoffrey of Monmouth, and the theological and legal speculation carried out by Geoffrey's own clerical coterie regarding the relation of sovereign power and Jews, led to my deep questioning of the dominant temporal paradigm of biopolitics as a sign of the modern, or as a static "arch-ancient thing," as Derrida would have it. The material and virtual events of the early twelfth century taught me that medieval Christian sovereignty fabricated itself on what can be understood as neighbors as collateral damage: the naming of Muslims as the enemy of medieval Christendom and designating European Jews as *servi* (or *homines sacri),* subject to the sovereign state of exception (the vicissitudes of expulsion being a recurring example of this across Western Christendom).

In Chapter 4, "Dead Neighbor Archives: Jews, Muslims, and the Enemy's Two Bodies," I look under the hood of the typological-machine of contemporary periodizations of sovereignty, especially in its turn to the messianic theology of the Apostle Paul (most notably in the work of Jacob Taubes, Giorgio Agamben, Alain Badiou, Kenneth Reinhard, Eric L.

Santner, and Slavoj Žižek), where the ghost of Carl Schmitt's work on political theology and sovereignty consistently hovers. My analysis traverses a deconstruction of two images: Benjamin's image of the chess-playing automaton, known as "the Turk," that introduces his "Theses on a Philosophy of History," and the Romanesque image of the Mystic Mill conjured by Taubes in his discussion of the political theology of Paul and in his critique of Schmitt. I show how their use of such images is surprisingly structured by medieval typological notions of sign and fulfillment. Despite their involvement in this medieval typological thinking, however, I further show how their works, and their close readers, such as Agamben, anxiously foreclose the "medieval," rather than addressing its collateral archives. The traumatic cost of this foreclosure of the medieval in contemporary theories of sovereignty and biopolitics is then exposed in a reading of two major treatises: *Against the Jews and their inveterate obstinacy* and *Against the Saracens [Islam] as a sect and heresy*, authored by Peter the Venerable (1122-60), powerful Abbot of the monastery of Cluny in Burgundy. I conclude by asserting "that in order for there to be a relation between philosophy and theology that is not a murderous typological one, we need to traverse the symbolic process whereby medieval Christian typology excarnated Jews and Muslims." Collateral archives are the archives of the excarnated—those archives made to die so that secularism can be made to live.

A major proof-text of contemporary debates over sovereignty is William Shakespeare's tragedy, *King Richard II*. Ernst Kantorowicz dramatically opened his study of the king's two bodies with his reading of that play, and most contemporary theorists, notably Eric L. Santner, have simply adopted his reading. In Chapter 5, "Tears of Reign: Big Sovereigns Do Cry," I read *King Richard II* past the famous deposition scene with its broken mirror (Act IV), at which point Kantorowicz and Santner stop, in order to explore the play's abundant archive of tears. The aim of the chapter is to show how contemporary discourses on sovereignty and biopolitics serve as ongoing sovereign border technologies between the

death in "to make live" and "to make die." I show how Shake-speare's archive of tears can provide a way of seeing collateral archives and their queer untimeliness in both medieval polit-ical theology and contemporary biopolitics.

In his groundbreaking book, *Homo Sacer: Sovereign Power and Bare Life* (1998), Agamben excavated the Roman juridi-cal notion of *homo sacer*, the one who could be killed without taint of homicide, but who could not be sacrificed. Chapter 6, "Undeadness and the Tree of Life: Ecological Thought of Sovereignty," explores what it would mean to diffract the cat-egory of *homo sacer* with a *collateral archive* of *res sacra* (a thing that may be cut, but may not be sacrificed). I return first to the fearful sovereign symmetry proposed by Michel Foucault—the classical sovereign who could "make die" and "let live," and the so-called modern biopolitical sovereign who can "make live" and "let die." The concept of *res sacra* offers a way of re-reading the historiography of two noted medieval artifacts devoted to a political theology of the Tree of Life: an early medieval stone sculpture called the Ruthwell cross and the 12th-century carved walrus ivory known as the Cloisters Cross. The carved stone trees speak of radical expo-sure to the state of exception, the scene of the Crucifixion. They were re-excavated and debated by German-Jewish art historians exiled at the Warburg Institute (London) in the 1930s and 1940s (and beyond to Ernst Kantorowicz's belated intervention in the debate in 1960s).[50] This splice asks how

---

[50] See Ernst Kitzinger, "Anglo-Saxon Vine Scroll Ornament," *An-tiquity* 10.37 (1936): 61–71; Fritz Saxl, "The Ruthwell Cross," *Jour-nal of the Warburg and Courtauld Institutes* 6 (1943): 1–19; Meyer Schapiro, "The Religious Meaning of the Ruthwell Cross," *Art Bulle-tin*, 26 (1944): 232–245; and Ernst H. Kantorowicz, "The Archer in the Ruthwell Cross," *Art Bulletin* 42 (1960): 57–59. On the emigra-tion of German Jewish art-historians in 1933, when the Nazis insti-tuted their race laws in the university see, Karen Michels, "Art His-tory, German-Jewish Immigrants, and the Emigration of Iconolo-gy," in *Jewish Identity in Modern Art History*, ed. Catherine M. Soussloff (Berkeley: University of California Press, 1999), 167–179,

these talking trees serve as aerials that transmit a trauma, such that it becomes transitive, or what Bracha Ettinger has called "transtraumatic."[51] Their transmission of the sovereign cut paradoxically opens up a linked border space between talking trees and German-Jewish scholars in exile. The cutting of ivory in the Cloisters Cross shows how sovereignty could be Judaized and Jews could be biopoliticized in this traumatic juncture of sovereignty and biopolitics in the twelfth century.[52]

Unlike the Rankean historian vilified by Benjamin in his "Theses on the Philosophy of History," my critique of medieval Christian sovereignty has embraced archives of collateral damage. These are, indeed, the archives of the "victors" cut out as dead time. But by reading the dead time of collateral archives, an infra-red exposure glows to reveal how Muslims and Jews came to be gathered up by medieval Christian sovereignty into categories of "enemy" and *servi*—the collateral damage of Christendom's sovereignty. The collateral archive matters, because it is on the paperwork of lawsuits, debt transactions, tax lists, chronicles, expulsion orders, romances and other fictions, that Christian sovereignty constituted itself on the naming of the enemy (Muslims) and the state of exception, declaring Jews (again) as *servi*, or slaves. My analysis is epistemological. Of course, Jews and Muslims did live peaceably at moments in Western Christendom. But Christian sovereigns always wielded the potential to name the en-

and Christopher S. Wood, "Art History's Normative Renaissance," in *The Italian Renaissance in the Twentieth Century* (Florence: Olschki, 2002), 65–92.

[51] Bracha L. Ettinger, *The Matrixial Borderspace*, ed. Brian Massumi (Minneapolis: University of Minnesota Press, 2006), 167. Her revisions of Lacanian psychoanalysis can productively open the boundaries between creaturely life and animal life defended by Eric L. Santner (see footnote 1).

[52] See also Chapter 2 in this volume, "Arthur's Two Bodies and the Bare Life of the Archives."

emy and call the state of exception (and they did so, as this collection demonstrates). It is the constitution of this sovereign potential for collateral archives that is the subject of this collection. I have dubbed this sovereign potential "excarnating" in order to show how Christian orthodoxies of incarnation and Real Presence from the eleventh century onward could only manifest themselves as a function of excarnating sovereignty directed against Muslim and Jews and those Christians who came to be labeled as unorthodox.

The final chapter of this collection, "Doing Dead Time for the Sovereign: Archive, Abandonment, Performance," returns to the question of the poetic history of the collateral archive and asks what performance might have to do with reading the collateral archive. The chapter questions the typology of empty and messianic time intrinsic to Benjamin's writing and raises a third term, "dead time," as intrinsic to the collateral archive and as an important component of the death in "to make live." I show how the ontology of dead time enabled the virtual fabrication of the panopticon, an apparatus that Foucault argued structured biopolitics by its production of the "population" and its surveillance. Mary Ann Doane, as we have seen, has defined dead time as that "in which nothing happens, time which is in some sense 'wasted,' expended without product."[53] Thus, dead time can be imagined as the close neighbor to medieval *acedia*. The "ambiguous negative value" of *acedia* provided me with a performative energy in 2003 for working with the inmates of Mountjoy Prison, Dublin to piece together the public exhibition, *Cell*. *Cell* is the performance of the collateral archive entangled among inmates, spectators, prison guards, and historian. Once entangled, even for a moment, the collateral archive is exposed in the infra-red of performance. This is not the "swallowing up" of divine violence performed on the Korah brothers, or the carnage that immobilized Niobe. Instead, it was a performance that for a moment takes place in the

[53] Doane, *The Emergence of Cinematic Time*, 160.

fleeting light of justice during the dead time of evening lock-down. The closing words of that essay provide my conclusion to this introduction: "It was indeed only a 'minor' interruption of the Panopticon, a refusal of the elision of dead time. We knew that after *Cell* each of us would return to marking our own dead time, but becoming 'minor' is a powerful means by which the spectacle of abandonment can be momentarily suspended by problematizing it by threading thought through space and time along coordinates different from the optics and scriptures of political theology."

Chapter 2

Transmedieval Mattering and the Untimeliness of the Real Presence

An incarnation, or a burial, I cannot say.
                    T. Tasso, *Jerusalem Delivered* (1581)

IT'S A BODY; IT'S FLESH; IT'S MATTERING

Vibrant matter glows in the Humanities.[1] It is quantum physics all the way down; there are not two physics, a mechanical Newtonian physics of inert matter for the macroscopic world, and a quantum one of dynamic matter for the microscopic. Time and space are not containers; they, too, are dynamic. And just like light, whose behavior as wave and

---

[1] This chapter originally appeared, in slightly different form, as Kathleen Biddick, "Transmedieval Mattering and the Untimeliness of the Real Presence" (Book Review Essay), *postmedieval: a journal of medieval cultural studies* 4.2 (2013): 238–252.

particle, confused burgeoning quantum physicists in the 1920s and 1930s, the discourse of vibrant matter, too, exhibits a duality: at times dynamic matter materializes in the humanities as a body, other times as flesh. Current debates over "body" and "flesh" are no less fierce than those over light and matter conducted back then among physicists including Niels Bohr, Albert Einstein, Werner Heisenberg.[2] Because these controversies over body and flesh constrain and enable what can be said about materialization, they matter. This review essay reads contemporary debates over mattering (body and flesh) through the apparatus of the Real Presence—that is, the orthodox insistence, fabricated in the eleventh century, on the material presence of the flesh and blood of the body of Christ in the sacrament of the Eucharist. This essay explores how the untimeliness of the Real Presence haunted medieval discourse then and contemporary theory now.

LANFRANC (1005–1089)[3]

Flesh is the Sacrament of the flesh and Blood is the sacrament of the blood. (*Caro, videlicet, carnis, et sanguis sacramentum est sanguinis.*)

Lanfranc, *On the Body and Blood*

Father Mark G. Vaillancourt wrote his Fordham doctoral dissertation (2004) on Guitmund of Aversa's contribution to the Eucharistic debate over the Real Presence waged in the eleventh century. Thanks to his recent translation, scholars

[2] We now know that Bohr was right, as technological developments in experimental physics are enabling a new empirical domain: experimental metaphysics. Karen Barad, *Meeting the Universe Halfway: Quantum Physics and the Entanglement of Matter and Meaning* (Durham: Duke University Press, 2007), 247–352.

[3] This section reviews, Lanfranc, *On the Body and Blood of the Lord* and Guitmund of Aversa, *On the Truth of the Body and Blood of Christ in the Eucharist*, trans. M.G. Vaillancourt, in *The Fathers of the Church: Medieval Continuation* 10 (Washington, DC: Catholic University of America Press, 2009).

without Latin proficiency can now read two treatises by Lanfranc and Guitmund crucial to this onto-epistemological controversy and study this crisis of mattering for themselves. Both medieval texts enjoyed a printed afterlife in the sectarian strife of the sixteenth century when the orthodoxy of the Eucharist and questions of sovereignty were at stake. In 1530 Erasmus printed Lanfranc's treatise (*De Corpore et Sanguine Domine*) and it is his edition that scholars will find reproduced in the *Patrologia Latina*. Vaillancourt translated the Erasmus edition with the corrections to that text established by Jean de Montclos.[4]

My focus here is on the treatise of Lanfranc of Bec. Abbot, theologian, jurist, he also served as justiciar and archbishop of Canterbury under William the Conqueror. He wrote his famous polemic on the orthodoxy of the Real Presence in the shadow of the Norman Conquest (1066).[5] In his famous treatise, *On the Body and Blood of the Lord*, composed around 1063, at which time he moved to William's newly founded ducal monastery at Caen, Lanfranc attacked the arguments of his contemporary Bérenger of Tours, who outspokenly questioned the Real Presence in the sacrament of the Eucharist. Lanfranc asserted the orthodoxy that "The Flesh is the Sacrament of the Flesh" (*caro, videlicet carnis . . . sacramentum est*).[6] Lanfranc's treatise goes beyond the stock litany of theological polemic—Bérenger as adversary of the Catholic Church (*catholicae Ecclesiae adversario*),[7] sacrilegious violator of oath

---

[4] Jean de Montclos, *Lanfranc et Bérenger: La controverse eucharistique du XIe siecle* (Louvain: Spicilegium Sacrum Lovaniense, 1971).

[5] For a concise and insightful summary of the Bérenger debate, see Jean de Montclos, "Lanfranc et Bérenger: les origines de la doctrine de la Transsubstantiation," in *Lanfranco de Pavia e l'Europa del secolo XI*, ed. G. D'Onofrio, Italia Sacra: Studi e Documenti di Storia Ecclesiastica 51 (Rome: Herder Editrice e Libreria, 1993), 297–326. See also Charles M. Radding and Francis Newton, *Theology, Rhetoric, and Politics in the Eucharistic Controversy 1078–1079: Alberic of Monte Cassino against Berengar of Tours* (New York: Columbia University Press, 2003).

[6] Lanfranc, *On the Body and the Blood*, 56.

[7] Lanfranc, *On the Body and the Blood*, 32.

(*sacrilegus violator*),[8] heretic (*esse haereticus*)—to pioneer an accusation of *treason* against him (*jurare perfidiam*).[9] Bérenger, in Lanfranc's opinion, not only challenged theological orthodoxy; he also traitorously undid the universalism of the Catholic Church, a universalism constituted by the flesh of Christ. To think against this sacramental flesh is to commit treason, because, according to Lanfranc's vision, the flesh of Christ is constitutively both sacramental *and* sovereign. The flesh of the Eucharist was thus, for Lanfranc, both a sacramental and a sovereign problematic. His accusation of treason brings into view both the sovereign body under threat and also the *homo sacer* (the one who may be killed without accusation of homicide, but who may not be sacrificed). Giorgio Agamben has argued that the murder of *homo sacer* and the treasonous murder of the sovereign are structurally undecidable. Treason against the sovereign (that is, killing the sovereign (*crimen laesae maiestatis*)) is never "just" an act of homicide, because it is always more than homicide: "it does not matter from our perspective, that the killing of *homo sacer* can be considered as less than homicide, and the killing of the sovereign as more than homicide; what is essential is that in neither case does the killing of a man constitute an offense of homicide."[10]

Lanfranc, instead, pinned sovereignty to the Real Presence. The body that becomes excessively present in the doctrine of the Real Presence is, not Christ, but the sovereign—the one who decides on the state of exception and the one who names the enemy. This was the political theology of the Real Presence; it also secreted biopolitics by constituting the exceptional category of the "Jew" as underwriter of the Real Presence and Muslims as *homines sacri* of Western Christendom.[11] The kernel of sovereignty needs to be understood,

---

[8] Lanfranc, *On the Body and the Blood*, 31.

[9] Lanfranc, *On the Body and the Blood*, 32.

[10] Giorgio Agamben, *Homo Sacer: Sovereign Power and Bare Life*, trans. Daniel Heller-Roazen (Stanford: Stanford University Press, 1998), 104.

[11] At the same time (c. 1063), Pope Alexander II also declared Mus-

then, as a biopolitical suture of Eucharistic and Jewish flesh.[12] Political theology and biopolitics are thus entangled phenomena in the Real Presence. Biopolitics is not a sign of the modern as most theorists assume. It does not supersede political theology. Put in Foucauldian terms: the classical sovereign (to make die and let live) and biopolitics (to make live and let die) constitute the impasse of sovereignty then and now.[13]

Consider some of the profound deformations of the Real Presence: space and time became entangled in transformations. Michal Kobialka, in his groundbreaking study *This is my Body: Representational Practices in the Early Middle Ages*, has argued that the newly constituted orthodoxy of the Real Presence was constitutive of new forms of medieval representation.[14] He tracks these changes by studying how Western Easter liturgies represented (or not) the body of Christ, which, according to the Gospels, was absent at the empty Easter tomb. Prior to the Eucharist crisis over the Real Presence in the tenth and early eleventh centuries, no cleric ever impersonated the risen Christ and spoke the gospel words (*Quem queritis*) to Mary Magdalene: *Whom do you seek?/*

lims the *homines sacri* of Western Christendom. Christians could spill the blood of Muslims without pollution. For an incisive discussion and references, see Tomaž Mastnak, *Crusading Peace: Christendom, the Muslim World, and Western Political Order* (Berkeley: University of California Press, 2002), 40–41.

[12] Kathleen Biddick, "Arthur's Two Bodies and the Bare Life of the Archive," in *Cultural Diversity in the British Middle Ages: Archipelago, Island, England*, ed. Jeffery Jerome Cohen (New York: Palgrave Macmillan, 2008), 117–134 (and also reprinted in this volume).

[13] The temporal coexistence I am arguing for changes the terms of Santner's discussion of Foucault's anguish at figuring out the sovereignty of the Holocaust and Esposito's response to Foucault. See Eric L. Santner, *The Royal Remains: The People's Two Bodies and the Endgames of Sovereignty* (Chicago: University of Chicago Press, 2011), 12–28.

[14] Michal Kobialka, *This is My Body: Representational Practices in the Early Middle Ages* (Ann Arbor: University of Michigan Press, 1999).

Jesus of Nazareth. He is not here. He has risen just as it was predicted. An angel-actor (clearly not Christ) would voice these words at a "stage-set" of an empty tomb. As the Church promulgated the doctrine of the Real Presence, Kobialka shows how the Easter liturgy, for the first time, came to embody the absent body at the tomb. A cleric "performed" the absent body of resurrected Christ. The material embodiment of the absent body, according to Kobialka, transformed medieval representational grids of space and time. What is also chilling to realize is that it is these very same Easter *Quem Queritis* scripts embodying the resurrected Christ that also materialize the personified body of the Jewish people, who were excoriated as deicides.

Take, for example, the famous play book of the abbey of Fleury, which scripts the performance of the *Quem Queritis* at the turn of the twelfth century.[15] What in the tenth century counted for three or four spare lines of liturgical performance now exploded into a script of 75 lines along with stage directions. Jews are personified at the opening of the script: "Alas! Wretched Jewish people, Whom an abominable insanity makes frenzied. Despicable nation."[16] Kobialka links this changing ontology of theatrical embodiment to changing doctrinal epistemologies of the Real Presence. The sovereign flesh and blood of the Real Presence profoundly reorganized the temporal and spatial coordinates of medieval representation. It constructed a dominant gaze organized around an absent body that was forced to materialize as flesh and blood within liturgical-theatrical space.

The drive to embody and "re-present" the absent body of Christ theatrically also exploded sculpturally in stony materi-

---

[15] The text of this Easter play is recorded in Latin and English in *Medieval Drama*, ed. David Bevington (Boston: Houghton Mifflin, 1975). See also, *The Fleury Playbook: Essays and Studies*, eds. Thomas P. Campbell and Clifford Davidson, Early Drama, Art, and Music Monograph Series 7 (Kalamazoo: Medieval Institute Publications, 1985), and Theresa Tinkle, "Jews in the Fleury Playbook," *Comparative Drama* 38.1 (2004): 1–38.

[16] *Medieval Drama*, ed. Bevington, 39.

alizations of flesh (human, animals, plants, insects, monsters) that changed the face of church architecture in Western Europe (but not in Byzantium as Kinoshita reminds us).[17] Take, for example, the monumental building program at the ducal abbey at Caen, over which Lanfranc presided from 1063–1070, just at the inauguration of the orthodoxy of the Real Presence. The earliest phase of this program featured only one nave capital sculpted with a human form. Within a generation, as Eucharistic orthodoxy became a disciplinary site, sculpted matter invaded Romanesque capitals and proliferated on monumental church porches.[18] To put this in quantum terms, the promulgation of the orthodoxy of the Real Presence was an entangled phenomena in which sovereignty, bread, wine, body, flesh, precious metal, textiles, stone, chisel, celibate clerics, texts, and Jews intra-acted and produced exceptional grids of space and time.

Lest contemporary theorists think that such transformational grids were reconfigured in secularization, a glance at contemporary debates over body and flesh shows the lingering afterlife of the Real Presence.[19] A primal theological scene imagined by the French Jesuit Henri de Lubac (1886-1991) emplots the narrative. In his influential book *Corpus Mysticum* (French edition 1944, English translation 2006), Lubac argued that medieval scholastic theologians reduced and transposed the three terms of the sacramental Eucharist (*corpus verum, corpus Christi, corpus mysticum*) to two terms by inserting a *caesura* before *corpus mysticum*, thus collapsing

---

[17] Sharon Kinoshita, "Re-viewing the Eastern Mediterranean," *postmedieval* 2.3 (2011): 381 (369–385).

[18] For the architectural program at Caen and discussion of its sculpture from the first building phases, see Eric Gustav Carlson, "The Abbey Church of St.-Etienne at Caen in the Eleventh and Early Twelfth Centuries," PhD diss., Yale University, 1968.

[19] Jean-Luc Nancy, *Corpus*, trans. Richard A. Rand (New York: Fordham University Press, 2008) and *Dis-Enclosure: The Deconstruction of Christianity*, trans. Bettina Bergo, Gabriel Malenfant, and Michael B. Smith (New York: Fordham University Press, 2008); Roberto Esposito, "Flesh and Body in the Deconstruction of Christianity," trans. Janell Watson, *Minnesota Review* 75 (2010): 89–99.

two bodies (*corpus verum* and *corpus Christi*) into one and attaching the *corpus mysticum* to the institutional church, much to the detriment, as he saw it, of sacramental economy.[20] Whether Lubac is right or wrong is not at issue here (some scholars question his plot); more important is how his story of reduction of three bodies to two serves as a resource for theories of the body and flesh now.

Exemplary for its exposition of premodern political theology is *The King's Two Bodies: A Study in Medieval Political Theology*.[21] Ernst Kantorowicz used the same *caesura*, borrowed from Lubac, to fabricate his secularizing model of sovereignty. The transposition of *corpus mysticum* from the Eucharist to the institutional church, Kantorowicz argued, enabled the theology of the *corpus mysticum* to mutate into a secular politics of sovereignty represented by the two bodies of the sovereign: his mortal royal body and his second eternal body. This narrative of Kantorowicz is, as we shall see, key to Eric L. Santner's book *The Royal Remains*.

More recently, Esposito also uses the self-same narrative of Lubac as a tool to periodize his own reading of flesh, a concept crucial to his project of affirmative biopolitics. Esposito rehearses that once medieval theologians detached the sacramental Eucharistic term *corpus mysticum* and attached it to the institutional Church, they immunized it as historical form and (with a glance toward Nancy) thus doomed new thinking on phenomenologies of the body. Further, as a medieval dogmatic-institutional form, the body, for Esposito, is no longer part of the theology of the incarnation and therefore not part of his affirmative biopolitics. Such a move enables Esposito to use flesh as a support and to distance his own affirmative biopolitics from the efforts of Jean-Luc Nancy to deconstruct Christianity by averting from the flesh to a renewed critical phenomenology of the body. Thus, we can see

[20] Henri de Lubac, *Corpus Mysticum: The Eucharist and the Church in the Middle Ages: Historical Survey*, trans. Gemma Simmonds and Richard Price (Notre Dame: University of Notre Dame Press, 2006).
[21] Ernst Kantorowicz, *The King's Two Bodies: A Study in Medieval Political Theology* (Princeton: Princeton University Press, 1957).

that Lubac's claim for a cut of three bodies to two has produced a discursive impasse between body and flesh in contemporary theory along with a complementary temporal impasse of medieval and modern. In an anxious effort to exit the impasse, theorists frequently fall back on fantasies of the messianic (as in the case of Esposito). I want to join a reading of Lanfranc with the work of a particle physicist, Karen Barad, because her concept of an apparatus helps us to understand how the doctrine of the Real Presence could matter and have an afterlife in contemporary discourse.

BARAD

> (A)pparatuses are not mere observing instruments but boundary-drawing practices—specific material (re)configurings of the world—which come to matter.
> Karen Barad, *Meeting the Universe Halfway*

Karen Barad, who holds a doctorate in theoretical particle physics and teaches as a Professor of Feminist Studies, Philosophy and History of Consciousness (University of California-Santa Cruz), clarifies the mattering at stake in the Real Presence. In *Meeting the Universe Halfway*, she succinctly reviews debates over mattering in feminist and Foucauldian studies and then turns to an erudite and passionate reading of the quantum mechanics of the philosopher-physicist Niels Bohr (1885–1962). She persuasively counters and re-defines the representational legacy of mechanical physics: agency, objectivity, intention, causality, and knowing. Further, she reads the thought-experiments of Bohr back into science in order to clarify some of the persisting arguments over quantum materialities. The result is a breathtakingly diffractive reworking of the relationship of discoursing and mattering, dynamism and agency. Barad opens up new paths for connecting feminist theory, science studies, and politics. Her notion of the apparatus also offers a way of thinking of the far-reaching mattering power of what I am calling the apparatus of the Real Presence.

Barad forwards three key arguments: (1) that the primary

ontological unit is phenomena: the "*ontological inseparabil-ity/entanglement of intra-acting agencies*";[22] (2) that the primary modality of dynamism is performance: "if agency is understood as an enactment and not something someone has, then it seems not only appropriate but important to consider agency as distributed over nonhuman as well as human forms";[23] (3) that apparatuses "enact agential cuts that produce determinate boundaries and properties of 'entities' within phenomena, where 'phenomena' are the ontological inseparability of agentially intra-acting components. That is, agential cuts are at once ontic and semantic."[24] Put another way, Barad posits no constitutive exterior to entanglements of discourse and matter. Key, instead, for Barad, is the work of apparatuses. These produce agential separability, an exteriority *within* phenomena: "If the apparatus is changed, there is a corresponding change in the agential cut and therefore in the delineation of object from agencies of observation and the causal structure (and hence the possibilities for 'the future behavior of the system') enacted by the cut."[25] An apparatus is no mere laboratory set-up and it is too simple to think of it as an assemblage of humans and non-humans. Instead, she carefully argues for an apparatus as an entangled state of agencies without intrinsic boundaries: "Apparatuses are not located in the world but are material configurations or refiguring of the world that re(con)figure spatiality and temporality as well as (the traditional notion of) dynamics (i.e., they do not exist as static structures, nor do they merely unfold or evolve in space and time.")[26]

The "cut" matters in Barad's argument. It produces differences within differences and is contingent with apparatuses, which are never simply human and historical. This notion (exteriority within) and nomenclature (cut) seemed to me, however, to veer, at times, into unexamined ontotheologies

---

[22] Barad, *Meeting the Universe Halfway*, 139, emphasis in original.

[23] Barad, *Meeting the Universe Halfway*, 214.

[24] Barad, *Meeting the Universe Halfway*, 148.

[25] Barad, *Meeting the Universe Halfway*, 175.

[26] Barad, *Meeting the Universe Halfway*, 146.

of generative violence. Bohr's engagement with the writings of his beloved fellow Danish philosopher, Søren Kierkegaard (1813–1855), can provide a clue to this question of ontotheology. Kierkegaard thought deeply about the cut of Abraham's covenant (circumcision) and the cut of sacrifice asked of Abraham (his beloved son, Isaac, on Mount Moriah). Bohr absorbed this infinite movement of renunciation explored by Kierkegaard and worked it into his physics: "the necessity of a final *renunciation* of the classical ideal of causality and a radical revision of our attitude towards the problem of physical reality."[27]

If we read *Meeting the Universe Halfway* not as a book but as an apparatus, then it becomes an obsidian blade, a steel knife, a diamond cutter, a laser beam that repetitiously performs the generative violence that joins feminist theory and feminist science studies. It is also a must-read for theologians, since it imagines mattering as an exteriority within without the god-trick of messianism. Barad's study enables us to see the Real Presence as a phenomenon, an apparatus.

BENNETT

> In a world of vibrant matter, it is thus not enough to say that we are "embodied."
>
> Jane Bennett, *Vibrant Matter*

Jane Bennett, Professor of Political Theory at Johns Hopkins University, exquisitely crafts a manifesto for vibrant matter and a vital materialist theory of democracy. She wants to "try to give voice to a thing-power" and her book can be read like the score for a concept opera in the style of Philip Glass.[28] Like Barad, she seeks to "detach materiality from the figures of passive, mechanistic, or divinely infused substances."[29]

---

[27] Cited in Barad, *Meeting the Universe Halfway*, 129, emphasis mine.

[28] Jane Bennett, *Vibrant Matter: A Political Ecology of Things* (Durham: Duke University Press, 2010), 2.

[29] Bennett, *Vibrant Matter*, xiii.

There are eight movements. Chapter One turns objects into things with thing-power, or actants (a term that she borrows from Bruno Latour), meaning a source of action human or non-human. Baruch Spinoza holds the baton and marks the conative (a striving or desire present in everybody) tempo: trash becomes a vital assemblage of things; Kafka's story of a broken-down spool of thread, called Odradek, embodies multiple ontologies;[30] the sample of Gunpowder Residue presented in trial proceedings works as a legal actant; and the phenomenon of mineralization becomes an architect of evolution. In the second movement (Deleuze and Guattari at the podium), Bennett complicates her theme. To speak of things is just too simple—they might be mistaken as some kind of pre-existing, individual form, when in fact vibrant matter is always becoming in groupings—assemblages—a key concept of Deleuze and Guattari: "assemblages are living, throbbing confederations that are able to function despite the persistent presence of energies that confound them from within."[31]

She exemplifies the great blackout of 14 August 2003, as an assemblage of non-human and human actants (electricity, power-lines, brush fires, corporations) that acted in disconcert to produce the grid failure. As a reprise she considers the question of intentionality and causality in assemblages and swerves to Jacques Derrida and his messianic account of the unfillable promise to account for drive in assemblages without insinuating intentionality and purposiveness.[32] My argument is not with Derrida, but with the way in which Bennett uses his concept of the messianic as a placeholder for the proliferation of unmarked political theologies in contemporary theory. When Bennett concluded, playfully, with "a kind of Nicene Creed" for vital materialists, I paused.[33] After all, an inaugural experiment of imperial political theology fabricated itself at the Council of Nicaea (325).

Chapters Three and Four offer two more examples of as-

[30] Santner also reads Odradek in *The Royal Remains*, 83–85.
[31] Bennett, *Vibrant Matter*, 23–24.
[32] Bennett, *Vibrant Matter*, 32.
[33] Bennett, *Vibrant Matter*, 122.

semblages of vibrant matter at work. Chapter Three address-es food as a conative body intra-acting with the complex bod-ies of American consumers (note that her typology of vibrant bodies is multiplying—conative bodies, proto-bodies, com-plex bodies). The question of the inanimate, in this case met-al, is the challenge of Chapter Four. Bennett staunchly de-fends the dynamic conative properties of metals, even though "they are not quite 'bodied'."[34] This meditation leads to the key question of Chapter Five: how to account for the intrinsic vitality of things without resorting to some mysterious value-added, for example, a soul? This question fascinated Ameri-can and European audiences in the period leading up to World War I. Bennett takes as her interlocutors Henri Berg-son and Hans Driesch with an important detour through Immanuel Kant. This chapter is on the verge of realizing that agency itself needs to be rethought, but Bennett pulls back from the edge. Chapter Six asks how narratives of intrinsic vitality of things linked up to an American "culture of life" produced policies prohibiting stem-cell research and brought on the war in Iraq.

At this intermission, Bennett leaves her reader asking: does Newton ever let go? Is it enough to change the sign on the matter of mechanical physics from inert to dynamic without rethinking fundamental epistemological and ontological con-cepts (discourse, causality, agency, knowing, power, identity, embodiment, objectivity, space and time)? Chapter Five opens with her genealogical loyalty toward a tradition of thinking inhabited by "Epicurus, Lucretius, Thomas Hobbes, Baruch Spinoza, Denis Diderot, Friedrich Nietzsche, Henry David Thoreau and others" (the "and others," as we have already noted, include Bruno Latour, Gilles Deleuze, Félix Guattari, Henri Bergson and Hans Driesch).[35] The genealogy intrigues for its exclusions. It skips from classical to early modern thinkers (forget Western medieval thinking of mat-tering by such as Bernard Sylvestris and Nicolas Oresme); then it pauses at Bergson and Driesch, who wrote just prior

[34] Bennett, *Vibrant Matter*, 56.
[35] Bennett, *Vibrant Matter*, 62.

to the quantum revolution of matter in the 1920s and 1930s. It then leaps over to theorists of the later twentieth century. With the exception of her passionate claim on dynamic matter, Bennett leaves most of the representationalisms of mechanical Newtonian physics in place. This framework hobbles her important effort to think the question of the concluding two chapters: what are the implications of vibrant materiality for political theory?

Bennett's project is too urgent to be lost to Newtonian representationalism and Barad's profound reworking of Newtoniasms based on her quantum knowledge of dynamic matter[36] (for a schematic summary of issues at stake) can be of great use. I propose a *postmedieval* Symposium that would bring Bennett and Barad together.[37] Imagine them intraacting with this list of Bennett's questions:[38] that discourse is for humans,[39] that non-linguistic things can't know,[40] that a parliament of things might undo the hard boundaries between human and non-human,[41] that vibrant matter might "cause" political outcomes.[42]

I would like to pose my own question to this proposed symposium: can there be a vital materialist psychoanalysis? Bennett broaches the psychoanalytic when she invokes the process of identification: "To put it bluntly, my conatus will not let me 'horizontalize' the world completely. I also identify with members of my species, insofar as they are bodies most

[36] For a schematic summary of issues at stake, see Barad, *Meeting the Universe Halfway*, 88–89.

[37] Barad, *Meeting the Universe Halfway*, 88–89.

[38] Please note that I have offered page references to where Barad takes up just these questions posed by Bennett.

[39] Bennett, *Vibrant Matter*, 2; Barad, *Meeting the Universe Halfway*, 146–153.

[40] Bennett, *Vibrant Matter*, 104; Barad, *Meeting the Universe Halfway*, 340–342.

[41] Bennett, *Vibrant Matter*, 104; Barad, *Meeting the Universe Halfway*, 58–59.

[42] Bennett, *Vibrant Matter*, 107; Barad, *Meeting the Universe Halfway*, 175–179.

similar to mine."[43] When she criticizes demystification, "that most popular of practices in critical theory" as always being about something human, Bennett forecloses her own powerful constitution of the "human" in *Vibrant Matter*.[44] The human is never given in advance as Barad argues.[45] How the human might be given is the quandary at stake in Santner's *The Royal Remains*.

SANTNER

> Political theology and biopolitics are, in a word, *two modes of appearance of the flesh* whose enjoyment entitles its bearers to the enjoyment of entitlements in the social space they inhabit.
>
> Eric L. Santner, *The Royal Remains*

Eric L. Santner is the Philip and Ida Romberg Professor of Modern German Studies at the University of Chicago. *The Royal Remains* is a love story, a *carniture*. Santner asks how humans might come to love the undead flesh of the king's second body that has taken up shelter, like an inflaming splinter, in modern bodies. This excessive matter lodged itself, when, during the French Revolution, the transfer of the second body of the King to the new bearers of sovereignty, the People, failed. Santner claims the French Revolution as his "historical index"—sign of the modern: "the task would be, in a word, to *incarnate* in some ostensibly new way, the *excarnated* principle of sovereignty."[46]

His allegory of this breakdown is Jacques-Louis David's *The Death of Marat* (1793).[47] As a failed cult object (Marat could not be converted into the *new* Real Presence of the

---

[43] Bennett, *Vibrant Matter*, 104.

[44] Bennett, *Vibrant Matter*, xiv.

[45] Barad, *Meeting the Universe Halfway*, 205–212. The work of psychoanalyst Bracha L. Ettinger, *The Matrixial Borderspace* (Minneapolis: University of Minnesota Press, 2006), offers a way of thinking of a vital materialist psychoanalysis.

[46] Santner, *The Royal Remains*, 92.

[47] Santner, *The Royal Remains*, 89.

Revolution), this painting inaugurates visual modernism. David brings this historical impasse to presence in the painterly void of the empty upper half of the canvas. This abstract space stands in for the missing and impossible representation of the People—a kind of "ectoplasmic substance of this haunting,"[48] or what Santner more closely defines as the "representational deadlock situated at the transition from royal to popular sovereignty."[49]

Santner unfolds his philosophy of the flesh in six chapters. Each one transposes a major debate in contemporary theory of sovereignty into a Lacanian psychoanalytic key.[50] Only those creatures that enter the symbolic space of the signifier matter. Up to the French Revolution, according to Santner, the sovereign was the one who decided on human signification in this field of immanence.[51] This is an unflinching account of the human (non-signifiers need not apply). Those thinkers, such as Spinoza and Deleuze, who have focused on the conatus, especially the conatus of "becoming animal," he calls practitioners of "*pantheism of flesh and nerve*" or "*biopolitical pantheism*."[52] Santner thus misses an opportunity to expand his analysis to include creatures that know and can and do become what I call *res sacra* (things which can be abandoned and destroyed by political theology and biopolitics), even if the things do not signify.[53] My concern with his stance can be rephrased: how can theorists of sovereignty raise questions in the psychoanalytic register in such a way that they do not consolidate that register, that is, decide on

[48] Santner, *The Royal Remains*, 93.

[49] Santner, *The Royal Remains*, 95.

[50] If readers are not familiar with the terms of this debate, Santner provides a clear guide and I will not attempt to define this extensive vocabulary here.

[51] Santner's concept of immanence: "immanence is itself an internally disordered space, one 'curved' by the presence in it of an element that belongs to neither nature and culture" (*The Royal Remains*, 209).

[52] Santner, *The Royal Remains*, 133–138, emphasis in original.

[53] Barad, *Meeting the Universe Halfway*, 340–342.

that register? The sovereign is the one who decides. How may psychoanalytic theorists remain open to a notion of psychoanalysis that is always differing from itself and, perhaps as my conclusion will suggest, a psychoanalytic theory in need of mourning its own sovereign trauma?

Most of all Santner is interested in the *fantasy* of sovereignty. In the first chapter he needs to distinguish his philosophy of the flesh from that articulated by Esposito in *Bíos* and he offers a trenchant critique of Esposito's formulation of immunization.[54] Because Esposito remains at the conceptual level of his dialectic, he cannot understand the *fantasy* of immunization: "there is, I think, still a great deal of work to be done before one can attach any sort of radical hope, let alone messianism, to a new thinking of the flesh."[55]

Santner also chastises Agamben for being too literal about the flesh (it is not what you think—that stuff underneath the skin) and, therefore, Agamben cannot discern fully what is at stake with the state of exception. Santner makes his first pass through defining what he means by the flesh: "It (the flesh) is, in a word, the peculiar substance that ultimately *drives* the political theologies of sovereignty and the science fictions of immunological monstrosities, two seemingly disparate traditions that in some sense converge in Hobbes' *Leviathan*."[56]

Chapter Two is devoted to a reading of Santner's "key guide," Ernst Kantorowicz's study *The King's Two Bodies* (1957). He shows how Kantorowicz's famous reading of the deposition of King Richard II in Act 4 of Shakespeare's tragedy by that name can be understood as the paradoxical exposure of the sovereign to the state of exception. Santner uses his reading to reformulate Agamben's concept of bare life: bare life does not involve the separation of zoê from bíos, as Agamben would have it; instead, it marks their jointure in a surplus of immanence, that surplus, the matter of the flesh.[57]

[54] Roberto Esposito, *Bíos: Biopolitics and Philosophy*, trans. Timothy C. Campbell (Minneapolis: University of Minnesota Press, 2006).
[55] Santner, *The Royal Remains*, 31.
[56] Santner, *The Royal Remains*, 19.
[57] Santner, *The Royal Remains*, 58.

When Richard is deposed what is left on stage is a fleshly organ without a body.

Paradoxically, Santner never addresses how Kantorowicz's text functions as its own *fantasy* of sovereignty written in the mid-1950s, written at the same time and under the same signifying pressures faced by the other interlocutors of Santner's study: for example, Lacan was lecturing on the psychoses (1955-1956); Francis Bacon was painting his study of Pope Innocent X; Carl Schmitt was publishing *Hamlet or Hecuba* (1956), Samuel Beckett was drafting his *Endgame,* which was first performed on 3 April 1957, just one month after the publication of the *King's Two Bodies.* Santner staunchly dismisses studies that have attempted to "deconstruct" or "historicize" Kantorowicz on the claim of his interest in the "underside of fantasy."[58]

To read Kantorowicz at the historiographical level, as Santner does, that is, as the underwriting of the *Royal Remains,* is to stop too soon. His reading misses a crucial opportunity for his love story: to love the undead flesh of the sovereign that resides at the heart of Kantorowicz's own fort/da game. Here is another side of Kantorowicz, what I like to think of as the "hole" in his immanence,[59] to be found in an article he published three years before his death.[60] In it he held a séance with his Warburg Institute colleagues (dead and alive) Ernst Kitzinger, Fritz Saxl, and Meyer Schapiro, each of whom had written on an early medieval carved stone cross, a "tree of life cross," known by the name Ruthwell Cross. Kantorowicz offered a midrashic reading—uncharacteristic of his research—of a disputed carved figure on the cross, known in the art historical literature as the "archer." Relying on the scholarship of Louis Ginzberg, a noted Talmudist and author of the multi-volume series *Legends of the Jews,* Kantorowicz argued that the archer represented Ishmael, son of Abraham's evicted concubine, Hagar. Christians

[58] Santner, *The Royal Remains,* 45–46.
[59] Santner, *The Royal Remains,* 210.
[60] Ernst Kantorowicz, "The Archer in the Ruthwell Cross," *Art Bulletin* 42.1(1960): 57–59.

imagined Muslims as sons of Hagar. A midrash of Ishmael as wilderness archer and wild man grew up around him. In this midrashic essay, Kantorowicz touches his own (suppressed) genealogy as a grandson of a noted Poznan rabbi, and his work as a young military attaché in Istanbul during World War I, where he supervised the German work on the Orient Express and went on to write a dissertation on Muslim craft guilds. Kantorowicz was interested in the Tree of Life. It appears as an entry in the index of *The King's Two Bodies*, "Tree, Inverted."[61]

The zombie flesh of the sovereign and psychoanalysis are closely bound. In Chapter 3 Santner traces how Freud, "philosopher of the flesh," in his insights into the libido and the death drive offers a new thinking that can be an endgame for the failed sovereign transference to the People during the French Revolution. Santner broaches a psychoanalytic theory of trauma (to be adumbrated in Chapter 6) with a beautiful analysis of Freud's writing on the fort/da game. What interests him about the nature of a traumatic tear and its naming is its undecidability:

> … the facilitation of human vitality within a field of representations is driven by an excess that has no proper place within that field; in every such "matrix" there remains a surplus. Freud's fundamental insight was that without that surplus element (the flesh in Santner's terms) we would never experience questions of meaning as being genuinely *meaningful*, as being *truly worth our while*.[62]

He concludes the chapter with a reading of Kafka's Odradek, a character, as we have seen, also read by Bennett in *Vibrant Matter*. More than a lively thing, Odradek, spool-creature, is for Santner another example of an organ without a body (kin to the deposed Richard II), a spectral materialization of the zombie flesh of the sovereign.

[61] Kantorowicz, *The King's Two Bodies*, 565.
[62] Santner, *The Royal Remains*, 73, emphasis in original.

But is Freud's theory of trauma more of a medievalism, rather than a modernism, as Santner robustly contends? Freud's exemplary example of traumatic repetition, cited at the opening of *Beyond the Pleasure Principle*, is drawn from Tasso's epic of the First Crusade, published in 1581. Readers of *Gerusalemme Liberata* (*Jerusalem Delivered*) will know that Freud truncated the account of the second wounding of Clorinda, a Muslim warrior, by the Christian Crusader, Tancred. When she speaks through the wound of the tree bludgeoned by Tancred (his second wounding of Clorinda), she lets Tancred know that she is not alone. Buried with her, she explains, are fellow martyrs (Saracens and French soldiers who have fallen in the fight). Tasso intended the wounded tree as the second burial-place for the Crusader archive—a poetic crypt that would silence once and for all the noisy ghosts of the First Crusade.[63] So successful was his encryption that Freud was deafened to the words of Clorinda's ghost who spoke as "dying of the dying voice" and so he repeated the Crusader trauma in his paradigm of Western trauma in *Beyond the Pleasure Principle*.[64] What happens when the trauma of the medieval theologico-political is foreclosed in the very theory of trauma? What happens when the theory of trauma is itself a traumatic crypt of medievalism?

Santner devotes Part Two of the *Royal Remains* (Chapters 4, 5, and 6) to exquisite readings of visual modernism (David's *Death of Marat* and the paintings of Francis Bacon) and two examples of literary modernism: the *Chandos Letter* by Hugo von Hofmannsthal, published in 1902, and *The Notebooks of Malte Laurids Brigge* by Rainer Maria Rilke, published in 1910. He joins these readings with critical studies of Deleuze and Esposito, both of whom have published on Bacon. He explores the resonances of Walter Benjamin with Rilke. These literary readings exemplify Santner's methodology: "what I have attempted to do in this study is also, in

[63] Kathleen Biddick, "Unbinding the Flesh in the Time that Remains: Crusader Martyrdom Then and Now," *GLQ: A Journal of Lesbian and Gay Studies* 13.2–3 (2007): 197–228.
[64] Santner, *The Royal Remains*, 160.

some sense, to bring together texts and figures that exhibit similar 'frequencies' of vital intensity, with the aim of clarifying just what it is that is vibrating, just *what sort of vital intensity* is at issue."[65] The frequencies, in the end, vibrate with love: "this is a love that is willing—that gathers the will and the courage—to endure the encounter with the flesh that twitches in an always singular fashion in the other."[66]

In contrast, the frequencies of the critiques advanced in Part Two (Bataille, Deleuze, Esposito and others) jolt like flesh caught in the tuner. The impasse comes, I argue, from the project's stranglehold on its "precise historical index." My reading of Lanfranc has sought to show the untimeliness of the flesh. It cannot support a historical index and a historical index cannot support the flesh. With great clarity Shakespeare understood such untimeliness of the flesh and staged it in Acts 4 and 5 of the tragedy of *King Richard II*. Kantorowicz and Santner exit the play after their analysis of the deposition scene of Act 3. In these crucial and under-analyzed final two acts, Shakespeare audaciously uncouples the Real Presence from sovereign flesh where it had been pinned for five centuries. The playwright also understood how the sovereign flesh could be and was re-constituted fantastically off stage in the Christian Crusader imaginary. In the closing lines of *King Richard II*, Bolingbroke vows to go on Crusade: "I'll make a voyage to the Holy Land, / To wash this blood off my guilty hand: / March sadly after; grace my mourning here. / In weeping after this untimely bier."[67] A decade prior to staging Shakespeare's tragedy, Clorinda had already whispered of the undecidability of the Crusader Imaginary, "An incarnation, or a burial, I cannot say."[68]

---

[65] Santner, *The Royal Remains*, xix, emphasis in original.
[66] Santner, *The Royal Remains*, 243.
[67] William Shakespeare, *King Richard II*, 5.6.49–52.
[68] Tasso, *Jerusalem Delivered* (1581), trans. Anthony M. Esolin (Baltimore: Johns Hopkins University Press, 2000), Canto 13, ll. 51–52.

Chapter 3

Arthur's Two Bodies and the Bare Life of the Archives

Truly the Jew is able to have nothing that belongs to himself, because whatever he acquires is not for himself but for the king, because they do not live for themselves but for others and so they acquire from others and not for themselves.

Henry de Bracton, *On the Laws and Customs of England*[1]

[1] "Iudaeus vero nihil proprium habere potest, quia quicquid acquirit non sibi acquirit sed regi, quia non vivunt sibi ipsis sed aliis et sic aliis acquirunt et non sibi ipsis": Henry de Bracton, *On the Laws and Customs of England* (*De Legibus et Consuetudinibus Angliae*), ed. George E. Woodbine, trans. Samuel E. Thorne, 4 vols. (Cambridge: Harvard University Press, 1968-1977), 4:208. Note that this oft-cited passage is an *addicio* to a section on warranty and Thorne publishes it (208n3). Thorne lists the manuscripts that contain this *addicio* in 1:417. The core of this treatise was written in the 1220s and 1230s and then was subsequently much revised according to Paul Brand, "The Age of Bracton," *Proceedings of the British Academy* 89 (1996): 65–89. The dating of this particular passage is in need of more scholarly work.

Thus a famous English legal tract of the thirteenth century defines the status of Jews.[2] This chapter seeks to write in between the singular body, "the Jew" (*Iudaeus*), and plural bodies embodied in the verb, "they live" (*vivunt*). It wagers that this medieval legal text (and others like it) needs to be folded into genealogies of contemporary sovereignty and biopolitics argued by the philosopher Giorgio Agamben.[3] Crucial to Agamben's understanding of biopolitics is the Roman juridical concept of *homo sacer*—that is, the one who cannot be sacrificed but may be murdered without penalty. Such a legal exception reduces the human body to what Agamben calls "bare life" (a "zone of indistinction" that shuttles back and forth between *zoe* and *bíos*), a biopolitical condition that, he argues, has now become the rule of contemporary sovereignty. Also intrinsic to sovereignty, according to Agamben, is the archive (the said and the unsaid) and by implication history itself. This chapter asks: What might the one *who may have nothing,* the Jew, a kind of *homo sacer* imagined by thirteenth-century English law, have to do with the constitution of Western sovereignty and its archives?

Medieval historians have already expended much painstaking scholarship on the juridical status of Jews under English law.[4] Rather than take sides in the debate over the question of their freedom or unfreedom, this chapter, instead, offers a biopolitical perspective on the question of Jews in the constitution of archive and constructions of temporality in Anglo-Norman England. My starting point is Geoffrey of Monmouth's *History of the Kings of Britain* (*Historia Regum*

---

[2] This chapter originally appeared, in slightly different form, as Kathleen Biddick, "Arthur's Two Bodies and the Bare Life of the Archives," in *Cultural Diversity in the British Middle Ages: Archipelago, Island, England*, ed. Jeffrey Jerome Cohen (New York: Palgrave, 2008), 117–134.

[3] Giorgio Agamben, *Homo Sacer: Sovereignty, Power and Bare Life,* trans. Daniel Heller-Roazen (Stanford: Stanford University Press, 1998) and *Remnants of Auschwitz: The Witness and the Archive,* trans. Daniel Heller-Roazen (New York: Zone Books, 1999).

[4] See note 35 below.

Britanniae, c. 1138, hereafter *HRB*).[5] This study refrains too from lively contemporary debates over the purported ethnic (Welsh, Breton, Anglo-Norman, or English) identifications and border writing at stake in Geoffrey's history. Hugh M. Thomas has offered a good overview of this scholarship in *The English and the Normans: Ethnic Hostility, Assimilation, and Identity 1066-c. 1220,* and rich examples of such border tracings may be found in the works of Jeffrey Jerome Cohen, Laurie A. Finke and Martin B. Shichtman, Patricia Clare Ingham, and Michelle Warren.[6] Instead, I am asking about the biopolitics of Geoffrey's invention of King Arthur as a "twin person," that is, one who is both mortally wounded (*letaliter vulneratus est)*[7] and yet lives—he is taken to be healed on the isle of Avalon ("qui illinc ad sananda vulnera sua in insulam Avallonis evectus").[8] Geoffrey's concept of a royal twin person offers, I argue, not only a formative biopolitical moment in the medieval fabrication of the king's two bodies (a juridical concept that would become central to medieval sovereignty), but also a stunning example of how mundane contemporary bureaucratic practices lodged themselves in such bio-

---

[5] Latin citations are from *The Historia Regum Britanniae of Geoffrey of Monmouth: I. Bern, Burgerbibliothek, MS 568,* ed. Neil Wright (Cambridge: D.S. Brewer, 1984) (hereafter Wright), and to enable comparisons for readers, I cite from the English translation, *History of the Kings of Britain,* trans. Lewis Thorpe (New York: Penguin, 1966) (hereafter Thorpe).

[6] Hugh M. Thomas, *The English and the Normans: Ethnic Hostility, Assimilation, and Identity 1066-c. 1220* (Oxford: Oxford University Press, 2003); Jeffrey Jerome Cohen, *Hybridity, Identity and Monstrosity in Medieval Britain: On Difficult Middles* (New York: Palgrave Macmillan, 2006); Laurie A. Finke and Martin B. Shichtman, *King Arthur and the Myth of History* (Gainesville: University of Florida Press, 2004); Patricia Clare Ingham, *Sovereign Fantasies: Arthurian Romance and the Making of Britain* (Philadelphia: University of Pennsylvania Press, 2001); and Michelle R. Warren, *History on the Edge: Excalibur and the Borders of Britain, 1100-1300* (Minneapolis: University of Minnesota Press, 2000).

[7] Wright, 132.

[8] Wright, 132.

political inventions. By tracing out the sovereign archival palimpsest of Geoffrey's text, it is possible to write a secret history of its spectral debt.

THE INFINITE LABORS OF THE ARCHIVE

> These duties (Master of the Exchequer Writing Office) need but few words to explain, but demand almost endless labors.
> Richard Fitz Nigel, *Dialogus de Scaccario*[9]

When in 1129 Geoffrey of Monmouth witnessed the first charter at Oxford to bear his signature, royal archivists were radically transforming their temporal capacities to monitor income and debt on a continuous annual basis.[10] Henry I (1100-1135) introduced new linking technologies designed to join the discrete bureaucratic activities of reviewing customary receipts (often in the form of notched wooden tallies) rendered by sheriffs with an efficient fiscal computation based on the principle of the abacus. Scribes recorded the royal sources of income and debt (county by county), as well as the names of creditors and debtors, on carefully prepared parchment rolls and then preserved these documents for ongoing consultation. By inaugurating the archival series known as the Pipe Rolls, the royal bureaucracy precociously embodied the temporal concept of "continuity" (from 1158 onward, the Pipe Rolls, are available in a virtually continuous series).[11] In his famous study, *The King's Two Bodies: A Study*

---

[9] "que quidem officia, licet paucis exprimantur verbis, infinitis tamen vix expleri possunt laboribus": Richard Fitz Nigel, Treasurer of the Exchequer (c. 1158) and former Archdeacon of Ely (c. 1160) wrote about the procedures of the Exchequer in the late 1170s; cited from Richard Fitz Nigel, *Dialogus de Scaccario: The Course of the Exchequer,* ed. and trans. Charles Johnson, with corrections by F.E.L. Carter and D.E. Greenway (Oxford: Clarendon Press, 1983), 26.

[10] For the charters witnessed by Geoffrey, see H.E. Salter, "Geoffrey of Monmouth and Oxford," *English Historical Review* 34 (July 1919): 382–385.

[11] Kathleen Biddick, "People and Things: Power in Early English

in *Medieval Political Theology,* Ernst Kantorowicz argued
that the fabrication of just such a notion of continuity was
crucial to the medieval imagining of the corporate, undying
body of the sovereign, the king's second body.[12]

The Pipe Rolls secured this temporal continuity through
its "scriptural" archival procedures (not even erasures were
allowed) described in the late 1170s by Richard Fitz Nigel but
already materially in evidence in the organization of the 1130
Pipe Roll.[13] The scribe first pricked and ruled each parchment sheet to be bound in Roll and then further broke down
the space of the page by labeling compartments in which
relevant information was to be entered (see Figure 1, overleaf). The Rolls were thus conceived as graphic modules that
cast a fiscal grid (with all the normalizing pretensions of such
coordinates) over the English counties (and, in 1130, the
Welsh territories of Pembroke and Carmarthen). Although
seeming to encode a diversity of local arrangements, the
bureaucratic practices embodied in the Rolls, in fact, actually

Development," *Comparative Studies in Society and History* 32
(1990): 3–23. The literature on the Pipe Rolls is enormous; basic
references may be found in my 1990 article. See, also, M.T. Clanchy,
From Memory to Written Record: England, 1066-1307 (Cambridge:
Harvard University Press, 1979). Note that Clanchy underscores the
use of the Domesday Book (bound as a book): "seems to have been
principally symbolic, like the regalia, since it cannot be shown that it
was frequently consulted at the time Fitz Neal was writing in c. 1179
(that is time of the composition of the *Dialogue of the Exchequer*)"
(122). The Pipe Rolls inaugurate the kind of continuous bureaucracy that is relevant to this discussion of Geoffrey of Monmouth.

[12] Ernst H. Kantorowicz, *The King's Two Bodies: A Study in Medieval Political Theology* (Princeton: Princeton University Press, 1957);
see Chapter 4 on continuity and corporations, but note that when
Kantorowicz discusses the importance of annual taxation (284–
291), he neglects to mention the Pipe Rolls. Ingham draws attention
to the resonance between Geoffrey's Arthur and Kantorowicz in her
Sovereign Fantasies, 4–5.

[13] The ruling and compartmentalizing of the parchment for the Pipe
Rolls is described in Nigel, *Dialogus de Scaccario,* 29–30.

worked to deterritorialize local difference.[14]

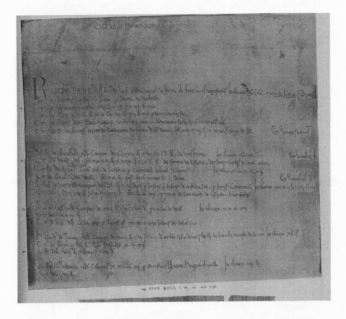

Figure 1. Public Record Office, Pipe Roll, 31 Henry I (1130), membrane 6. Source: Charles Johnson and Hilary Jenkinson, *English Court Hand: A.D. 1066-1500* (Oxford: Clarendon Press, 1915), Plate IV.A.

The earliest preserved Pipe Roll (but not the *inaugural* roll of this accounting system) from 31 Henry I (1130) can be studied as a map tracing out the archival coordinates of the archdeaconal milieu of Geoffrey of Monmouth (see Figure 1).[15] Walter the Archdeacon (Geoffrey's mentor, provost of

[14] For discussion of how such deterritorialization and reterritorialization worked in both archive and in the landscape of settlement, see Biddick, "People and Things."

[15] *The Pipe Roll of 31 Henry I* (Michaelmas 1130), transcribed by Rev. Joseph Hunter for the Record Commission in an edition of 1833 and reprinted (London: H.M. Stationery Office, 1929), hereafter cited as *PR*.

his Oxford college of St. George, and purported owner of the ancient book upon which Geoffrey based his "translation") appears in the 1130 Pipe Roll (hereafter PR) charged with a large sum of 180 marks (equivalent to the cost of the farm of the town Stamford that year) for a plea (*pro placitum*) between himself and Restold, the former sheriff of the county.[16] Walter paid roughly half of his charge (sixty-eight shillings), and his balance owing was recorded for future audit. This brief entry does two things: it locates Walter enmeshed in the royal justice system, and it inscribes him in the continuous archival discipline of the Pipe Rolls, since the payment of his outstanding balance can be checked annually. Although it is impossible to know the exact nature of Walter's business with the former sheriff, the greedy competition of the archdiaconate for court fees was already established by this date.[17]

An older intellectual contemporary of Geoffrey, Adelard of Bath, also appears in the 1130 Pipe Roll. Scribes record his pardon, by courtesy of royal writ, of a murder fine (4 shillings, 6 pence) levied against the hundreds of the county of Wiltshire.[18] Renowned Arabist and author of treatises on the abacus and astrolabe, Adelard has been associated with the new computational technologies used in generating the Pipe Rolls, and some historians place him as a clerk in the Exchequer and thus intimately involved with its archival disciplines.[19] Historians have also speculated that the very form of

[16] *PR,* 3. Restold was sheriff of Oxfordshire between 1122 and 1127: Judith A. Green, *English Sheriffs to 1154,* Public Record Office Handbooks 24 (London: H.M. Stationery Office, 1970), 70.

[17] Jean Scammell, "The Rural Chapter in England from the Eleventh to the Fourteenth Century," *English Historical Review* 86 (1971): 1–21.

[18] *PR,* 22.

[19] For basic work on Adelard of Bath, see Charles Burnett, *Adelard of Bath: An English Scientist and Arabist of the Early Twelfth Century* (London: Warburg Institute Surveys and Texts, 1987), 14; Charles Homer Haskins, *Studies in the History of Mediaeval Science* (Cambridge: Harvard University Press, 1924), 20–42; and Reginald L. Poole, *The Exchequer in the Twelfth Century* (Oxford: Clarendon,

the Pipe Rolls, a *rotulus* (roll), and not the folded quire of parchment typical of the construction of the book (*libellus*), bears the traces of the contacts that Adelard and those like him had with Spanish Jews educated in Arabic sciences and for whom the roll would be a familiar format for writing.[20] Geoffrey of Monmouth undoubtedly had Adelard in mind when he praised the astronomical computations and prognosticating studies undertaken at the Caerlon college of the two hundred philosophers:

The city also contained a college of two hundred learned men, who were skilled in astronomy and the other arts, and who watched with great attention the courses of the stars and so by their careful computations prophesied for King Arthur any prodigies due in his time.

[preterea ginnasium ducentorum phylosoforum habebat qui astronomia atque ceteris artibus eruditi cursus stellarum diligenter obseruabant et prodigia eorum temporum ventura regi Arturo veris argumentis predicebant.][21]

The Pipe Rolls of 1130 also map the coordinates of King Henry's royal control over Jews. The reader of the Pipe Rolls can track Henry as he used his arrogated sovereign right over Jews in England to broker indebtedness. For instance, Richard, son of Giselbertus, owed the king 200 marks of silver for

1912), 44, 50–53, 56–57.

[20] There are elusive discussions of Jewish and Arabic influences on the actual roll format of the Pipe Rolls in Clanchy, *From Memory to Written Record,* 108–110, and Poole, *Exchequer,* 52–57. For an overview, see Brigitte Bedos-Rezak, "The Confrontation of Orality and Textuality: Jewish and Christian Literacy in the Eleventh and Twelfth Century in Northern France," *Rashi 1049-1990,* ed. Gabrielle Sed-Rajna (Paris: Les Editions du Cert, 1993), 541–558, and Jeremy Johns, *Arabic Administration* in *Norman Sicily* (Cambridge: Cambridge University Press, 2002), 1–10.

[21] Thorpe, 227; Wright, 110.

the help that the king gave him against his debt to the Jews.[22] Rubi Gotsche (the Pipe Roll rendering of the name of Rabbi Yosi of Rouen) and other Jews, to whom Ranulf, Lord of Chester, was indebted, are recorded as owing ten marks for the help of the king regarding the count's debts.[23] The largest fine (£2,000, or 13.25 percent of the total fees demanded by the royal treasury for the year) in the 1130 Pipe Roll is levied against the Jews of London for killing (*interficerent*) a sick man.[24] Rabbi Yosi of Rouen is among those Jews listed defraying this fine and he is the earliest *rav* or master to be linked to Rouen, the capital of Normandy and a center of Jewish learning distinguished enough to have been visited by Abraham Ibn Ezra around 1149.[25] The entries discussed so far show how the Pipe Rolls inscribed clerics like Geoffrey of Monmouth with archival practices that fabricated continuity and also bore the material traces of forms of knowledge and writing practices gained by contact of the Anglo-Norman court with Muslims and Jews.

During the 1130s, as Geoffrey was composing the *HRB,* his archdiaconal circle was also busy confecting its own archival innovations. Their work took the form of inventing new legal archives.[26] The *Leges Edwardi Confessoris* (hereaf-

---

[22] *PR,* 53.

[23] *PR,* 149.

[24] *PR,* 149. The total for different forms of income and the overall totals for the 1130 Pipe Roll are tabulated by Judith A. Green, *The Government of England under Henry I* (Cambridge: Cambridge University Press, 1986).

[25]Norman Golb, *The Jews in Medieval Normandy* (Cambridge: Cambridge University Press, 1998), 225. For a discussion of the Jewish population in England in the mid-twelfth century, see Kevin T. Streit, "The Expansion of the English Jewish Community in the Reign of King Stephen," *Albion* 15 (1993): 177–192. Important also is the collection of essays *The Jews of Medieval Britain: Historical, Literary and Archaeological Perspectives,* ed. Patricia Skinner (Woodbridge: Boydell & Brewer, 2003).

[26] Indeed, later versions of the *Leges Edwardi Confessori* (hereafter *LEC*) written at the end of the twelfth century interpolated extracts from Geoffrey's *HRB*: see Walter Ullmann, "On the Influence of

ter, *LEC*), composed most likely at Lincoln around 1136 (remember that Walter of Oxford, Geoffrey's mentor, was an archdeacon of Lincoln), claimed to record the *laga Edwardi* (law at the time of Edward the Confessor). The opening of the tract constructs a deterritorializing fiction of continuity.[27] It tells how in 1070 William the Conqueror summoned English nobles (*Anglos nobiles*), twelve from each county, and asked them to declare (*edicarent*) the rules of their laws and customs (*incidentes legem suaram et consuetudinum*).[28] Upon hearing them, William with the advice of his barons authorized them (*et sic auctorizate sunt legis Regis Aedwardi*).[29] The modern editor of the *LEC*, Bruce R. O'Brien, shows this text to be an imposture: "the *Leges Edwardi* is not a translation of Old English laws, nor is any part of it derived from a preconquest English legal text, as is the case with all the other codes. When the author does use another source, it is like those used in *Leges Henrici Primi*, a Frankish work."[30]

The *LEC* describes the king boldly as the vicar of the highest King (Christ) (*rex autem, qui vicarius summi Regis est*).[31] Such a legal vision of royal embodiment resonates with

Geoffrey of Monmouth on Legal History," *Speculum Historiale: Geschichte im Spiegel von Geschichtsschreibung und Geschichtsdeutung*, eds. C. Bauer, L. Bohn, and M. Muller (Freiburg: Verlag Karl Alber, 1965), 258–276.

[27] This section is indebted to the following study: Bruce R. O'Brien, *God's Peace and King's Peace: The Laws of Edward the Confessor* (Philadelphia: University of Pennsylvania Press, 1999). O'Brien dates the composition of the *LEC* to around 1136 (49) and thinks Lincoln the most likely place for its composition (53). His argument for it being the product of archdiaconal circles is persuasive. This treatise enjoyed great popularity during the twelfth century (at least six manuscripts in three versions survive). For a perceptive overview of law texts drawn up in the twelfth century, see Patrick Wormald, *The Making of English Law: King Alfred to the Twelfth Century*, 2 vols. (Oxford: Blackwell, 1999), 1:465–476.

[28] *LEC*, 192–193.

[29] *LEC*, 192–193.

[30] *LEC*, 29.

[31] *LEC*, 174–175.

the contemporary theology of kingship articulated by the author of the *Norman Anonymous,* a collection of treatises attributed to William Bona Anima, Archbishop of Rouen (1079-1110) or his archdiaconal circles.[32] Among his associates, the Archbishop of Rouen could count leading English churchmen: Lanfranc, William Giffard (Bishop of Winchester), and Gerard (Archbishop of York). William had been a monk at Bec, an abbot at Caen, and also a sometime supporter of the abbey of Fecamp (archival material from which abbey ended up bound with Geoffrey's *History* in the Bern manuscript).[33] As archbishop of Rouen, William was also acquainted with Norman dukes and kings including Henry I, who spent more than half his reign in Normandy. Under the archbishop's watch, Crusader bands from Normandy entered Rouen in the autumn of 1096 and massacred the Jews of the city who refused baptism.[34] In his treatises, William Bona

---

[32] The articulation of notions of the king's body in the *Norman Anonymous* (Cambridge, Corpus Christ College MS Lat. 415) were of great interest to Kantorowicz, *King's Two Bodies,* 42–92. The authorship has been worked out by George H. Williams and has been widely accepted: *The Norman Anonymous of 1100 A.D.: Towards the Identification and Evaluation of the so-called Anonymous of York,* Harvard Theological Studies 18 (Cambridge: Harvard University Press, 1951). Sections of the key tract 024Af on the theology of kingship have been translated by Oliver O'Donovan and Joan Lockwood O'Donovan, *From Irenaeus to Grotius: A Sourcebook in Christian Political Thought* (Cambridge: William B. Eerdmans, 1999), 250–259.

[33] Williams, *The Norman Anonymous,* 102–127, offers biographical details of William Bona Anima. It should be noted that Norman Cantor disagreed with this attribution in *Church, Kingship and Lay Infrastructure in England* (Princeton: Princeton University Press, 1958), 181–185. The fact that the tract came from a tightly enmeshed Anglo-Norman archdiaconal circle is not disputed. For the entanglement of this circle, see M. Brett, *The English Church under Henry I* (Oxford: Oxford University Press, 1975), 9. Wright describes the Fecamp materials bound in Bern, Burgerbibliothek, MS. 568, xxviii–xxxi.

[34] Golb, *Jews in Medieval Normandy,* 117.

Anima intertwined his theology of kingship (the king as vicar of Christ) with his speculations on the king's two bodies. William conceived of the king as a *gemma persona:* a twin person. When Geoffrey imagined Arthur as a *gemma persona* with a personal body that could be mortally wounded and a theological body that could not die, he echoed the legal and theological concepts circulating among Anglo-Norman canons in the earlier part of the twelfth century.

As a legal treatise, *LEC* is also noteworthy for setting a European precedent for defining the legal status of the Jew as property of the king:

> It should be known that all Jews, in whichever kingdom they may be, ought to be under the guardianship and protection of the liege king; nor can any one of them subject himself to any wealthy person without the license of the king, because the Jews themselves and all their possessions are the king's. But if someone detains them or their money, the king shall demand (them) as his own property if he wishes and is able.[35]

---

[35] *LEC,* 185; O'Brien, *God's Peace,* 184. Gavin Langmuir succinctly summarizes the implications of this clause in his essay "The Jews and the Archives of Angevin England: Reflections on Medieval Anti-Semitism," *Traditio* 19 (1963): 183–244. He observes: "we thus seem to be confronted with a clearly degraded legal status of Jews in England by about 1135, well before similar continental developments, and it should doubtless be seen as a result of the early strength of the English government" (200). Much subsequent debate about this clause has floundered on the status of property in twelfth-century England. See, for instance, Paul R. Hyams, "The Jews in Medieval England," in *England and Germany in the High Middle Ages,* eds. Alfred Haverkamp and Hanna Vollrath (London: Oxford University Press, 1996), 181–185. For an important continental perspective, see William Chester Jordan, "Jews, Regalian Rights, and the Constitution in Medieval France," *AJS Review* 23 (1998): 1–16. No historians have asked how this clause might have been *constitutive* of shaping notions of property. For an important discussion of the historiographical debate over the concept of property in twelfth-century England, see John Hudson, "Anglo-Norman Land Law and

[Sciendum est quod omnes Iudei, in quocumque regno sint, sub tutela et defensione Regis ligii debent esse; neque aliquis eorum potest se subdere alicui diviti sint licencia Regis, quia ipsi Iudei et omnia sua Regis sunt. Quod si aliquis detinuerit eos vel pecuniam eorum, requirat rex tanquam suum proprium, si vult et potest.]

LEC was a potent archival invention. It deterritorialized the Anglo-Saxon legal archive in order to territorialize the king as a twin body and to produce Jews as a juridical category. *LEC* elides Jews and their possessions with the king's double body. We have already seen the capacity of the king to "possess" the possessions of the Jews in the 1130 Pipe Rolls where the king exercised his rights to administer the debt of the Jews through various appeals by both Christians and Jews. Such legal appeals over debt cost money, and thus the king "doubled" his juridical control over debt. A half century later, in the next generation of English law books, pleas of debts would be very precisely defined as belonging to the king's two bodies, that is his crown (*corona*) and his dignity (*dignitas*) so claimed Ranulf Glanvill, Chief Justiciar, in *The Treatise on Laws and Customs of the Realm of England:* "pleas concerning the debts of laymen also belong to the crown and dignity of the lord king" ("placitum quoque de debitis laicorum spectat ad coronam et ad dignitatem domini Regis").[36]

Several decades ago, in his important discussion of *LEC,* Gavin Langmuir observed how this clause on possession of Jews, in its departure from Carolingian discourses, marked a break in the "rightlessness" of the Jews in medieval Europe. This break coincides, I argue, with cleaving the king's body into two persons in contemporary legal (*LEC*) and literary

the Origins of Property," in *Law and Government in Medieval England and Normandy* (Cambridge: Cambridge University Press, 1994), 198–223.

[36] *The Treatise on Laws and Customs of the Realm of England commonly called Glanvill,* ed. and trans. G.D.G. Hall, 2nd edn. (Oxford: Oxford University Press, 1993), 116 (with a note on further reading by M.T. Clanchy).

(*HRB*) texts. So far, I have been tracing the dispersed strands of archival technologies threaded through this cleavage: 1) the deterritorialization of geographic regions and local time through the Pipe Rolls that gridded space and marked time as a continuity for fiscal surveillance and dispersed over that grid the juridical right of the king over the debts of the Jews; and 2) the deterritorialization of the laws of the different Anglo-Saxon kingdoms through the fiction of the *LEC*.[37] Through this strategy, the law tract produced the juridical category of the Jew, over which category the king exercised sovereign right. This is not coincidence. The "it should be known" (*sciendum quod*) of the clause on Jews is intertwined with the "was established for this" (*hoc constitutus est*) of the king's body as the vicar of the highest king (*vicarius summi Regis est*).

THE TEARS OF THE ARCHIVE

> . . . the King ordered Ambrosius Merlin to explain just what the battle of the Dragons meant. Merlin immediately burst into tears. He went into a prophetic trance and then spoke as follows.[38]
>
> Geoffrey of Monmouth, *The History of the Kings of Britain*

In his important essay on the contexts and purposes of the *HRB*, John Gillingham emphasized the role of history as the sign of civilization in the twelfth century: "to be without history was the mark of the beast. Yet the Britains had virtu-

---

[37] Jeffrey Jerome Cohen points to precisely this kind of deterritorialization process in his discussion of Geoffrey of Monmouth in *Hybridity, Identity and Monstrosity*: "Geoffrey's revisionist historiography employed a dual strategy: explosive recovery of Britain's full history, and silent passing over of the richness of the English past" (68). Here I would simply deepen this observation to say that Geoffrey deterritorializes an Anglo-Saxon past to fabricate a *continuous* history.

[38] Thorpe, 171. "precepit rex Ambrosio Merlino dicere quid prelium draconum portendebat. Mox ille in fletum prorumpens spiritum hausit prophetie et ait": Wright, 74.

ally no history."[39] So far this chapter has suggested that the accomplishment of *HRB* was not simply to provide such a history, as Gillingham has observed, but rather to render it as a *continuous* archival event—a consecutive and orderly narrative ("actus omnium continue et ex ordine perpulcris orationibus").[40] In so doing the *HRB* enmeshes itself in the kinds of contemporary archival practices so far considered. At the same time Geoffrey's history also recounts what the neatly ruled membranes of the Pipe Rolls foreclosed and what the fictions of legal continuity the *LEC* suppresses—the violence of founding this sovereignty in and through archival continuity, and thus, the violence of founding the king's second body, the body that cannot die. Put in other words, *HRB* enacts the violence of traversing what Agamben has called the sovereign zone of indistinction:

> sovereign exception is the fundamental localization (Ortung), which does not limit itself to distinguishing what is inside from what is outside, but instead traces a threshold (the state of exception) between the two, on the basis of which outside and inside, the normal situation and chaos, enter into those complex topological relations that make the validity of the juridical order possible.[41]

I now want to consider how Geoffrey casts this "taking of the outside" as massacre. He brackets his history with tales of massacres, and he uses the Latin cognates of *caedes* (carnage, slaughter) to form the brackets. The *HRB* opens with two massacres in which the patricide Brutus and his Trojans

---

[39] John Gillingham, "The Context and Purposes of Geoffrey of Monmouth's *History of the Kings of Britain*," *Anglo-Norman Studies* 13 (1990-1991): 99–118, 105. Laurie A. Finke and Martin B. Shichtman emphasize Geoffrey's exercise in rendering the scattered into a "coherent narrative" in *King Arthur and the Myth of History* (38). I am urging that we deepen this observation to apprehend the implications of a *continuous* narrative.

[40] Thorpe, 51; Wright, 1.

[41] Agamben, *Homo Sacer*, 19.

slaughter unarmed (*inermis*) Greeks:

> the Trojans were fully equipped; their enemies were vir-
> tually unarmed. Because of this the Trojans pressed on all
> the more boldly and the slaughter that they inflicted was
> very heavy. They continued to attack in this way until al-
> most all the Greeks were killed and they had captured
> Antigonus (brother of Pandrasus, king of the Greeks) and
> his comrade Anacletus.[42]

> [Nam Troes armis muniti erant, certeri uero inermes.
> Unde audatiores insistentes cedem miserandam infer-
> ebant nec eos hoc modo infestare quieuerunt donec cunc-
> tis fere interfectis Antigonum et Anacletum eiusdem so-
> tium retinuerunt.][43]

The Trojans then treacherously launch their second attack.
By ruse, they enter the Greek camp during the night and slay
the sleeping (once again, unarmed) soldiers in their tents.
Brutus "beside himself with joy" (*fluctuans gaudio*) surveyed
the carnage (*caedis*) in the morning light.[44] Geoffrey uses
cognates for *caedes* for the last time in *HRB* to describe the
fatal battle between Mordred and Arthur:

> In the end, when they had passed much of the day in this
> way, Arthur, with a single division in which he had post-
> ed six thousand, six hundred and sixty-six men, charged
> at the squadron where he knew Mordred was. They hack-
> ed away through with their swords and Arthur continued
> to advance, inflicting terrible slaughter as he went. It was
> at this point that the accursed traitor was killed and many
> thousands of men with him.[45]

---

[42] Thorpe, 58
[43] Wright, 4.
[44] Thorpe, 61; Wright, 7.
[45] Thorpe, 261.

[Postquam autem multum diei in hunc modum duxerunt, irruit tandem Arturus cum agmine uno, quo sex milia et sexcentos sexaginta sex posuerat, in turmam illam ubi Modredum sciebat esse et uiam gladiis aperiendo eam penetrauit atque tristissimam cedem ingessit. Concidit namque proditor ille nephandus et multa milia secum.][46]

Geoffrey not only brackets his history with massacre, he closely binds slaughter and prophecy. The Saxon massacre of the unarmed British nobility at the council meeting at the Cloister of Ambrius[47] precipitates the events that lead up to the prophecies of Merlin. The story is familiar. Merlin, a "fatherless" child from the union of a woman and an incubus, is on the verge of becoming a kind of inverted Passover sign, because King Vortigern wishes to sprinkle his blood on the collapsing foundations of a massive defensive tower. Merlin halts the proceedings and orders an archaeological excavation—"iube fodere terram";[48] archaeology and the archive are also closely bound.[49] When King Vortigern asks Merlin to explain the fighting dragons uncovered by this excavation, Merlin first bursts into tears, and then his spirit is prophetically seized.

Geoffrey is careful to fashion an archival pedigree for Merlin's prophecies. He informs his reader that he has translated them from British to Latin, and he sends his edition by letter to Alexander, Bishop of Lincoln. Geoffrey thus aligns Merlin's prophecies (as he has aligned his history, *HRB*) with the "sayable" of the archive and thus with the imagined continuity of archival utterance. His painful and awkward suturing of massacre and prophecy seems to work feverishly: I, Geoffrey, recognize the violent foundational moment of the

[46] Wright, 131.
[47] Thorpe, 164–165.
[48] Wright, 73.
[49] Jacques Derrida, *Archive Fever: A Freudian Interpretation*, trans. Eric Prenowitz (Chicago: University of Chicago Press, 1995), 92: "As we have noted all along, there is an incessant tension here between archive and archaeology."

archive, but nevertheless I love the archive. What is the "un-sayable" of the archive that beats in the pulse of Geoffrey's fever? Like a Derrida before Derrida, Geoffrey prompts us to think about the relations of archivization and anarchiviza-tion: "the anarchive, in short the possibility of putting to death the very thing, whatever its name, which *carries the law in its tradition:* the archon of the archive, the table, *what* carries the table and who carries the table, the subjectile, the substrate, and the subject of the law."[50]

SONGS OF THE UNSAYABLE

If the reader listens closely, the unsayable of Geoffrey's ar-chive floats in the Whitsun air above King Arthur's crown-wearing feast at Caerlon, a momentous event assembled at a center of scholarship and music. Geoffrey unabashedly lures his readers with descriptions of the musical glory of this occasion at which the assembled clergy processed "chanting in exquisite harmony" (*miris modulationibus precinebat*),[51] and organ music filled the naves of the churches where Ar-thur and his queen celebrated their coronal sovereignty. In twelfth-century England, Pentecost (an understudied liturgi-cal feast of tongues and one aptly focused on by Geoffrey, the wizard of translation) was a powerful communal event dur-ing which local clergy paraded with their parishioners to the cathedral church where they were obliged to make oblations. In large dioceses that covered several counties, such as Lin-coln, to which Oxford belonged, the bishop allowed Pente-costal processions to congregate at Eynsham, where the men of Oxfordshire received an indulgence equivalent of the trek to Lincoln.[52] Important to this feast, and of special meaning

---

[50] Derrida, *Archive Fever,* 79.

[51] Thorpe, 228; Wright, 111.

[52] M. Brett, *The English Church Under Henry 1* (Oxford: Oxford University Press, 1975), 162–164. For comments (all too brief) on Pentecostal liturgical dramas at Barking Abbey, England and at Rouen in Normandy (they include the use of doves that figure in Geoffrey's procession), see Diane Dolan, *Le drame liturgique de*

for crown-wearing ceremonies with their special quasi-liturgical royal garments, was the singing of the hymn, *Te Deum*. This early medieval hymn is redolent with the images of processing martyrs robed in white garments washed by the precious blood of Christ.

The imagery and performance of Christian feast of Pentecost doubled and interacted with a concurrent Jewish celebration, the Feast of Weeks (Shavuot), a harvest festival of first fruits that commemorated the giving of the Torah. At Shavuot, Jewish families presented young schoolboys for induction into the yeshiva.[53] Israel Jacob Yuval has traced the traumatic festal intersections of Pentecost and Shavuot in his readings of the Mainz memorials in the *Hebrew Chronicles of the Crusades*, which commemorate the Jewish martyrdoms there when Crusader bands, intent on forced baptism, attacked the Jews of Mainz during the feast of Pentecost/Shavuot.[54] When Ashkenaz *paytanim* (liturgical poets) subsequently mourned this slaughter in liturgical hymns, they did so by imagining an archival device capable of recording and remembering traumatic events. They drew upon the Midrashic image of the *porphyrion* (royal purple cloak) and

Pâques en Normandie et en Angleterre au moyen age, Publications de L'Universite de Poitiers Lettres et Sciences Humaines 16 (Paris: Presses Universitaires de France, 1975), 130.

[53] Naomi Seidman has drawn attention to the narrative of Pentecost (Acts 2) as a site of doubling and difference that inflects the translation of Jewish-Christian difference: *Faithful Renderings: Jewish-Christian Difference and the Politics of Translation* (Chicago: University of Chicago Press, 2006), 21–24. For a description of the excavations of the "school of the Jews" at Rouen, see Golb, *Jews in Medieval Normandy*, 154–169, 563–576.

[54] Israel Jacob Yuval, *Two Nations in Your Womb: Perceptions of Jews and Christians in Late Antiquity and the Middle Ages* (Berkeley: University of California Press, 2006), 135–204. Note that Caroline Walker Bynum's recent publication on the theology of blood addresses a later period—the long fifteenth century (1370s to 1520s)—in areas mostly east of the Rhine: *Wonderful Blood: Theology and Practice in Late Medieval Northern Germany and Beyond* (Philadelphia: University of Pennsylvania Press, 2007).

attributed to it the capability of precise transcribing: "every drop of blood of Jews killed by Gentiles is recorded in a divine 'ledger' in the form of a scarlet garment."[55] This splattered woven textile, an archive of trauma, reverberates with the words of Isaiah 63:2: "why is thy apparel red, and thy garments like his that treads in the wine press?"

Muffled echoes of this proof text resound in the *Te Deum*, the liturgical hymn that would have been intoned at Arthur's Pentecostal crown-wearing. The proof text also baffles one of Merlin's prophecies:

> a man shall wrestle with a drunken Lion, and the gleam of gold will blind the eyes of the onlookers. Silver will shine white in the open space around, causing trouble to a number of winepresses. Men will become drunk with the wine which is offered to them; they will turn their backs on Heaven and fix their eyes on the earth.

> [Amplexabitur homo leonem in vino et <fulgor> auri oculos intuentium excecabit. Candebit argentum in circuitu et diversa torcularia vexabit. Imposito vino inebriabuntur mortales postpositoque caleo in terram respicient.][56]

This verse from Isaiah can also be found incised on an artifact possibly contemporary with Geoffrey's composition of Merlin's prophecies—the remarkable ivory processional cross, known as the Cloisters Cross, or the Bury St. Edmunds' Cross.[57] The central front medallion of this exquisitely carved

---

[55] In *Two Nations,* Yuval traces the complicated Ashkenazic reworkings of this motif in the post-1096 liturgical hymns, 92–109.

[56] Thorpe, 184; Wright, 83.

[57] See Elizabeth C. Parker and Charles T. Little, *The Cloisters Cross: Its Art and Meaning* (New York: Harry N. Abrams, 1994), who publish the inscriptions of the cross and offer detailed bibliography; see also Thomas Hoving, *King of the Confessors* (New York: Simon and Shuster), revised in 2001 as an e-book available for download at http://www.ebooks.com/ebooks/book_display.asp?IID=118433. The Cloister Cross is untimely. Here I offer an argument for an earlier

cross depicts Moses raising the Brazen Serpent surrounded by figures bearing tituli intended to develop the typology of the scene. The prophet Isaiah bears a scroll carved with the familiar verse: "Why then is thy apparel red and thy garments like theirs that tread in the winepress" (Isaiah 63:2).[58]

Taken together as an ensemble, the numerous titular inscriptions of the Cloisters Cross foreground the problem of translation. The Cross is exceptional for featuring the earliest representation of the dramatic scene recounted in the Gospel of John in which Caiaphas, the Jewish High Priest, and Pontius Pilate, the colonial governor, debate the wording of the titulus to be affixed to the head of Christ's Cross. The studied depiction of this scene renders the specific inscription of the titulus on the Cloisters Cross even weightier. The artist has changed the gospel text from "Jesus of Nazareth, King of the Jews," to read "Jesus of Nazareth, King of the Confessors." This change invokes, I argue, the overtones of the *Te Deum* hymn, a hymn of confessors, sung during the liturgical processions of Easter and at Pentecost: "Te deum laudamus te dominum confitemur" ("We praise you, God, we confess you to be Lord").

The dating of the Cloisters cross is disputed. Some scholars attribute it to the abbacy of Anselm of Bury (1121-1148); others consider its anti-Semitic typology more relevant to the abbacy of the illustrious Abbot Samson (1188-1211), whose office is associated with the massacre of the Jews in Bury St. Edmunds. The earlier date gains support when the convergence of the archival projects of the Cloisters Cross and

dating. In Chapter 6, I argue that the Cloisters Cross can also be attributed to the Becket Circle (c. 1170). See also Norman Searle, "The Walrus-Ivory Cross in the Metropolitan Museum of Art: the Masterpiece of Master Hugo of Bury?" in *Suffolk in the Middle Ages* (Dover: Boydell Press, 1986), 81–98. Under Anselm (1123), Bury obtained the privilege that should the monastery become the seat of a bishopric it would be served only by monk-bishops. With its immunities from the diocesan at Norwich, the monastery at Bury functioned as a bishopric manqué (Brett, *English Church,* 61).

[58] Parker and Little, *Cloisters Cross,* 244–245.

Geoffrey of Monmouth is considered along with early-twelfth-century schism of the "Jewish" pope.[59] That schism ended in 1138 (around the time that Geoffrey was composing his *History*) with the death of Anacletus II (Peter Pierleone of Rome) who was the great-grandson of a converted Jew.[60] During this schism, Peter the Venerable and Bernard of Clairveaux championed the antipope, Innocent II. Geoffrey of Monmouth invoked this schism when he cast "Anacletus" as the comrade of Antigonus, son of Pandrasus, King of the Greeks. It is Anacletus whom Brutus forces into betraying the Greek camp. Anselm of Bury, as papal legate, was in Normandy in 1119 when the Pierleone family served Pope Calixtus at the Council of Rheims and caused a scandal among northern prelates. Oderic Vitalis recounted the racializing comments made by prelates attending the council at Rheims. They were offended by the Pierleone physique and their irredeemable family history of usury.[61] When Innocent II, the antipope, traveled from Rome to France to secure support, he celebrated Easter at St. Denis in 1131 at which time he received a delegation of Parisian Jews bearing a Torah scroll. The Jews of Rouen also offered Innocent II gifts upon his triumphant arrival in that city.

Geoffrey's *HRB* and the Cloisters Cross converge distinctively on problems of translation, continuity, and archive.

---

[59] Anselm of Bury waged an unpopular campaign to establish the Immaculate Concepcion as an official feast. This feast was approved in a Legatine Council held in London in 1129: *Councils & Synods with Other Documents Relating to the English Church, Part II. 1066-1204*, ed. Frederick K. Maurice Powicke (Oxford: Clarendon University Press, 1981), text no. 134:750–754; Brett, *English Church*, 82, 190.

[60] Innocent II secured the support of Peter the Venerable of Cluny, Bernard of Clairveaux, and Abbot Suger. The death of Anacletus II in January 1138 brought an official end to the schism. Mary Stroll, *The Jewish Pope: Ideology and Politics in the Papal Schism 1130* (Leiden: Brill, 1987); Golb, *Jews in Medieval Normandy*, 198–202.

[61] Dominique Iogna-Prat, *Order and Exclusion: Cluny and Christendom face Heresy, Judaism, and Islam (1000-1150)*, trans. Graham Robert Edwards (Ithaca: Cornell University Press, 2002), 320–322.

Both projects grapple with translation as a form of conversion. As it purports to translate an ancient British book, the *HRB* converts its British source into an archive—a continuous Latin history. The Cloisters Cross probes the limits of the archive and of conversion. Rather than translate the titulus of Pilate according to the gospel text "Jesus of Nazareth, King of the Jews," it edits those words to read in the Latin and Greek inscriptions: "Jesus of Nazareth, King of the Confessors" (*Rex confessorum*; *Basileos examolisson*). The Hebrew version of this phrase inscribed on the titulus marks the "untranslatable" since this line on the titutlus is a cipher of misoriented upside down letters.[62] The Cross accomplishes what Dominique Iogna-Prat has analyzed as a new impulse of this period, not simply to denounce the execution of the "King of the Jews" (a common trope of anti-Judaic polemic dating from early Christianity), but to demonstrate the ongoing, "continuous" nature of Jewish deicide.[63]

A contemporary Jewish archival project, the *porphyrion*, hovers at the edges of the Cloisters Cross. It is just such a processional cross that would have accompanied the dramatic liturgies of Easter and Pentecost at Bury and that embodied the problems of translation, continuity, and archive with which Geoffrey of Monmouth grappled as he imagined Arthur's Whitsun crown-wearing. The twin-person of a sovereign Arthur fabricated by Geoffrey—his personal body that could be mortally wounded and his theological body that

---

[62] Parker and Little, *Cloisters Cross,* 69–75, discuss the inscriptions on the titulus at length. Judith Olszowy-Schlanger treats the knowledge and practice of Hebrew in pre-expulsion England in her essay "The Knowledge and Practice of Hebrew Grammar among Christian Scholars in Pre-Expulsion England: The Evidence of 'Bilingual' Hebrew-Latin Manuscripts," in *Hebrew Scholarship and the Medieval World,* ed. Nicholas De Lange (Cambridge: Cambridge University Press, 2001), 107–130. For the question of the untranslatable Jew and Christian concepts of translation and conversion, see Seidman's excellent chapter on conversion and translation from Jerome to Luther in her *Faithful Renderings,* 115–152.

[63] Iogna-Prat, *Order and Exclusion,* 279.

could not die—was confected, I have argued, out of an archival project enmeshed in the fantasies of translation based on the stability of the signified, on archive as continuity, and on radical possession of that which was untranslatable, "the Jew." The "infinite" bureaucratic labors of recording and preserving the fiscal data in the sayable archive of the Pipe Rolls, the juridical allocation of sovereign rites over Jews, the Pentecostal processions that traversed diocesan space to "confess" at the metropolitan cathedral, the infinite realms imagined by Geoffrey formed the flesh of Arthur's second body. The painstakingly fabricated and complexly rendered corporate flesh of the sovereign's second body remains indebted to the bare life of the unsayable shadow category constituted by this archival project of the twelfth century: the singular archival Jew (*Iudaeus*) who, nevertheless, lived in the plural (*vivunt*).

Chapter 4

Dead Neighbor Archives
Jews, Muslims, and the Enemy's Two Bodies

MESSIANIC PEARLS

In the wake of World War II, students of European sovereignty began to ask more urgently what new thinking could
unbind politics from sovereignty and its annihilating legacy
of internment camps and killing fields.[1] How can the power
constitutive of sovereignty—to suspend the law to produce
the state of emergency and to name the enemy (who is *not*
the neighbor?)—be undone epistemologically?[2] An ongoing

[1] This chapter originally appeared, in slightly different form, as
Kathleen Biddick, "Dead Neighbor Archives: Jews, Muslims, and the
Enemy's Two Bodies," in *Political Theology and Early Modernity*,
eds. Graham Hammill and Julia Reinhard Lupton (Chicago: University of Chicago Press, 2012), 124–142.
[2] The prominent German legal scholar of sovereignty, Carl Schmitt,
famously argued for these two criteria of the sovereign in his diptych of works: *Political Theology: Four Chapters on the Concept of*

search for an antidote has turned contemporary theorists to theology and psychoanalysis as resources for a "cure."[3] A recent reading of the Epistle of Paul to the Romans by the noted theorist, Giorgio Agamben, for example, has inspired him to argue for an unsovereign mode of temporality— messianic time—in which sovereign juridical conditions are transformed such that justice performs without the law, yet, paradoxically without abolishing it.[4] He visualizes messianic

Sovereignty, trans. George Schwab (Chicago: University of Chicago Press, 1985), and *The Concept of the Political*, trans. George Schwab (Chicago: University of Chicago Press, 1996). For discussion of the murderous effects of sovereignty, see Giorgio Agamben, *Remnants of Auschwitz: The Witness and the Archive*, trans. Daniel Heller-Roazen (New York: Zone Books, 1999) and his *State of Exception*, trans. Kevin Attell (Chicago: University of Chicago Press, 2005). For the epistemological stakes in separating out European sovereignty from slavery, see Kathleen Davis, *Periodization and Sovereignty: How Ideas of Feudalism and Secularization Govern the Politics of Time* (Philadelphia: University of Pennsylvania Press, 2008). For my own thoughts on this important work by Davis, see my review of her book at *The Medieval Review*, http://hdl.handle.net/20-27/spo. baj 9928.0904/006/.

[3] Recent discussions of sovereignty and messianic time include Alain Badiou, *Saint Paul: The Foundation of Universalism*, trans. Ray Brassier (Stanford: Stanford University Press, 2003); Jacob Taubes, *The Political Theology of Paul*, trans. Dana Hollander (Stanford: Stanford University Press, 2004); Giorgio Agamben, *The Time that Remains: A Commentary on the Letter to the Romans*, trans. Patricia Dailey (Stanford: Stanford University Press, 2005); Kenneth Reinhard, Eric L. Santner, and Slavoj Žižek, *The Neighbor: Three Inquiries in Political Theology* (Chicago: University of Chicago Press, 2005); Eleanor Kaufman, "The Saturday of Messianic Times (Agamben and Badiou on the Apostle Paul)," *South Atlantic Quarterly* 107 (2008): 37–54. For the traumatic temporality of sovereignty, see Davis, *Periodization and Sovereignty*. The potential of neighbor love as a way of undeadening sovereignty is explored in *The Neighbor* and in Eric L. Santner, *On the Psychotheology of Everyday Life: Reflections on Freud and Rosenzweig* (Chicago: University of Chicago Press, 2001), and his *On Creaturely Life: Rilke, Benjamin, Sebald* (Chicago: University of Chicago Press, 2006).

[4] Agamben, *The Time that Remains*, passim, especially 98, 107.

time as a pearl inside an oyster. Just as the bivalve secretes its nacre around an irritant, so messianic time contracts around *chronos* (empty chronological time) and brings forth *kairos*, the time of the singular occasion that "seizes" chronos.[5] Agamben's pearl also exemplifies the centrality of figural thinking to his understanding of messianic time. In messianic figuralism, the type (for example, Adam, or an oyster) and its antitype (Messiah, or a pearl) no longer stand in the "biunivocal" figural relation (Agamben's word) as they once did in the figural exegesis of the Middle Ages; instead, according to him, "the messianic is not one of two terms in the typological relations, it is the relation itself" *and* it is decisive.[6] Students of Carl Schmitt (1888–1985), the brilliant and troubling theorist of sovereignty, will hear in Agamben's rhetorical decisiveness echoes of Schmitt, who famously stated that the sovereign is the one who "decides" on the suspension of the law and the naming of the enemy.[7] Even as Agamben hopes to undo modern sovereignty, formally he participates in what I call typological decision, an act which embodies a historically Christian view of sovereign authority.

Schmitt also claimed that the sovereign exception in jurisprudence is analogous to the miracle in theology.[8] Schmitt was not the first to grasp this political-theological toggle between exception and miracle. Thomas Hobbes, whom Schmitt read closely, astutely observed in his *Leviathan* that one man's miracle is another man's plague, in other words,

---

[5] Agamben, *The Time that Remains*, 68–69.

[6] Agamben, *The Time that Remains*, 69, 74. For the temporal implications of medieval typological figuralism, see my study *The Typological Imaginary: Circumcision, Technology, History* (Philadelphia: University of Pennsylvania Press, 2003).

[7] Schmitt, *Political Theology*, 1; Schmitt, *Concept of the Political*, 26. Please note that in this chapter I do not intend to deal with Schmitt's typology of the enemy in his *Theorie des Partisanen* (Berlin: Dunckat and Humblot, 1963), trans. G.L. Ulmen, *Theory of the Partisan* (New York: Telos Press, 2007).

[8] Schmitt, *Political Theology*, 36.

the toggle can be deadly.[9] It is in this gap between the exception and the miracle that Eric L. Santner has proposed neighbor-love as an antidote to the sovereign naming of the enemy. In his words, neighbor-love is the "'miraculous' opening of a social link based on the creaturely deposits left by the [sovereign] state of exception that, as Freud indicates, *structurally haunts* the subject in and through the formation of the superego."[10] Santner contends that the past at issue in contemporary theories of messianic time and the miraculous is a traumatic past: "the element of the past that is at issue has the structural status of *trauma*, a past that in some sense never fully took place and so continues to insist in the present precisely as drive destiny, the symptomal torsion of one's being in the world, one's relation to a capacity to use the object-world."[11]

In this chapter I want to address something that, from my perspective as a trained medievalist, troubles me in these accounts of messianic and miraculous antidotes to sovereignty. In Agamben's conceptualization, medieval figural thinking is something to be overcome in the messianic; for Santner, who thinks temporality through trauma (sovereignty, he reminds us, is itself a mode of temporality),[12] it could be that the medieval has not yet arrived, and that it always already arrived in the death drive (those implacable forms of repetition compulsion). I am interested in how the messianic and miraculous as conceived by Agamben and Santner seem to

---

[9] On Thomas Hobbes's seeing that one man's miracle is another man's plague, see his *Leviathan*, eds. G.A.J. Rogers and Karl Schuhmann (Bristol: Thoemmes Continuum, 2003), 344–351; for instance, regarding Moses and Pharaoh, Hobbes writes: "And when he [Pharaoh] let them goe at last, not the Miracles persuaded him, but the plagues forced him to do it" (347). Hobbes discusses the sovereign "decision" of the miracle at 350–351.

[10] Santner, *On Creaturely Life*, 75.

[11] Santner, *The Neighbor*, 126.

[12] Santner insightfully observes that sovereignty is a mode of temporalization, but somehow, I think, he fails to work through the implications: Santner, *Psychotheology*, 60–61; Santner, *On Creaturely Life*, 66–67.

contract around each other.[13] What happens, this chapter asks, if the messianic and the miraculous are thought in parallax (looking at the same object from two separate vantage points)—does a medieval enemy lodge in the blind-spot of Agamben's messianic; does the despot (the excess of the sovereign) haunt Santner's miracle-making?[14] I answer these questions in the affirmative, showing how the figure of the undead Muslim recurs in the various philosophers and theologians whose arguments support Agamben's and Santner's claims. The undead Muslim as the irritant around which the pearls of messianic time slowly accrete is thus the subject of my study. In what follows, I examine how contemporary messianic thinkers have unconsciously laminated as "dead neighbors" the traumatic irritants productive of the messianic pearl. In order for a messianic pearl to glow miraculously (as Agamben and Santner would wish it to), the new thinking of today needs to engage, I argue, in an act of neighbor-love, whereby it embraces the untimely, undead excarnations of a history of typological damage.[15] Otherwise, I caution, these traumatic dead neighbors remain undead and driven in the drive of critical theories of sovereignty.

THE UNDEAD TURK

Let me open my archive of indigestible remainders with a brief investigation of what is arguably the most famous mod-

---

[13] In so doing it joins with the project of Davis, *Periodization and Sovereignty*.

[14] For the fantastical over-proximity of notions of the despot and the sovereign forged in the Enlightenment, see Alain Grosrichard, *The Sultan's Court: European Fantasies of the East*, trans. Liz Heron (New York: Verso, 1998). The psychoanalytic discourse of neighbor-love, routed through the concept of the Thing ("excessive presence and radical absence") echoes the discourse of the despot in uncanny ways (see note 3 for references).

[15] I take this notion of the indigestible remainder from Santner, *Psychotheology*, 29. He discusses the indigestible remainder as a hard kernel that can be "neither naturalized nor historicized."

ern thesis of messianic time, that is, Walter Benjamin's first thesis in *On the Philosophy of History*, completed in Paris in the winter of 1940 just as the Wehrmacht was breaking through the last line of French defenses. This renowned text reads as follows:

> The story is told of an automaton constructed in such a way that it could play a winning game of chess, answering each move of an opponent with a countermove. A puppet in Turkish attire and with a hookah in its mouth sat before a chessboard placed on a large table. A system of mirrors created the illusion that this table was transparent from all sides. Actually, a little hunchback who was an expert chess player sat inside and guided the puppet's hand by means of strings. One can imagine a philosophical counterpart to this device. The puppet called "historical materialism" is to win all the time. It can easily be a match for anyone if it enlists the services of theology, which today, as we know, is wizened and has to keep out of sight.[16]

Benjamin's striking image draws upon a famous automaton fabricated in the late eighteenth century.[17] This chess-playing machine, dubbed "the Turk," wended its sensational way through the salons of Vienna, Paris, London, and on to New York.

---

[16] Walter Benjamin, "Theses on the Philosophy of History," in *Illuminations: Essays and Reflections*, ed. Hannah Arendt, trans. Harry Zohn (New York: Schocken, 1968), 253 [253–264].

[17] For Benjamin's links to the essay by Edgar Allan Poe, see Joshua Robert Gold, "The Dwarf in the Machine: A Theological Figure and its Sources," *Modern Language Notes* 121 (2006): 1220–1236. The essay by Edgar Allan Poe, "Maelzel's Chess Player," *Saturday Literary Messenger*, April 1836, 318–26, is available at http://www.eapoe.org/works/ESSAYS/MAELZEL.HTM. For general information about this eighteenth-century automaton, see Tom Standage, *The Turk: The Life and Times of the Famous Eighteenth-Century Chess-Playing Machine* (New York: Walker and Company, 2002).

Figure 1. Joseph Freiherr zu Racknitz, *Über den Schachspieler des Herrn von Kempelen und dessen Nachbildung,* plate III, *The Turk—small man acting as director of the Turk* (Leipzig und Dresden, 1789). Photography: The Library Company of Philadelphia.

The Turk inspired Benjamin's dialectical image of the relations between historical materialism—philosophy in the guise of a Turkish puppet—and theology—the hunchbacked dwarf hidden in the machine. In a fine illustration (see Figure 1) of just one of the many efforts made during the eighteenth century to crack the illusionist gimmick of the Turk, the artist, you will observe, exposes the mechanical gears of this automaton as well as the hiding space where, it was speculated, the human agent (imagined by Benjamin as a "buckliger Zwerg," a hunchbacked dwarf) sat and pulled the strings of the puppet, whose gloved hand moved across the chessboard as it played with a contender from the audience.

Benjamin had become acquainted with the Turk through a brilliant essay by Edgar Allan Poe (via its translation by Baudelaire). In 1836 Poe had attended a few performances of the chess-playing machine in Richmond, Virginia. Like many before him, Poe tried to figure out its secret workings. In his subsequent publication on the phenomenon, Poe meticulously observed the Turkish puppet, also known popularly as the "oriental sorcerer." Here is an excerpt from his eyewitness description:

> The external appearance and, especially, the deportment of the Turk, are when we consider them as imitations of life, but very indifferent imitations. The countenance evinces no ingenuity, and is surpassed, in its resemblance to the human face, by the very commonest of wax-works. The eyes roll unnaturally in the head, without any corresponding motions of the lids or brows. The arm, particularly, performs its operations in an exceedingly stiff, awkward, jerking, and rectangular manner.

Poe's concise sketch captured what contemporary theorists would term the *undeadness* of the Turkish puppet. Santner, in his two recent studies *On the Psychotheology of Everyday Life* (2001) and *On Creaturely Life* (2006), defines undeadness as follows: "an internal alienness that has a peculiar sort of vitality and yet belongs to no form of life."[18] The undeadness of the chess-playing automaton with its undecidability between what Poe called the "oriental human" and "pure machine" also fascinated Benjamin. He used this undecidability to imagine a transformative temporality, which he called a *Jetzt-Zeit*, a messianic time, in which the undead Turk would be animated and the hunch of the dwarf would be straightened.[19] Historical materialism, Benjamin believed, had the capacity to read a "unique experience with the past" as it flashed in the present.

Benjamin based his concept of the miraculous and messianic *Jetzt-Zeit* on a structure of sign and fulfillment. He

---

[18] Santner, *Psychotheology*, 36.
[19] For an interesting exploration of Benjamin's *Jetzt-Zeit*, see Cesare Casarino, "Time Matters: Marx, Negri, Agamben, and the Corporeal," *Strategies* 16 (2003): 185–206.

hoped that his new philosophy of historical materialism would reconstitute this semiotic structure of the theological miracle. By imagining the dwarf who pulls the Turk's strings specifically as a "hunchbacked dwarf," he further intensified the theological overtones of his dialectical image. Those readers of Benjamin familiar with the Book of Leviticus (21:20), would know that among the list of those blemished chosen people forbidden to make bread offerings to God were included the "crookbacked or dwarf" (according to the King James Bible); the "bucklig oder verkümmert" (according to Martin Luther); and most significantly "ein Buckliger oder ein Zwerg," according to the German translation of the Hebrew text of Leviticus undertaken in the mid-1920s by Martin Buber and Franz Rosenzweig, renowned German-Jewish interlocutors of Benjamin.[20] Students of Leviticus also know that in close proximity to Chapter 21 is to be found the famous proof-text of neighbor-love. In Leviticus 19:18–34, God enjoins his chosen people to love their neighbor as themselves. Benjamin's dialectical image of the new thinking of messianic time thus juxtaposes the ghostly visual and acoustical effects of an undead Muslim and the scriptural echoes of a blemished Jew banned by God from ritual acts of sacrifice—but enjoined, nonetheless, to practice neighbor-love.

MACHINES WITHIN MACHINES

For medieval scholars, Benjamin's Turk does not look much different from Christian figural machines eschewed, as we have already seen, by Agamben. In his depiction and discussion of the typological wheel of fortune, Jeffrey Librett has noted that each rotation of the typological gears—from literal, then to figural, and around again to truth—is always reversible and doubled.[21] As the typological wheel turns, the

---

[20] Martin Buber and Franz Rosenzweig, *Die Schrift*, 13 vols. (Berlin: Verlag Lambert Schneider, 1926-1938), 3:91.

[21] Jeffrey S. Librett, *The Rhetoric of Cultural Dialogue: Jews and Ger-*

figura, the Christian, is always at excarnating risk of becoming Jewish (again), becoming the *littera*, the Jew: "the literal can always come to seem the mere figure of what figures it, which is henceforth rendered literal (or in any case, ... it can always come to seem the figure of something else, one knows not what)."[22] What this Christian reading machine radically forecloses is becoming Muslim; such an incarnational possibility is not even entertained. In order to stop the typological spin that could render the becoming-Jewish of the Christian, or (even more fearful) the becoming-Muslim of either Christian or Jew, the Christian typologist has to decide.

It is just such a typological decision, I argue, that joins medieval typology to the form of sovereignty analyzed by Schmitt. He who decides typology, then, is just like the sovereign, thus typology and sovereignty are closely bound. With Schmitt's political theology in mind (and Benjamin knew Schmitt's work), let us take another look at Benjamin's Turk. In his first thesis, you will recall, Benjamin described how the automaton produced its illusions through a "system of mirrors" (*ein System von Spiegeln*). Recent theoretical discussions of Benjamin's notion of *Jetzt-Zeit*, messianic time, especially by Agamben, function, I think, illusionistically, just like the system of mirrors that had rendered the chess-playing automaton believable to its viewing public. In their play of illusionary reflections these contemporary theoretical texts almost manage to vanish the medieval gears of the typological reading machine that are peeking out from Benjamin's image. The typological relation, as we have seen, is key to Agamben's argument about messianic time as a cure for sovereignty; he claims, as you will recall, that it is the typological relation (the relation of *littera* and *figura*) that *suspends* the sovereign's decision and offers a release, or perhaps an unplugging, from its undead existence. Agamben further asserts that it is the very typological *relation* itself that trans-

mans from Moses Mendelssohn to Richard Wagner and Beyond (Stanford: Stanford University Press, 2000); his typological wheel of fortune is found at 21.

[22] Librett, *Rhetoric*, 13.

forms temporality from *chronos* (the empty, mechanical time of typological decision) to *kairos*, messianic time.[23] For Agamben there can be no reversibility of the *littera* and *figura*; like a sovereign Agamben thus determines the figurality of messianic time.

MYSTIC GRINDINGS

Figure 2. Capital: The Mystic Mill (twelfth century). Vézelay Basilica, France. Photograph: Art History Images.

Agamben is not alone in his figural decisionism, and I want to offer two more examples of such decisionism drawn from

[23] Agamben, *The Time that Remains*, 74.

contemporary commentary on messianic time and miracles. In my first example, a stony piece of medieval sculpture crops up as an indigestible remainder of messianic thinking. Like pebbles in a shoe, this carving irritates Jacob Taubes's study, *The Political Theology of Paul*. Taubes, a professor of Jewish Studies and Hermeneutics at the Free University of Berlin and an interlocutor of Carl Schmitt, gave the lectures upon which this book is based in 1987 at Heidelberg, just a few days before his death from cancer. The frontispiece to the English translation features a photograph of one of the famous nave capitals of the Romanesque church at Vézelay, Burgundy (see Figure 2). The iconography of the carving renders the typological theme of the Mystic Mill. Moses (the *littera*, or type, of Paul) pours grain into the chute of a mill.

As its gears grind, Paul, apostle and *figura*, stooped in the corner of the capital, catches the refined flour in a sack. The sculpture, which dates to the third decade of the twelfth century, was carved at a time when Vézelay was a contested node in the monastic network of the abbey of Cluny, arguably the greatest abbey of Western Christendom. Cluny and the popes who reigned over Christendom in the late eleventh and twelfth centuries were closely bound. Less than a generation before the Vézelay carving, the Cluniac Pope, Urban II, had traveled to Burgundy to call the First Christian Crusade, in 1095. In 1144, Bernard of Clairveaux stood on the church steps at Vézelay to preach the Second Christian Crusade against Muslims.[24]

Why is this particular photograph of a medieval sculpture from the church at Vézelay set as the frontispiece to Taubes's

---

[24] The typological rhetoric of such sculptural programs has been elucidated by Rachel Dressler in her study of the West Façade of Chartres Cathedral, a sculptural ensemble contemporaneous with Vézelay. See Rachel Dressler, "*Deus Hoc Vult*: Ideology, Identity, and Sculptural Rhetoric at the Time of the Crusades," *Medieval Encounters* 1 (1995): 188–218. Dressler observes and annotates how "typological thinking was deeply ingrained in medieval Christianity and led to the use of an Old Testament paradigm as part of recruiting and victory rhetoric during the First Crusade" (195).

amazing midrashic reading of Paul and of the political theology of Carl Schmitt, with whom Taubes actually met in 1978 to discuss Paul? It should be noted that the same picture of this Vézelay capital had also appeared on the 1969 cover of an influential study of Paul the Apostle by Gunther Bornkamm, the Heidelberg New Testament scholar. At the moment in his lecture in which Taubes reflected on Chapter 9, Verse 13, of Paul's *Epistle to the Romans* ("As it was written, Jacob have I loved but not Esau"), he produced the photograph of the Vézelay sculpture for his audience and informed them that he received this copy of the "marvelous picture" from his friend, Jan Assmann (Egyptologist extraordinaire and scholar of religious studies). Taubes went on to say that he treasured the picture and carried it around in his bag, because "with the naïveté of the medieval stonemason, it says everything for those who know how to read."[25] Digressing, Taubes then linked the sculpture at Vézelay with a famous contemporaneous commentary by Suger, abbot (1122–51) of St.-Denis, Paris. To expound on the grand architectural refurbishments of his abbey, Suger wrote an account with the rather bureaucratic title, "What Was Done Under His Administration" (*de rebus in administratione sua gestis*), the purpose of which was to itemize the considerable costs incurred by the building program. Folded into Suger's laundry list of expenditures can be found a theological gloss to the typological themes represented in a complex sequence of stained-glass roundels designed for the ambulatory of St.-Denis. Here is the text that Taubes extracted from Suger's typological commentary on the Mystic Mill and recited at his seminar:

One of these [roundels], urging us onward from the material to the immaterial, represents the Apostle Paul turning a mill, and the Prophets carrying sacks to the mill. The verses of this subject are these: "By working the mill, thou, Paul, takest the flour out of the bran. / Thou makest

[25] Taubes, *Political Theology*, 38–39.

known the inmost meaning of the Law of Moses. / From so many grains is made the true bread without bran, / Our and angels' perpetual food."[26]

This short poem epitomizes the medieval Christian typological relation. Paul fulfills Moses, and the grain that will be baked into the sacred wafer of the Eucharist fulfills the Mosaic Law (from command to comestible).[27] After attentively describing the sculpture of the Mystic Mill and its typological relations, Taubes decisively concluded his ruminations with a vehement disavowal of medieval typology: "Of course, this is not *my* Paul [original emphasis]. . . . What I have to say about Moses and Paul is naturally something else."[28] With this emphatic assertion, I argue, Taubes decides on typological decisionism. He seems to be saying, "I know that this medieval Christian typology of Paul is a stony, indigestible exegetical fragment (an always doubled and reversible relation), but

[26] Taubes is citing from the translation by Erwin Panofsky, *Abbot Suger on the Abbey Church of St.-Denis and its Art Treasures* (Princeton: Princeton University Press, 1946), 74–75. The original text in Latin reads: "Tollis agendo molam de furfure, Paule, farinam. Mosaicae legis intima nota facis. Fit de tot granis verus sine furfure panis, Perpetuusque cibus noster et angelicus." For background on Vézelay, see Kirk Ambrose, *The Nave Sculpture of Vézelay: The Art of Monastic Viewing* (Toronto: Pontifical Institute for Medieval Studies, 2006) and Kevin D. Murphy, *Memory and Modernity: Viollet-le-Duc at Vézelay* (University Park: Pennsylvania State University Press, 2000).

[27] The "truth" of such fulfillment exploded on the sculpted tympanum of the main entry to the church at Vézelay, which grandiosely depicted the theme of Christ commissioning the Apostles to world mission. On the lintel of this tympanum all the Pliny-like monsters, those one-eyed, elephant-eared creatures inhabiting the edge of the world, march inexorably toward Christian conversion. The literature on this innovative portal is voluminous; it is best to start with the critical commentary by Dominique Iogna-Prat, *Order and Exclusion: Cluny and Christendom Face Heresy, Judaism, and Islam (1000–1150),* trans. Graham Robert Edwards (Ithaca: Cornell University Press, 2002), 267–274.

[28] Taubes, *Political Theology of Paul,* 39.

I, Jacob Taubes, decide on the meaning of Paul." Put another way, Taubes offers his reader an example of the indigestible remainder of medieval Christian typology. Taubes encounters this indigestible remainder in the form of a chunk of sculpted stone and then decides it away, thus repeating by foreclosure, as I shall unfold for you shortly, the excarnating Christian battle over the semiotics of miracle-making inscribed in the Vézelay capital.

Before turning to an analysis of the medieval crusade about meaning-making, especially meaning-making and miracles, I want to offer the promised second example of typological decisionism at work in the contemporary understanding of political theology. This example moves us from a medieval stone to the accusation of "getting medieval" through magic that surfaced in the treatise, *The Star of Redemption* (1920), by the German-Jewish philosopher, Franz Rosenzweig.[29] In the *Star*, Rosenzweig, like his interlocutor Benjamin, explicated his vision of a new philosophy capable of reconstituting the miracle in modernity. He argued that the semiotic structure of prefiguration and fulfillment was necessary for miracle-making and further asserted that, because the Quran lacked such a semiotic structure, Islam was incapable of miracle-making. His appraisal of Islam, not atypical of scholarship in the 1920s, has, nevertheless, broad implica-

---

[29] Franz Rosenzweig, *The Star of Redemption*, trans. Barbara E. Galli (Madison: University of Wisconsin Press, 2005), 127–129. For the question of Islam in Rosenzweig, see '*Innerlich bleibt die Welt eine*': *Ausgewählte Texte von Franz Rosenzweig über den Islam*, ed. Gesine Palmer (Bodenheim: Philo Verlag, 2002) and, more broadly, the brilliant essay by Suzanne Marchand, "Nazism, 'Orientalism,' and Humanism," in *Nazi Germany and the Humanities*, eds. Wolfgang Bialas and Anson Rabinbach (Oxford: Oneworld Publications, 2007), 267–305. In his essay, "Miracles Happen: Benjamin, Rosenzweig, Freud, and the Matter of the Neighbor," in *The Neighbor*, 83n12, Eric Santner notes that Rosenzweig excluded Islam from the semiotic structure of the miracle based on prefiguration and fulfillment (the typological relation).

tions.[30] Medievalists will recognize that Rosenzweig repeats almost verbatim the terms of the twelfth-century Christian polemic against Islam. That polemic, which justified the declaration of Muslims as the enemy (*hostes*) of Christendom, excluded Islam from the semiotics of miracle-making. Put another way, this polemic foreclosed Muslims from the symbolic order. Muslim bodies thus became the site where incarnation could not occur and thus became the site of excarnation.[31] Moreover, to designate Muslim magic and sorcery, Cluniac monks used the word *mechanicum*.[32]

These examples drawn from Taubes and Rosenzweig persuade me that the undeadness of Christian typological decisionism has insinuated itself into the heart of contemporary political theology and its theories of the philosophical and psychoanalytic miracles—the purported "cure" of messianic time. Taubes and Rosenzweig repeat a traumatic medieval battle over semiotics in which an imperializing Christendom excarnated Jews and Muslims as neighbors and declared

[30] Gil Anidjar offers a different reading of Franz Rosenzweig in *The Jew, The Arab: A History of the Enemy* (Stanford: Stanford University Press, 2003), 87–98. For an important meditation relevant to this argument, see the recent essay by Anne Norton, "Call me Ishmael," in *Derrida and the Time of the Political*, eds. Pheng Cheah and Suzanne Guerlac (Durham: Duke University Press, 2009), 158–176.

[31] Walter Benjamin, a reader of Rosenzweig, echoes him in thesis sixteen of *On the Philosophy of History*. There Benjamin separated a redemptive philosophy (historical materialism) from the undeadness of the mechanical world (semiosis from mechanics): "This historical materialist leaves it to others to be drained by the whore called 'Once upon a time' in historicism's bordello. He remains in control of his powers, man enough to blast open the continuum of history" (Benjamin, "Theses," 262).

[32] See Iogna-Prat, *Order and Exclusion*, 107–108, for a compelling discussion of the use of the Latin word *mechanicum* to designate a sorcerer and the scribal slippage that at times rendered this word as "manicheum" (after the heresy); see also Ellie Truitt, "*Trei poete, sages dotors, qui mout sorent di nigromance*: Knowledge and Automata in Twelfth-century French Literature," *Configurations* 12 (2004): 167–193.

them political enemies (*hostes*). If an aim of contemporary theory is to release the undeadness of sovereignty, then it is necessary, I argue, to lay bare the gears that drive its traumatic, theoretical core.

CHRISTIAN MIRACLES AND THE MECHANICS OF FORECLOSURE

Let me recap briefly the kind of excarnational fantasies impelling medieval polemics at Cluny—the same kinds of fantasies that have crept unconsciously into contemporary theories of messianic time.[33] Such polemics are well known to medieval scholars, so I shall only offer a brief sketch here. Peter the Venerable, abbot of Cluny (1122-1160), launched

---

[33] Around the time of the Second Crusade (1144), Peter the Venerable took up "the sword of the divine word" (in a kind of semiological Star Wars) to slay the enemies of Christendom, Jews and Muslims. As his secretary, Peter of Poitiers, famously put it in a letter to Peter: "You are the only one of our generation, who, with the sword of Divine words, slaughtered the three greatest enemies of holy Christianity, the Jews, the Heretics, and the Saracens, in order to humble the satanic pride and arrogance which rise up against the greatness of God": Peter of Poitiers, *Epistola*, ed. Reinhold Glei, in *Petrus Venerabilis Schriften zum Islam*, Corpus Islamico-Christianum, Series Latina (Altenberg, 1985), 1:228. The original Latin reads: "Solus enim vos estis nostris temporibus, qui tres maximos sanctae Christianitas hostes, Iudaeos dico et haereticos ac Saracenos, divini verbi gladio trucidastis et humiliare omnem arrogantiam et superbiamdiaboli 'extollentem se adversus altitudem dei'." Other treatises by Peter the Venerable cited in this essay include *Adversus Iudeorum inveteratam duritiem*, ed. Yvonne Friedmann, Corpus Christianorum, Continuatio Medievalis 58 (Turnhout: Brepols, 1985), hereafter cited as *AJ*, and Peter the Venerable, *Contra sectam Sarracenorum*, ed. Reinhold Kritzeck, and *Peter the Venerable and Islam* (Princeton: Princeton University Press, 1964). For helpful background on Peter the Venerable and Islam see, John V. Tolan, *Saracens: Islam in the Medieval European Imagination* (New York: Columbia University Press, 2002), and Kenneth M. Setton, "Western Hostility to Islam and Prophecies of Turkish Doom," *Memoirs of the American Philosophical Society* 201 (Philadelphia: American Philosophical Society, 1992).

the semiotic crusade against Jews and Muslims in two treatises written in the 1140s: "Against the Jews and their inveterate obdurancy" and "Against the Saracens [Islam] as a sect and heresy."[34] A noteworthy aspect of these polemics was his pioneering use of translated excerpts from the Talmud to argue against Jews and his citations from his commissioned Latin translation of the Quran to attack Muslims (known as Saracens according to popular twelfth-century Christian nomenclature). He intertwined these polemics with Cluniac theories of the Eucharist as the "always and ever" incarnating miracle and also as an "always and ever" incarnating institution.[35] The Eucharistic miracle, as Peter the Venerable theorized, provided the philosophical grounds for foreclosing Jews and Muslims from semiosis and rendering them excarnated bodies.

This is how Peter's argument about semiosis works. He argued that it was only through "signs" (*signa*) that Christianity converted the world, and the world for Peter meant the *nomos* of the earth, *oceans included*.[36] Peter launched his

[34] R.I. Moore briefly reflects on some of the problems of analyzing the pincer-like movement of Christendom's naming the enemy's two bodies (Jews in Europe and Islam in the West) in the second edition of his famous study, *The Formation of a Persecuting Society: Power and Deviance in Western Europe, 950–1250* (New York: Blackwell, 1987; 2nd edn., 2007). The first edition, which appeared in 1987, did not mention Muslims as the targets of a persecuting imaginary and the reflections in the 2007 edition do not really grapple with the stakes of omission.

[35] David Bates, "Political Theology and the Nazi State: Carl Schmitt's Concept of the Institution," *Modern Intellectual History* 3 (2006): 415–422.

[36] Cited in Iogna-Prat, *Order and Exclusion*, 299. See also Carl Schmitt, *The Nomos of the Earth in the International Law of the Jus Publicum Europaeum*, trans. G. L. Ulmen (New York: Telos Press, 2003). I am arguing against Schmitt's ahistorical thesis of the ocean as the "free space," free of Christendom; see his Chapter 1, "The First Global Lines," 86–100. The citation is from *AJ*, 1466–1473: "Totum vero orbem dixi, quia licet gentiles vel Sarraceni super aliquas eius partes dominatum exerceant, licet Iudei inter Chris-

attack from what he called a "congruent place" where his church (Cluny) and the church as a whole (*corpus verum*) conjoined or hinged at the altar of sacrifice, where the monk-priests of Cluny consecrated the bread and wine of the Eucharist. The altars of Cluny served as a sacrificial machine for Christendom (for example, when a professed Cluniac monk died, the monastery would commemorate him with the consecration of thirty hosts per day for a one-month period, which amounted to nine hundred Masses).[37] Peter understood the Eucharist semiotically. He conceived of the Eucharist as an exclusive sign (*signum incommunicatum*) and a perpetual miracle (*miracula*) once and always (*semel et semper*), as he designated the temporality of the miracle in Latin.[38] As the sign of typological truth, the Eucharist once and always fulfilled the Hebrew Scriptures. By implication the perpetual miracle of the Eucharist, as conceived by Peter, foreclosed the typological relation between Jews and Christians by deciding it once and always, since the sacrifice never ceased. Typology thus becomes a perpetual form of Christian sovereignty. By virtue of their power over signs (the Eucharist being the exclusive sign), Christians ruled the world: "because the Christian of the world is not converted to Christ without boundless signs" ("quod Christianus orbis absque signis immensis ad Christum conversus non est").[39]

Peter acknowledged that there had been miracles in the Hebrew dispensation—those performed by Moses in front of Pharaoh being examples—but these miracles were weak and superseded by the miraculous *signa* of Christ and the ongo-

---

tianos et ethnicos lateant, non est tamen aliqua vel modica pars terrae, non Tyrenni maris nec ipsius oceani remotissime insulae, quae vel domininantibus vel subiectis Christianis non incolantur, ut verum esse appareat quod scriptura de Christo ait: Dominiabitur a mari usque ad mare et flumine usque ad terminus orbis terrae."

[37] Iogna-Prat, *Order and Exclusion*, 236.

[38] This discussion is inspired by Iogna-Prat, *Order and Exclusion*, 182–218. Iogna Prat observes that Peter the Venerable's "sociology of Christendom was in the first instance a semiology" (257).

[39] *AJ*, 4, 1541ff.

ing miracle-workings of his apostles and his Christian disciples through time, even down to the monk-priests of Cluny. As for Islam, Peter vociferously denied its access to miracles. According to Peter's concept of miraculous semiosis, Mohammed could be neither a miracle-worker nor a prophet. Peter drew a sharp distinction between Muslim fabulation and *mechanicum* (the arts of sorcery and magic) and the true miracle modeled on the transformation of substance in the Eucharist.[40] Islam, in Peter's eyes, could only triumph by virtue of armed force and seduction.

Peter the Venerable's targeting of Jews and Muslims as enemies of medieval Christendom in his two polemics was nothing less than a semiological declaration of war. The Eucharist was the perfected, perpetual sign through which Christendom ruled land and sea. With the Eucharist, typological relations between the Hebrew Scriptures and the Christian New Testament were miraculously fulfilled once and always, foreclosing any possibility of an ongoing Jewish semiosis, or miracle-making. Islam was utterly bereft of semiotic capacity—its Quran, according to Peter, being only the confabulation of the Talmud and early heretical Christian writings. The Cluniacs, or *Ecclesia Cluniacensis*, under the leadership of Peter the Venerable, fabricated the institutional materiality of the Eucharist in their great Romanesque building programs (the church at Vézelay being an example). They sought to globalize the sign of "the republic of the Christian Church" and conflated the stone of the church altar, the *fabrica* of the Eucharist, with the church as a corporate institution, thus materializing sacred space as a new category. Peter worked to expel Islam from the semiotic *and* geographical space he fabricated and he effectively disincarnated Muslims as dead neighbors, the indigestible remainder of his political theology.

For Peter the Venerable, the perpetual miracle of Eucharistic decision and the monstrosity of undeadness (Islam) are conjoined. We can detect this joining at work in a famous

[40] *AJ*, 4, 1360–1954.

Cluniac sculptural artifact, the main portal to the church of St. Lazare in Autun (see Figure 3). The tympanum featured a novel example of Christ throned in majesty. The following sovereign inscription is chiseled on the border of the mandorla: "I alone dispose of all things and crown the just, those who follow crime I judge and punish."[41] In the right-hand corner of the central register of the tympanum, the leviathan rears up from the portals of hell. The sovereign miracle and the pestilential and monstrous are thus closely bound on the tympanum at Autun.

Figure 3. Tympanum: Punishments of the Damned (twelfth century). Autun Cathedral, France. Art History Images.

I want to jump from this medieval leviathan to its early-modern neighbor, the Leviathan depicted by Thomas Hobbes

[41] The Latin text of the inscription reads: "Omnia dispono solus meritos corono quos scelus exercet me judice poena coercet." For detailed photographs and mapping of the sculptural program of the tympanum, see Denis Grivot and George Zarnecki, *Giselbertus: Sculptor of Autun* (New York: Orion Press, 1961). For basic bibliography and debates over interpretation, see Linda Seidel, *Legends in Limestone: Lazarus, Gislebertus and the Cathedral at Autun* (Chicago: University of Chicago Press, 1999).

in the famous engraved frontispiece of *Leviathan* (1660) (see Figure 4), which can be productively read as a version of a Romanesque portal or threshold to his treatise. We know that Hobbes based his startling depiction of a composite, artificial, sovereign body, the Leviathan, on an optical device he most likely viewed during his stay in Paris in the late 1640s.

Figure 4. Title page of Thomas Hobbes's *Leviathan* (1651). The British Library, London. HIP/Art Resource, New York.

The Franciscan polymath, François Niceron, had perfected an anamorphic optical device at that time. To entertain and instruct his audiences, Niceron used fifteen images of Ottoman Sultans as the segments of representation that he resolved into the face of Louis XIII (see Figure 5).[42] Inscribed

---

[42] For a detailed study of optical devices known by Hobbes and their influence on the design of his frontispiece, see the following review essay: "The Title Page of *Leviathan*, seen in Curious Perspective," in Noel Malcolm, *Aspects of Hobbes* (Oxford: Clarendon Press, 2002), 200–233. The engraving of the "Ottoman sultans" can be found on table 49 of J.-F. Niceron's *La Perspective curieuse* (1638) and is

then in Hobbes's frontispiece is a paradoxical miracle that produces the Western sovereign through the mechanically manipulated images of Muslim "despots"—the despot being a Western fantasy of an excarnated Muslim sovereign.[43]

Figure 5. Anamorphic figure of Ottoman Sultans coalescing into bust of Louis XIII. From Jean-François Niceron, *La Perspective curieuse* (1638), plate 69. Bibliothèque nationale de France.

illustrated in Malcolm, *Aspects of Hobbes*, fig. 4.

[43] For the disincarnating Western discourse of the despot, see Grosrichard, *The Sultan's Court*; Guy Le Thiec, "L'Empire ottoman, modèle de monarchie seigneuriale dans l'œuvre de Jean Bodin," in *L'Oeuvre de Jean Bodin: Actes du colloque tenu à Lyon à l'occasion du quatrième centenaire de sa mort*, eds. Gabriel-André Pérouse, Nicole Dockés-Lallement, and Jean-Michel Servet (Paris: Honoré Champion Éditeur, 2004), 55–76; Lucette Valensi, *The Birth of the Despot: Venice and the Sublime Port*, trans. Arthur Denner (Ithaca: Cornell University Press, 1993); and Barbara Fuchs, *Mimesis and Empire: The New World, Islam, and European Identities* (Cambridge: Cambridge University Press, 2001).

IN THE TIME THAT REMAINS

Just as Jacob Taubes produced the traumatic kernel of messianic time in the form of the Romanesque capital from Vézelay, his lectures gathered in *The Political Theology of Paul* also, paradoxically, provide an opening onto ways of disassociating from this typological undeadness. In his introductory remarks made at Heidelberg, Taubes mentioned his teacher, Gershom Scholem, and Scholem's famous study of Sabbatai Sevi (1626–76), the self-proclaimed Jewish Messiah who converted to Islam and ended up residing at the Sultan's court in Istanbul. Taubes dramatically asks his audience, "Are we obliged to descend with him [*Sabbatai Sevi*] into this world of the abyss, Islam?"[44]

Let us pause at this question. In his recent and provocative study entitled *The Jew, The Arab: A History of the Enemy*, Gil Anidjar tries to answer Taubes's query. Anidjar urges scholars to think how the "consistent evacuation of the significance of the theological ('a force without significance' in Scholem's own phrase) repeats the evacuation of the Muslim from the Jews in the double figure of the Messiah—the Messiah and the Muslims, the Messiah and the Mussulman—and that it remains, indeed, in force."[45] According to Anidjar's critique, theories of messianic time, as currently understood and argued, especially by Giorgio Agamben, universalize the indigestible remainder of Christian typology as the dead Muslim neighbor, as the Mussulmen of the Nazi camps, which Agamben sees as the sovereign's final decision.

I promised at the opening of this essay that I would try to conjure a threshold in the contemporary theory of political theology through which the untimely and undead could pass. I have been arguing that in order for there to be a relation between philosophy and theology that is not a murderous typological one, we need to traverse the symbolic process whereby Christian typology excarnated both Jews and Muslims. The monastic fantasy of the signifier that seized Peter

---

[44] Taubes, *Political Theology*, 9.
[45] Anidjar, *The Jew, the Arab*, 161.

the Venerable, which foreclosed semiosis to Islam, assigning it to a mechanical world of gears, and superseded semiosis for Jews, remains in force, I claim, in Benjamin's first thesis on the concept of history. Indeed, I further contend that it is the Christian fantasy of the force and seduction of Islam and the supersession of Judaism that gives political theology today its incarnational consistency. Is it time for contemporary political theology to descend into its own abyss haunted by the dead neighbors that its typological machine has ground out? By rendering this machine inoperative, we can begin to ask what the untimely of typological time might look like.

Chapter 5

Tears of Reign
Big Sovereigns Do Cry

Hamm: What's he [Nagg] doing?
Clove: He's crying.
Hamm: Then he's living.

Samuel Beckett, *Endgame*[1]

---

[1] Samuel Beckett, *Endgame: A Play in One Act* (London: Faber and Faber, 1958); http://samuel-beckett.net/endgame.html. The play was first performed April 3, 1957, one month after Ernst Kantorowicz published his classic *The King's Two Bodies: A Study in Medieval Political Theology* (Princeton: Princeton University Press, 1957). It is useful to place the two texts alongside each other. This chapter originally appeared, in slightly different form, as Kathleen Biddick, "Tears of Reign: Big Sovereigns Do Cry," in *bodily fluids* [special issue], eds. Kamillea Aghtan, Michael O'Rourke and Karin Sellberg, *Inter/Alia: A Journal of Queer Studies* 9 (2014): 15–34.

Contemporary theorists of sovereignty and biopolitics might learn from the popular culture of zombies and its performance of the living and the living dead.[2] Zombie fictions are creatively re-animating dead zones of sovereignty imagined by theorists as "bare life" (Giorgio Agamben) or the undead "flesh" of the sovereign (Santner).[3] Zombies are transubstantiating quickly: from the zombie apocalypse of *Zombieland* (Columbia Pictures, 2009) with its Grail quest for the last Twinkie, to the now miraculous re-animation of the living dead—the subject of the novel *Warm Bodies* (2012) by Isaac Marion, now released as a film (Summit Entertainment, 2013). Imagined as a remake of Shakespeare's *Romeo and Juliet*, *Warm Bodies* stages a love-story between the living and the living dead and in so doing questions the sovereign construction of the borders between friend (the living) and enemy (the living dead). The zombies and humans of *Warm Bodies* slowly re-learn language and re-enter a world of tears (such tears are the medium of the argument that follows).

Over the past fifty years, theorists of sovereignty have spun—as feverishly as their counterparts in comics, film, and TV—science fictions of the living and the living dead. The classic study of premodern sovereignty, *The King's Two Bodies: A Study in Medieval Political Theology* (1957) by Ernst Kantorowicz, founds the narrative. He traced how premodern jurists came to imagine the sovereign as a creature with two bodies, one living and temporal, one eternally un-

---

[2] Modeled on Donna Haraway's famous "Cyborg Manifesto," see Sarah Juliet Lauro and Karen Embry, "A Zombie Manifesto: The Non-Human Condition in the Era of Advanced Capitalism," *Boundary 2* 35 (2008): 85–108, and *Better off Dead: The Evolution of the Zombie as Post-Human*, eds. Deborah Christie and Sara Juliet Laura (New York: Fordham University Press, 2011).

[3] Giorgio Agamben, *Homo Sacer: Sovereign Power and Bare Life*, trans. Daniel Heller-Roazen (Stanford: Stanford University Press, 1998), 104; Eric L. Santner, *The Royal Remains: The People's Two Bodies and the Endgames of Sovereignty* (Chicago: University of Chicago Press, 2011).

dead. Subsequent sovereign science fictions spun from Kantorowicz—by Michel Foucault, Giorgio Agamben, Roberto Esposito, Eric Santner, to name just a few authors—matter because they try to draw the line between the living and the living dead as a *temporal* marker: once upon a time there was the sovereign power to make die and let live (clean cuts between the living and the dead) and then came modern biopolitics, the power to make live and let die (the impasse of the living and the living dead).[4] Consider a recent installment of

[4] This essay engages in debates raised by recent publications by Eric L. Santner and Graham Hammill, both of which revisit in contrasting ways the question of political theology: Eric L. Santner, *The Royal Remains* and Graham Hammill, The *Mosaic Constitution: Political Theology and Imagination from Machiavelli to Milton* (Chicago: University of Chicago Press, 2012). Hammill's study offers a persuasive critique of the corporeal literalization of the metaphor of the king's two bodies. Likewise, Jacques Lezra rethinks the politico-philosophical conditions of present democracy by questioning the incarnations of the king's two bodies: *Wild Materialism: The Ethic of Terror and the Modern Republic* (New York: Fordham University Press, 2010). See further my own critique of sovereignty and messianic thinking: "Dead Neighbor Archives: Jews, Muslims and The Enemy's Two Bodies," in *Political Theology and Early Modernity*, eds. Julia Reinhard Lupton and Graham Hammill (University of Chicago Press, 2012): 124–142 (and also reprinted in this volume). These studies engage the so-called classics of political theology: Carl Schmitt, *Political Theology: Four Chapters on the Concept of Sovereignty*, trans. of *Politisches Theologie* (1922) by George Schwab (Chicago: University of Chicago Press, 1985); Walter Benjamin, *The Origin of the German Tragic Drama*, trans. John Osborne (London: New Left Books, 1977); Samuel Weber, "Taking Exception to Decision: Theatrical-Theological Politics: Walter Benjamin and Carl Schmitt," in *Walter Benjamin 1892-1940 zum 100. Geburtstag*, ed. Uwe Steiner (New York: Peter Lang, 1992), 123–138; Giorgio Agamben, *Homo Sacer*; Michel Foucault, *The History of Sexuality, Vol. 1: An Introduction*, trans. Robert Hurley (New York: Random House, 1978), 145, *Society Must Be Defended: Lectures at*

such sovereign science fictions, Eric Santner's *The Royal Remains: The People's Two Bodies and the Endgames of Sovereignty* (2011). Drawing upon Kantorowicz's narrative of the king's two bodies, Santner represents modernity as sovereignty's apocalyptic zombieland. The modern citizen-subject, according to his argument, is seized by a fantastic excess of alien flesh—the undead residue of the failed transference at the time of the French Revolution of the medieval sovereign's second body (the immortal one) into the modern body politic of the People.

This chapter argues that these processes of transference and periodization in contemporary theory need to be understood as sovereign border technologies. Kantorowicz drew the hard line when he presented the king's two bodies as a product of the secularizing (read also, modernizing) *transference* of the corporate sacramental body of the Catholic Church (*corpus mysticum*) into the corporate notion of juridical royal embodiment. Kantorowicz intimates that this "transfer" was what psychoanalysts would call today "transference," in that Tudor jurists fabricating the juridical fantasy of royal zombie embodiment did so "unconsciously rather than consciously."[5] Kantorowicz thus positioned himself fantastically as the "one who knows" classic sovereignty, and scholars have been transferring to his text ever since.[6] What

---

the College de France, 1975-76, eds. Mauro Bertani and Alessandro Fontana, translated by David Macey (New York, 2003), 239–263, and also *Discipline and Punish: Birth of the Prison,* trans. By Alan Sheridan (New York: Random House, 1977); and Roberto Esposito, *Bíos: Biopolitics and Philosophy,* trans. Timothy Campbell (Minneapolis: University of Minnesota Press, 2008).

[5] Kantorowicz, *The King's Two Bodies,* 19.

[6] For a study of Kantorowicz that is sensitive to these issues of institutional transference, see Alain Boureau, *Kantorowicz: Stories of a Historian,* trans. Stephen G. Nichols and Gabrielle M. Spiegel (Baltimore: Johns Hopkins University Press, 2001). Kathleen Davis points to the traumatic medievalisms of sovereignty. For insight into this uncanny persistence of sovereignty in these purported acts

this institutional transference has foreclosed, I argue, is the queer imbrication of classical sovereignty (to make die) and biopolitics (to make live)—the living and the living dead.[7] Such temporal foreclosure results, I believe, in the *fetish of modernity* among the disciples of Kantorowicz. Their tracts profess their faith in biopolitics as the sign of modernity; at the very same time, they must painfully disavow the disturbing evidence for untimely traumatic entanglements of classical sovereignty and biopolitics. This impasse is not much fun, as Tim Dean has pointed out in his recent essay on the "Biopolitics of Pleasure."[8]

This chapter asks, then, how to rethink the living and the living dead, the theoretical impasse of political theology and biopolitics, such that critique is not dismissed as "mere" historicism or, alternatively, as a misguided effort to separate out symbolic fiction from fantasy?[9] How, then, to argue for

of deconstruction, see her *Periodization and Sovereignty: How Ideas of Feudalism and Secularization Govern the Politics of Time* (University of Pennsylvania Press, 2008). For my review of Davis's book in *The Medieval Review*, see here: https://scholarworks.iu.edu/dspace/bitstream/handle/2022/6531/09.04.06.html.

[7] For how this is staked out in discursive terms, see Kathleen Biddick, "Unbinding the Flesh in the Time that Remains: Crusader Martyrdom, Then and Now," *GLQ* 13.2-3 (2007): 197–225, and also Biddick, "Dead Neighbor Archives" (in this volume).

[8] Tim Dean, "The Biopolitics of Pleasure," *South Atlantic Quarterly*, 111 (Summer 2012): 477–495.

[9] The periodization of sovereignty has closed down in unfortunate ways more lively modes for re-imagining Lacanian psychoanalysis and temporality. For inspiration in this creative effort see the reconfigurative work of the Lacanian psychoanalyst and artist, Bracha L. Ettinger, *The Matrixial Borderspace* (Minneapolis: University of Minnesota Press, 2006), esp. 167 for a compelling example of the ways in which she reconfigures temporality. Her revisions of Lacanian psychoanalysis can productively open the boundaries between creaturely life and animal life defended by Santner. I also have in mind the rich critique of temporalities engaged by queer

what I perceive as the queer untimeliness the living and the living dead, the untimeliness of political theology and biopolitics?

AN ARCHIVE OF TEARS

Kantorowicz opened his study of the king's two bodies with his now famous reading of William Shakespeare's tragedy, *King Richard II*. He concentrated exclusively on the famous deposition scene (Act IV) in which Richard, stripped of his regalia, calls for a mirror and shatters it upon glimpsing his reflection. According to Kantorowicz, Shakespeare's tragedy eternalized the metaphor of the king's two bodies. Subsequent theorists (notably Santner) also truncate their readings of the play at the mirror scene and argue along similar lines. But why do Kantorowicz and Santner exit the play at Act IV? There is more, I argue, to Shakespeare's performance of sov-

theorists, such as Carolyn Dinshaw, "Touching on the Past," in *The Boswell Thesis: Essays on Christianity, Social Tolerance, and Homosexuality*, ed. Mathew Kuefler (Chicago: University of Chicago Press, 2006), 57–73; Elizabeth Freeman, *Time Binds: Queer Temporalities, Queer Histories* (Durham: Duke University Press, 2010); Carla Freccero, *Queer/Early/Modern* (Durham: Duke University Press, 2006); Biddick, "Unbinding the Flesh"; and Michael Uebel, "Opening Time: Psychoanalysis and Medieval Culture," in *Cultural Studies of the Modern Middle Ages*, eds. Eileen A. Joy, Myra J. Seaman, Kimberley K. Bell and Mary K. Ramsey (New York: Palgrave, 2007), 269–274. The question of the medieval as the unconscious of contemporary theory grows more pressing and is taken up in a special cluster of essays, "The Medieval Turn in Theory," ed. Andrew Cole, *The Minnesota Review* 80 (April 2013): 80–158. On the same problem, see also Bruce Holsinger, *The Premodern Condition: Medievalism and the Making of Theory* (Chicago: University of Chicago Press, 2005) and *The Legitimacy of the Middle Ages: On the Unwritten History of Theory*, eds. Andrew Cole and D. Vance Smith (Durham: Duke University Press, 2010). See my review of Cole and Smith's volume in *The Medieval Review* here: https://scholarworks.iu.edu/dspace/bitstream/handle/2022/9063/10.09.12.html.

ereignty in *King Richard II*.[10] By the end of the play (the fifth
scene of Act V), Shakespeare has transformed Richard into a
human crying machine.[11] In so doing Shakespeare is staging,
I argue, the temporal imbrication of classical sovereignty (to
make die) and biopolitics (to make live). Richard's tears enable us to engage the question: how might an excess of tears
breach the sovereign borders drawn (as we have seen) by the
transference and periodization of contemporary theorists?[12]

[10] Citations from *King Richard II* are taken from *The Norton Shakespeare*, 2nd edn., ed. Stephen Greenblatt (New York: W.W. Norton,
2008).

[11] Here is the text for the human crying machine (*King Richard II*,
Act V, Scene 5, ll. 43–60):

> [*Music*]
> Ha; ha; keep time! how sour sweet music is,
> When time is broke and no proportion kept.
> So is it in the music of men's lives.
> And here have I the daintiness of ear
> To check time broke in a disorder'd string;
> But for the concord of my state and time
> Had not an ear to hear my true time broke.
> I wasted time, and now doth time waste me,
> For now hath time made me his numb'ring clock.
> My thoughts are minutes, and with sighs they jar
> Their watches on unto mine eyes, the outward watch
> Whereto my finger, like a dial's point,
> Is pointing still, in cleansing them from tears.
> Now sir, the sound that tells what hour it is
> Are clamorous groans that strike upon my heart,
> Which is the bell. So sighs and tears and groans
> Show minutes, hours and times. But my time
> Runs posting on in Bolingbroke's proud joy,
> While I stand fooling here, his Jack o' the clock.

[12] Richard II was rumored to be "sodomitical" in his lifetime and
Lancastrian propaganda emplotted his alleged sodomitical perversi-
ty to justify his deposition after the fact: Sylvia Federico, "Queer
Times: Richard II in the Poems and Chronicles of Late Fourteenth-
Century England," *Medium Aevum* 79 (2010): 25–46. Judith Brown

King Richard II offers me an archive of tears with which to explore how historians might *see* through sovereign scenes and see *through* them.[13] Try this in your home archive. First, blind yourself with tears: "Deep down, deep down inside, the eye would be destined not to see but to weep. For at the very moment they veil sight, tears would unveil what is proper to the eye."[14] Tears stage scenes of fleshly encounter. They are inside and outside at the same time. Such teary folding offers a way of rethinking a biopolitics of sovereignty founded as it is in fantasies of embodiment.[15] But please be advised, my archive of tears is not, however, intended to produce a history of tears. Scholars such as Elina Gertsman, Marjory E. Lange, Kimberly Christine Patton, Tom Lutz, and Peter Schwenger (to name just a few) have ably traced such genealogies.[16] Nor am I trying to write a history of religious com-

offers a beautiful meditation on Richard's queerness in her essay "Pretty Richard (in Three Parts)," in *Shakesqueer: A Queer Companion to the Complete Works of Shakespeare*, ed. Madhavi Menon (Durham: Duke University Press, 2011), 286–301.

[13] David Michael Kleinberg-Levin, *Sites of Vision: The Discursive Construction of Sight in the History of Philosophy* (Cambridge: MIT Press, 1997), 197.

[14] Jacques Derrida, *Memoirs of the Blind: The Self-Portrait and Other Ruins,* trans. Pascale-Anne Brault and Michael Naas (Chicago: University of Chicago Press 1993), 126. See also these beautiful meditations on tears: John D. Caputo, *The Prayers and Tears of Jacques Derrida* (Bloomington: Indiana University Press, 1997) and Anais N. Spitzer's chapter on tears in her study, *Derrida, Myth and the Impossibility of Philosophy* (New York: Continuum, 2011), 24–45.

[15] See Paul A. Kottman, *A Politics of the Scene* (Stanford: Stanford University Press, 2008). Kottman urges that students "reorient our understanding of politics by making the dramatic scene (or, better, scenes) a fundamental category of political life" (7).

[16] Two of my favorite essays in the bibliographic vale of tears are Lance Duerfahrd, "Afterthoughts on Disability: Crying at William Wyler's *Best Years of Our Lives*," in *On the Verge of Tears: Why the Movies, Television, Music, Art, Popular Culture, and the Real World*

punction and its gift of tears, since we already have good studies of such phenomena in the work of medievalist, Sandra J. McEntire, and also in Gary Kuchar's investigation of Catholic recusant poetry of religious sorrow in early modern England, a literature of sighs and tears.[17] Instead, I am asking how tears might be a media that queers the fantasy of sovereign decision and the naming of the enemy (the basic ingredients of sovereignty, according to Carl Schmitt)?[18]

Make us Cry, eds. Michele Byers and David Lavery (Newcastle-upon-Tyne: Cambridge Scholars Publishing, 2010), 50–66, and Éamonn Dunne and Michael O'Rourke, "Miller's Idle Tears" (unpublished paper): https://www.academia.edu/6919392/Millers_Idle_Tears. For an introduction to a bibliography on tears, see the following studies: *Crying in the Middle Ages: Tears of History*, ed. Elina Gertsman (New York: Routledge, 2012); Marjory E. Lange, *Telling Tears in the English Renaissance* (New York: Brill, 1996); Tom Lutz, *Crying: The Natural and Cultural History of Tears* (New York: Norton, 1999); Kimberley Christine Patton and John Stratton Hawley, *Holy Tears: Weeping in the Religious Imagination* (Princeton: Princeton University Press, 2005); and Peter Schwenger, *The Tears of Things: Melancholy and Physical Objects* (Minneapolis: University of Minnesota Press, 2006). For discursive reflections, see Slavoj Žižek, *The Fright of Real Tears: Krzysztof Kieslowski Between Theory and Post-Theory* (London: British Film Institute, 2001). I have also benefited from the beautiful essay by Annika Thiem, "Adorno's Tears: Textures of Philosophical Emotionality," *Modern Language Notes* 124 (2009): 592–613.

[17] Sandra J. McEntire, *The Doctrine of Compunction in Medieval England: Holy Tears* (Lewiston: Mellen Press, 1990); Gary Kuchar, *The Poetry of Religious Sorrow in Early Modern England* (Cambridge: Cambridge University Press, 2008).

[18] The prominent German legal scholar of sovereignty, Carl Schmitt, famously argued for these two criteria of the sovereign in his diptych of works: *Political Theology: Four Chapters on the Concept of Sovereignty* and *The Concept of the Political*, trans. of *Der Begriff des Politischen* by George Schwab (Chicago: University of Chicago Press, 1996).

SO SIGHS AND TEARS AND GROANS /
SHOW MINUTES, HOURS AND TIMES

When it comes to *King Richard II*, critical readings, as I have already noted, crescendo with the scene of the shattered mirror in Act IV. More recently, scholars have begun to claim, contra Kantorowicz, that Shakespeare was not eternalizing the metaphor of the king's two bodies in *Richard II,* but rather that he was de-sacramentalizing it.[19] They argue that Shakespeare was intent on removing the corporate concept of the king's two bodies from any pretensions to an eternal register.[20] More specifically, Kuchar has recently read *King Richard II* as Shakespeare's intentional de-sacramentalizing parody of contemporary Jesuit-influenced recusant literature of devotional tears.

Eternalizing, de-sacramentalizing—these are the binaries of counter-discourses that, I argue, miss Shakespeare's powerful staging of another political scene in Act V: the transformation of Richard into a human crying machine. By Act V, Scene 5, the audience already knows that assassins are on their way to Richard's prison cell. Meanwhile, Richard ticks away. He recounts to the audience how his heavy groans have become the mechanical gears that strike his heart, which now peals the hourly chime. He observes how his hands mark each minute as they metronomically wipe the tears from his clock-face. In fabricating this human crying machine, Shakespeare mobilizes a mechanical metaphor in order to point to what he imagines as the "escapement" of sovereignty.

---

[20] For reflections on de-sacramentalization, see Regina Mara Schwartz, *Sacramental Poetics at the Dawn of Secularism* (Stanford: Stanford University Press, 2008); Gary Kuchar, *Poetry of Religious Sorrow* and also his *Divine Subjection: The Rhetoric* of *Sacramental Devotion in Early Modern England* (Pittsburgh: Duquesne University Press, 2005); and David Womersley, *Divinity and State* (Oxford: Oxford University Press, 2010).

In Elizabethan clock talk (of which geeky Shakespeare was enamored) the escapement is a generic term used to describe the mechanisms that transfer energy to an oscillating lever that produces the stepped increments registered on the minute and hour hands of the clock (see Fig. 1). For Elizabethans the escapement consisted of a crown wheel (a gear shaped like a crown) driven by a weight and checked by pennon-like gears mounted on a vertical shaft, known as a verge. The verge would eventually be refined into a lever called a deadbeat. By turning the king into a human clock Shakespeare is staging sovereignty, likewise, as an oscillating lever, a verge, a deadbeat. In Act V, Shakespeare uses Richard's tears as the lever. This lever oscillates discontinuously between the mortal body of the king and the imagined eternal corporate body of sovereignty. When we read this scene, we begin to wonder why Shakespeare devoted so much time to imagining sovereignty as a toggle, and also, why Kantorowicz read past this uncanny image of Richard as a weeping clock.

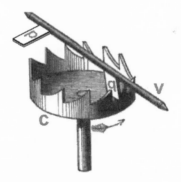

Figure 1. The Verge Escapement of a mechanical clock, where C=crown wheel, v=verge, and p and q are the pennon-like gears. Source: Wikimedia Commons.

My method for exploring this conundrum is to *juxtapose* Shakespeare's staging of a sovereign time bomb in Act V with the better-known scene of the shattered mirror (Act IV), so beloved by Kantorowicz. Just before Richard calls for the mirror in Act IV, he cries out to the audience that his tears blind him. These blinding tears offer up to him a kind of x-ray vision—he suddenly announces that he now is able to see himself surrounded by a pack of traitors. Hounded by this pack, Richard proceeds to gaze into the mirror and then to shatter it. Might we then ask whether Richard is shattering the traitors to which his x-ray vision has given him painful access?

I am going to pause here and ask readers to do something that might seem strange. I am asking them to pick up the pieces of this broken glass, because I think Shakespeare is using these splinters deliberately to recall images of the heated late medieval debate over the orthodoxy (or not) of the Real Presence (the transubstantiation of bread and wine into Christ's flesh and blood) in the sacrament of the Eucharist. The orthodox guarantee of the Real Presence in the Eucharist was closely bound, indeed pinned, by polemicists (as I shall unfold below) to the embodiment of the sovereign. Orthodox versions of the Real Presence and sovereignty were closely bound. By the later medieval period, theological debates over the doctrine of the Real Presence of the Eucharist revolved around optics. As Heather Phillips and other scholars have noted, optics and mathematics had deeply permeated theological speculation by the fourteenth century.[21] Shakespeare's much noted fascination with optics and the special effects he conjures in *Richard II* need to be understood not only technically, but also theologically. A school of late medieval univer-

---

[21] See the important essay by Heather Phillips, "John Wyclif and the Optics of the Eucharist," in *From Ockham to Wyclif*, ed. Anne Hudson and Michael Wilks, Studies in Church History, Subsidia 5 (Oxford: Basil Blackwell, 1987), 245–258. See also David Aers, *Sanctifying Signs: Making Christian Tradition in Late Medieval England* (Notre Dame: University of Notre Dame Press, 2004), 53–66, and Dallas G. Denery II, *Seeing and Being Seen in the Later Medieval World: Optics, Theology and Religious Life* (New York: Cambridge University Press, 2005).

sity scholars, conversant in optics and mathematics, rejected the doctrine of transubstantiation based on their scientific studies. John Wyclif (1320-1384, Oxford University), for example, used the science of optics throughout his treatise, *De Eucharistia* (1380), in order to deny the orthodoxy of transubstantiation of the Real Presence by opening up the gap between *nudum sacramentum* (that is, the bare bread and wine of the sacrament of the Eucharist) and *res sacramenta*, the virtual presence of Christ in the sacrament. Wyclif reasoned as follows: "The body of Christ is more clear and resplendent than the sun ... and at every point of the host there is the figure, *Mukephi* (a word he drew from Muslim optical treatises—the Arab work *mukāfi'* is the word for a parabola or parabolic section)."[22] He thus imagined the host as an optical device composed of myriad paraboloid mirrors, which focused the divine body of Christ like a burning mirror. Wyclif used optics to refuse the binary logic of the doctrine of the Real Presence and called that logic a form of idolatry.

In the mirror scene of *King Richard II*, it is as if the politics of sovereignty and Eucharistic optics become mirror images of each other. Richard, recall, had seen through his tears in Act IV to perceive the traitors surrounding him.[23] And indeed, Shakespeare's play is first and foremost a play about treason. The word treason and its variants (treason, traitor, and treachery) occur most frequently in *King Richard II* compared to any of his other plays. This hinging of treason with resonant images of Eucharistic optics in Act IV feels crucial to me for understanding what Shakespeare is trying to

---

[22] Cited in Phillips, "John Wyclif and the Optics of the Eucharist," x.

[23] Christopher Pye richly reflects on the theatricality of grief and treason and invites us to think of tear blots as well as inky blots: "The Betrayal of the Gaze: *Richard II*," in Christopher Pye, *The Regal Phantasm: Shakespeare and the Politics of the Spectacle* (New York: Routledge, 1990), 82–105. My analysis draws together theological debates over the Real Presence and the question of treason.

do in the play regarding political theology. At this juncture, Kantorowicz's reading seems particularly unhelpful. In a book of over 500 pages in length, treason is a subject inexplicably absent from his discussion of sovereignty. He mentions treason a total of only six times. Even when discussing the play of *Richard II*, he merely alludes to treason, without any analysis. When he comes to his final doxological chapter devoted to Dante, whom he praised as the singular humanistic embodiment of sovereignty (self-crowned crown and self-mitred—a kind of anamorphic image of Richard II), Kantorowicz keeps his silence regarding the stunning and leaky corporeality of treason lodged at the very heart of the *Commedia*.[24] Readers of the *Inferno* will recall that at the zero-point of the *Inferno*, in the neighborhood (or ghetto) he dubbed *Judecca*, Dante encounters Satan half-trapped in the frozen lake of his tears (lesser traitors are fully frozen in the lake "like straw in glass").[25] The emperor of the *Inferno* ('lo imperador del doloroso regno," l. 28) is eternally condemned to gnawing on the traitors of Caesar (Cassius and Brutus) and on Judas (the traitor of Christ), whose bodies cram the trinity of his mouths. Neither this imperial cannibal nor the bodies on which he gorges are able to speak—and for once,

[24] Intimates of the Stefan George circle (of whom Kantorowicz was a loyal member from the 1920s to the death of Stefan George in 1933) might have read such acclamations of Dante as a secret tribute to their Master, Stefan George, who was known to costume himself as Dante in laurels. For photographs and discussion of such, see Robert E. Norton, *Secret Germany: Stefan George and His Circle* (Ithaca: Cornell University Press, 2002). The text of Dante's *Inferno*, Canto 34 may be found at the Princeton Dante Project: http://www.princeton.edu/dante/. See John A. Scott, "Treachery in Dante," in *Studies in the Italian Renaissance: Essays in Memory of Arnolfo B. Ferruolo*, eds. Gian Paolo Biasin, Albert N. Mancini, and Nicolas J. Perella (Naples: Società Editrice Napoletana, 1985), 27–39.

[25] "la dove l'ombre tutte era coperte / e transparien come festuca in vetro": *Inferno* XXXIV, ll. 11–12.

Dante does not ventriloquize.[26] When Dante beholds this awful sight of infernal sovereignty incorporating treason (literally), he evokes for his readers a profound sense of what Eric Santner has called "undeadness": "It was not death, nor could one call it life / Imagine, if you have the wit / what I became, deprived of either life."[27] Amidst the flap of Satan's wings and the rain of his tears, attentive readers might also hear the rustle of documents from the 1302 treason trial of Dante and his three co-defendants, whom Florentines judged guilty and condemned to exile.[28]

Kantorowicz, I speculate, disavows treason in his study of sovereignty, because the question of treason was so biographically traumatic for him. On April 20, 1933, shortly after the Nazi Party had barred Jews from civil service (under the new Law for the Restoration of Professional Civil Service), he, who in 1930 had been appointed to a professorship in medie-

---

[26] See Sylvia Tomasch, "Judecca, Dante's Satan and the Displaced Jew," in *Text and Territory: The Geographical Imaginary in the European Middle Ages*, eds. Sylvia Tomasch and Sealy Gilles (Philadelphia: University of Pennsylvania Press, 1998), 247–267.

[27] "Io non mor' e non rimasi vivo / pensa oggimai per te, s'hai fior d'ingegno / qual io divenni, d'uno e d'altro privo": *Inferno* XXXIV, ll. 25–27.

[28] See Randolph Starn, *Contrary Commonwealth: The Theme of Exile in Medieval and Renaissance Italy* (Berkeley: University of California Press, 1982). Starn lists the seven counts against Dante and three named co-defendants brought forth by the court (70–71). They range from forgery (tampering with public documents) to incitement of rebellion. Neither Dante nor his co-defendants appeared in court or responded to the subsequent bans declared against them. On 27 January 1302, the court, following the legal fiction of *ficta litis contestatio* (simulated trial), sentenced each of them to exile for two years. On 10 March 1302, the court sentenced Dante and fourteen others under communal ban to death by fire. These legal proceedings expose the vertiginous convergence of accusations of forgery, incitement to rebellion (treason), and ban, since those banned from the commune were regarded as the "enemy" (*hostes*).

val history at the University of Frankfurt, wrote decisively to the Minister of Science, Art and Education to inform the Minister forthwith that he would be suspending his summer teaching duties.[29] Among the reasons Kantorowicz offered for this decision, was his shock that he, who had fought heroically for Germany in World War I and who had published an acclamation of a national Germany in his bestselling history, *Kaiser Friedrich der Zweite* (1927), was being treated like a "traitor" (Landes-verräter) because of his Jewish descent.[30]

Treason would prove to be neuralgic for Kantorowicz throughout his career, but not so for his scholarly admirers. In *Discipline and Punish* (1978), Michel Foucault uncannily sutured his hectic and much celebrated opening tableaux of the execution of a regicide in Paris in 1757 with his enthusiastic (booster) endorsement of Kantorowicz's major work, *The King's Two Bodies: An Essay in Political Theology*, which had been recently translated into French. Giorgio Agamben, another critical commentator on Kantorowicz's theory of the king's two bodies, argued for the twinning of the execution of a regicide with the killing of a *homo sacer*: "it does not matter from our perspective, that the killing of *homo sacer* can be considered as less than homicide, and the killing of the sovereign as more than homicide; what is essential is that in neither case does the killing of a man constitute an offense of homicide."[31] Agamben is arguing here for the undecidability

---

[29] The literature on Kantorowicz is copious also, and I cite here (again) an insightful starting point: Boureau, *Kantorowicz: Stories of a Historian.*

[30] The text of this letter is reproduced in Eckhart Grünewald, *Ernst Kantorowicz und Stefan George: Beiträge zur Bibliographie des Historikers bis zum Jahre 1938 und zu seinem Jugendwerk "Kaiser Friedrich der Zweite,"* Frankfurter Historische Abhandlungen 25 (Wiesbaden: F. Steiner, 1982), 114–115.

[31] Foucault, *Discipline and Punish*, 28; Agamben, *Homo Sacer*, 102. Agamben comments directly on the *King's Two Bodies* in his *State of*

of the sovereign and *homo sacer*. Agamben's insight enables an understanding of how Kantorowicz unwittingly articulated such undecidability in his letter of resignation (he, a hero, is being treated like traitor, and because of his Jewish ancestry he is deemed *homo sacer* by the new Nazi race laws). It is precisely this catastrophic undecidability that his great study of sovereignty, *The King's Two Bodies*, forecloses.

Shakespeare, in contrast, searched for the lever between royal treason and bare life, the sovereign and *homo sacer*, politics and theology. He is trying to rethink the zombie franchise of the late sixteenth century. I have already noted his exploration of such a lever when he stages Richard II as a human-clock, but he also plays with this lever in Scene 4 of Act V through his theatrical choices for staging the assassination of Richard. Rather than work with the commonly accepted Tudor account of Richard's demise as death by starvation, Shakespeare chose to use Holinshed's competing version of his death by assassination. Holinshed's account, as scholars have noted, deliberately echoes the medieval narrative describing the assassination of the Archbishop of Canterbury, Thomas Becket, by King Henry II.[32] The bare bones of that twelfth-century story are as follows: A king wishes his adversary dead and his henchmen take matters into their own hands and execute the deed.[33] In a play filled with allu-

Exception I, trans. Kevin Attell (Chicago: University of Chicago Press, 2005), 83–84.

[32] Lister M. Matheson, "English Chronicle Contexts for Shakespeare's Death of Richard II," in *From Page to Performance: Essays in Early English Drama,* ed. John A. Alford (East Lansing: Michigan State University Press, 1995), 195–219.

[33] See Victor Houliston, "Thomas Becket in the Propaganda of the English Reformation," *Renaissance Studies* 7 (1993): 43–70; A.G. Harmon, "Shakespeare's Carved Saints," *Studies in English Literature* 45 (2005): 315–331; and Robert E. Scully, "The Unmaking of a Saint: Thomas Becket and the English Reformation," *Catholic Historical Review* 86 (October 2000): 579–602.

sions to optical illusions, the special effects of which so en-amored Elizabethans, Shakespeare renders the assassination of Richard II as a kind of temporal anamorphosis.[34] The audience sees the death of Richard II unfold on stage, howev-er, when heard acoustically awry, the audience hears another temporal moment, the assassination of Thomas Becket in 1170.

When the reader takes up a perspective glass to view Richard's assassination—and a perspective glass is an optical device used by Elizabethans to correct, or bring into proper perspective, the anamorphic puzzles of the type posed by painters and by dramatists, such as Shakespeare—or, alterna-tively, if readers physically move their vantage point, as Hol-bein invited viewers to do in his famous anamorphic painting *The Ambassadors*, so they could view the death's-head lurk-ing there, then what comes into view in the assassination scene is a surprise. The correction of Shakespeare's temporal anamorphosis reveals none other than Lanfranc of Bec (c. 1005-1089)—abbot, jurist, scholar and court prelate, justiciar, and subsequently Archbishop of Canterbury under William the Conqueror. In the shadow of the Norman conquest of England, Lanfranc wrote his famous polemic on the ortho-

---

[34] The Oxford English Dictionary (OED) defines anamorphosis as follows: "a distorted projection or drawing of anything, so made that when views from a particular point, or by reflection from a suitable mirror, it appears regular and properly proportioned." See also Pye, "Betrayal of the Gaze"; Allan Shickman, "The 'Perspective Glass' in Shakespeare's *Richard II*," *Studies in English Literature* 18 (Spring 1978): 217–228, and "'Turning Pictures' in Shakespeare's England," *The Art Bulletin* 59 (March 1977): 67–70; Ernest Gilman, *The Curious Perspective: Literary and Pictorial Wit in the Seven-teenth Century* (New Haven: Yale University Press, 1978), 88–127; Robert M. Schuler, "Magic Mirrors in *Richard II*," *Comparative Drama* 38 (2004): 151–172; and Alison Thorne, *Vision and Rhetoric in Shakespeare: Looking Through Language* (New York: St. Martin's Press, 2000).

doxy of the Real Presence.[35] In his famous treatise, *De corpo-ra et sanguine Domini adversus Berengariam*, composed when he moved to the newly-founded ducal monastery at Caen in 1063, Lanfranc attacked the arguments of his con-temporary Berengar, who outspokenly questioned the Real Presence in the sacrament of the Eucharist (the materializa-tion of the flesh and blood of Christ upon the words of Eu-charistic consecration). Lanfranc asserted the orthodoxy that "The Flesh is the Sacrament of the Flesh."[36] The high stakes of this theological controversy—its conflicts between inter-pretation, criticism, identity, and realism—have been well studied.[37] What interests me from the point of view of Shake-

---

[35] An English translation of Lanfranc's *Liber de corpora et sanguine Domini* (c. 1063) may be found in *The Fathers of the Church: Medie-val Continuation*, Vol. 10, trans. Mark G. Vaillancourt (Washing-ton, DC: Catholic University of America, 2009), hereafter called Lanfranc. Vaillancourt keys his English translation to the Latin text of the *Patrologia Latina*, ed. J-.P. Migne, 161 vols. (Paris, 1857-1866), 150:407–442. For a concise and insightful summary of the Bérenger debate see, Jean de Montclos, "Lanfranc et Bérenger: les origines de la doctrine de la Transsubstantiation," *in Lanfranco de Pavia e L'europa del secolo XI*, ed. Giulio D'Onofrio (Italia Sacra: Studi e Documenti di Storia Ecclesiastica), Vol. 51 (Rome: Herder Editrice e Libreria, 1993), 297–326. The citation is from Lanfranc, 56. See also, Charles M. Radding and Francis Newton, *Theology, Rhetoric, and Politics in the Eucharistic Controversy, 1078-1079: Alberic of Monte Cassino against Berengar of Tours* (New York: Columbia University Press, 2003).

[36] "caro, videlicet carnis . . . sacramentum est": Lanfranc, 56.

[37] The literature is copious and I cite here a few exemplary studies: Brian Stock, *The Implications of Literacy: Written Language and Models of Interpretation in the Eleventh and Twelfth Centuries* (Princeton: Princeton University Press, 1983), 252–314; Michal Kobialka, *This is My Body: Representational Practices in the Early Middle Ages* (Ann Arbor: University of Michigan Press, 1999); Brigitte Miriam Bedos-Rezak, "Medieval Identity: A Sign and a Concept," *American Historical Review* 105.5 (December 2000): 1489–1533; David Aers and Sarah Beckwith, "Eucharist," in *Cultur-*

speare's interest in treason and the Real Presence, is how Lanfranc's treatise goes beyond the stock litany of theological polemic—Berengar as adversary of the Catholic Church,[38] sacrilegious violator of oath,[39] heretic[40]— to pioneer an accusation of *treason* against him.[41]

Berengar, in Lanfranc's opinion, not only challenged theological orthodoxy; he also traitorously undid the universalism of the Catholic Church, a universalism constituted by the flesh of Christ.[42] To think against this sacramental flesh is to commit treason, because, according to Lanfranc's vision, the flesh of Christ is constitutively both sacramental *and* sovereign. The flesh of the Eucharist, thus, for Lanfranc was both a sacramental and a sovereign problematic. His accusation brings into view both the sovereign body under threat of treason and also that of *homo sacer* (the one who may be killed without accusation of homicide, but who may not be sacrificed). In the gap in between the visible and the invisible, in which Berengar had meditated provocatively on the unhistorical nature of Christ's flesh, Lanfranc, instead, sutured sovereign law and in so doing paradoxically immunized universal flesh of Christ as a sovereign body politic. Thus, a biopolitics of the flesh needs to account for this "unhistori-

al Reformations: Medieval and Renaissance in Literary History, eds. Brian Cummings and James Simpson (Oxford: Oxford University Press, 2010), 153–156; and Amy Nelson Burnett, "The Social History of Communion and the Reformation of the Eucharist," *Past and Present* 211 (2011): 77–119.

[38] "catholicae Ecclesiae adversario": Lanfranc, 29.

[39] "sacrilegus violator": Lanfranc, 31.

[40] "esse haereticus": Lanfranc, 32.

[41] "jurare perfidiam": Lanfranc, 40.

[42] For a recent consideration of Lanfranc on universalism (his resurrection of Augustinian themes), see Patrick Healy, "A Supposed Letter of Archbishop Lanfranc: Concepts of the Universal Church in the Investiture Contest," *English Historical Review* CXXI.494 (December 2006): 1385–1407.

cal" twining of the sacred flesh and sovereignty across the normalized divides of medieval and modern in an effort to re-conceive biopolitics of the flesh as a traumatic scene that expands and sediments as it maintains a deadly kernel, a medieval suture of flesh to sovereignty. Such a suture precludes any linear periodization of political theology and biopolitics. The suture also inverts Kantorowicz's metanarrative of political theology and sovereignty in which sacramental flesh gives way to a secularized body politic. In contrast to Kantorowicz's normalization of Shakespeare as an agent of eternalizing the king's two bodies. I have argued, instead, that the playwright stages theatrical scenes in order to expose the suture of sacramental flesh to sovereign law. The theatrical exposure does not attempt to undo sacramentality and sovereignty, but to expose their traumatic suture.

But does Shakespeare stop at this stage of critique or does he go further and offer a meta-theatrical critique of representation as a drive toward Real Presence—or put another way, as a way of rethinking the zombie franchise of the sixteenth-century? The tears of Richard's Queen Isabella offer another archive of tears for exploring the relations between Shakespeare's critique of the sovereignty of Real Presence and his ontology of the theater. Shakespeare uses Queen Isabella to remake the widely known medieval liturgical theater of the Easter story, known as *Quem Queritis* ("Whom do you seek?"). According to this Gospel story, Mary Magdalene discovers the empty Easter tomb and then encounters a gardener, the resurrected Christ, who asks her "Whom do you seek" and then admonished Mary Magdalene not to touch him (*Noli me tangere*). In his ground-breaking study, entitled *This is my Body: Representational Practices in the Early Middle Ages* (1999), medievalist and theater-historian Michal Kobialka has argued that changing orthodox epistemologies of the Real Presence were constitutive of medieval forms of representation. He tracks these changes by studying how Western Easter liturgies represented (or not) the dead body of Christ, which according to the Gospels, was absent at the empty

Easter tomb. Prior to the Eucharistic crisis over the Real Presence, in the tenth and early eleventh centuries, no cleric ever impersonated the Risen Christ and spoke the Gospel words to Mary Magdalene. An angel-actor, clearly not Christ, would voice these words at the "stage-set" of an empty tomb. The angel addresses her tersely: "Whom do you seek?/ Jesus of Nazareth. He is not here. He has risen just as it was predicted."[43] By the end of the eleventh century, as the Church promulgated and disciplined the doctrine of the Real Presence, Kobialka shows that the body of the resurrected Christ is represented for the first time in the Easter performance of the *Quem Queritis*. In the twelfth-century versions, Christ now appears on stage before Mary Magdalene in the guise of gardener. He enacts the *Noli mi tangere* scene recounted in Gospel of John.

Such a material, theatrical embodiment of the absent, resurrected Christ transformed, according to Kobialka, the medieval representational grids of space and time. What is also chilling to realize, (and this is a link that Kobialka does not really develop), is that it is these very same *Quem Queritis* scripts of the later twelfth century that materialize the personified body of the Jewish people, who are excoriated as deicides. Take for example, the famous playbook of the abbey of Fleury, which scripts the performance of the *Quem Queritis* at the turn of the twelfth century.[44] What in the tenth

---

[43] Michal Kobialka, *This is My Body: Representational Practices in the Early Middle Ages* (Ann Arbor: University of Michigan Press, 1999). Kobialka discusses the *Quem Queritis* trope described in the *Regularis concordia* based on British Library MS Cotton Faustina B III, f. 189, on pages 72–99.

[44] The text of this Easter play is recorded in Latin and English in *Medieval Drama*, ed. David Bevington (Boston: Houghton Mifflin, 1975), 39–44. See also *The Fleury Playbook: Essays and Studies*, eds. Thomas P. Cambell and Clifford Davidson (Kalamazoo: Medieval Institute Publications, 1985), and Theresa Tinkle, "Jews in the Fleury Playbook," *Comparative Drama* 38 (2004): 1–38. Shakespeare played with the "quem queritis" trope in several plays, as Cynthia

century counted for a three or four spare lines, had now exploded into a script of seventy-five lines along with stage directions. Jews are personified at the opening of the *Quem Queritis* script: "Alas! Wretched Jewish people, Whom an abominable insanity makes frenzied. Despicable nation." As the script unfolds, the risen (theatricalized) Christ appears to Mary Magdalene and asks her the famous question recorded in the Gospel of John: "Woman, why do you weep, Whom do you seek?" At the moment of recognition, in the famous *noli mi tangere* scene, Christ instructs Mary Magdalene not touch him.

Kobialka links this changing ontology of theatrical embodiment to changing doctrinal epistemologies of the Real Presence at the open of the twelfth century. The details of the epistemological change are important. Early medieval Christians had imagined the flesh of the Eucharist as a ternary flesh intertwining the *corpus verum* (that was the historical Christ), *corpus mysticum* (that was the Eucharist), and *corpus Christi* (that was the Church). With the promulgation of the doctrine of transubstantiation the sacramental flesh was reduced to a binary. The *corpus verum* dropped out; the Universal Church came to be regarded as the *corpus mysticum*; the *corpus Christi* became the Eucharist. This chiasmic reduction from a ternary to binary epistemology resulted in the (death) drive to represent the absent resurrected Christ theatrically and, as art historians tell us, in other media. Witness, for example, the eruption of human forms in Romanesque sculpture. The monumental Romanesque building program at the ducal abbey at Caen, over which Lanfranc presided from 1063-1070 (just at the inauguration of the orthodoxy of the Real Presence), featured only one capital sculpted with a human form. Within one generation, as that orthodoxy be-

Lewis outlines in "Soft Touch: On the Renaissance Staging and Meaning of the 'noli me tangere' Icon," *Comparative Drama* 36 (2002): 53–73.

came the subject of disciplinary enforcement, sculpted humanoid forms would come to populate Romanesque capitals, as well as monumental porches of those churches.[45] Kobialka offers a trenchant insight into these new representational modes of embodiment: "Whereas in the corporeal and mystical approaches [that is, ternary], the body of Christ was silent, now the silent body was to speak the language of theological pedagogy that delimited the space of representation by consolidating the structures of belonging."[46] This binary sacramental flesh profoundly reorganized the temporal and spatial coordinates of medieval representation and forced a dominant gaze to organize itself around a body that is forced to materialize within theatrical space.

FRESH AGAIN, WITH TRUE LOVE'S TEARS

So what does Shakespeare's politics of the scene have to do with Kobialka's genealogy of changing forms of medieval representation? Kobialka imagines the Renaissance stage as the teleological endpoint of such theatrical pedagogy involved in the coerced materialization of the Real Presence in the form of an actor. I disagree with Kobialka's teleology, and I think Shakespeare would too. And now let me explain why. Shakespeare rewrote the medieval Easter *Quem Queritis*

[45] For a major study of the building program at Caen and discussion of its sculpture from the first building phases, see Eric Gustav Carlson, "The Abbey Church of Saint-Etienne at Caen in the Eleventh and early Twelfth Centuries," Ph.D. diss., Yale University, 1968, 296.

[46] Kobialka, *This is My Body*, 157. My argument disagrees with that of Wolfgang Iser, who wrote: "In this context the persona appears as a kind of empty space, and the filling of this space is what constitutes the thrust of the play": *Staging Politics: The Lasting Impact of Shakespeare's Histories*, trans. David Henry Wilson (New York: Columbia University Press, 1993). Instead, I am arguing that Shakespeare attempts to keep the empty space open and uses the sense of seeing through tears to do so.

trope self-consciously in several of his plays, and, most notably in King Richard II in order to unpin sovereignty from the
Real Presence, to re-imagine the boundaries of the living and
living dead configured in the eleventh century.

In Act III, scene 4 of *Richard II*, Shakespeare opens his re-
staging of the *Quem Queritis* trope.[47] Richard's queen, Isabella, still uninformed of her husband's recent capture by his
usurper, Bolingbroke, but fearing the worst, seeks respite in a
garden accompanied by her attendants. Shakespeare sets the
stage reminiscent of the medieval horotolanus scene of the
Quem Queritis in which Mary Magdalene and the two other
Mary's hasten to the tomb before which the apostles John
and Peter puzzle over the absence of Christ's body and the
presence of the discarded shroud. Mary then encounters a
gardener who reveals himself to her as the resurrected Christ.
In Shakespeare's scene, the tidings of the gardener to Isabella
(staged as a kind of Mary Magdalene) are not about resurrection. *Instead, the gardener informs the queen of a kind of anti-
transfiguration* in which Richard is described as "depressed
he is already / and disposed 'tis doubt he will be" (III.4.68–
69). The scene closes with the gardener's promise to plant a

---

[47] Kuchar, *The Poetry of Religious Sorrow*, 48–53, construes Shakespeare's "Quem Queritis" scene as a parody and a de-sacralizing
move. To complicate the performance of Queen Isabella, recall her
biopolitics as a presumably Virgin Queen: born 9 November 1389;
wed to Richard II at the age of 7 (1 November 1396); separated at
age 10 by his abdication and imprisonment (1399); and then wid-
owed by the ripe age of 11. See Helen Ostovich, "'Here in this garden': The Iconography of the Virgin Queen in Shakespeare's *Richard II*," in *Marian Moments in early modern British Drama*, eds.
Regina Buccola and Lisa Hopkins (Burlington: Ashgate, 2007), 21–
34. The scene of the kiss also reminds us that both Anglican and
continental Protestant Eucharistic liturgies removed the "kiss of
peace" offered in the congregation after the Communion: see Craig
Koslofsky, "The Kiss of Peace in the German Reformation," in *The
Kiss in History*, ed. Karen Harvey (Manchester: Manchester University Press, 2005), 18–35.

memorial bush of rue on the spot where the tears of the weeping queen fell. In this pseudo-*Quem queritis* scene, Shakespeare thus imagines the tears of Magdalene/Isabella not as redemptive, but as memorial, and in so doing, he inters, but not disrespectfully, important representational strands of twelfth-century versions of the *Quem Queritis* trope that had constituted themselves, as I have already noted, around the materialization of the absent body.

Shakespeare is rewriting the garden scene. But, are his moves those of desacralization as Gary Kuchar has argued in his own intriguing reading of these *Quem Queritis* stagings in *Richard II*? To ponder this question, let us see how Shakespeare further pursues staging the *Quem Queritis* scene in Act V, Scene 1. By this moment in the play, Richard has already deposed himself and is about to wend his way through the streets of London to the Tower. His queen and her attendants await him along the parade route. Isabella is now cast as Mary Magdalene on the verge of encountering the resurrected Christ. She wishes, on catching sight of him, that she, like the Magdalene, could wash Richard "fresh again with true-love tears" (V.1.10) as Mary Magdalene has once washed the feet of Christ with her tears. But Shakespeare's staging of their encounter inverts, once again, aspects of the medieval *Quem Queritis* script. Isabella sees in Richard not a resurrected body, as Mary Magdalene did in the Gospel stories, but, instead, a zombie: "Thou map of honour, thou King Richard's tomb" (V.1.12). Richard turns to Isabella and speaks the word of Christ addressed to the Magdalene on Easter morning: *Noli flere* (do not weep): "Join not with grief, fair woman" (IV.1.16). Shakespeare then crosses out the subsequent scene of *Noli me tangere*, although it is a scene that he did know well and staged in *All's Well that Ends Well.*

Importantly, in *Richard II*, Shakespeare does not defer the touch refused by the Gospel *Noli me tangere*; instead, he has Richard and Isabella kiss before their final separation. Their substitution of a kiss for the refusal of touch (*Noli me tangere*) has been read as a parodic sign of de-sacralization on Shakespeare's part. But, I ask, do we misrecognize this kiss as a touch? Does this kiss touch upon something different? Richard speaks: "One kiss shall stop our mouths, and dumbly part" (V.1.95). Shakespeare takes this image, "stop our mouths," from the New Testament, namely, Paul's Epistle to Titus (1:11), where Paul rails against what he called the "circumcision party" in Corinth, and he uses an imperative Greek form of the verb, *epistomizo*, meaning "to stop the mouth." It is the word used in Greek to put the bit in the horse's mouth, to insert the mouthpiece on the flute. Shakespeare uses the phrase several times in his plays with menacing connotations. Thus, though Richard and Isabella do touch, and indeed, kiss each other on the mouth, it is kiss of violence, a silencing, a touch that is not a touch—a touch that produces untouchability.

I think Shakespeare is doing two things here. First, I think he is deliberately un-staging the risen Christ in this scene in order to open up the third term of the *Quem Queritis*: the absent, silent body of the resurrected Christ. The unspoken words of the *Noli me tangere* in Act V, Scene 1 honor the silent body of the absent Christ without forcing that body "to speak the language of theological pedagogy that delimited the space of representation by consolidating the structures of belonging."[48] By staging a touch that does not touch—the kiss as a form of torture, that stops the mouth—Shakespeare, I think, is not desacralizing nor resacralizing, but he is asking us all to reconsider a post-Real Presence in which the living dead do not underwrite the living. Just as in *Warm Bodies*, and its staging of a love between the living and the living dead, Shakespeare asks us to think again, what is touch, what is absent silence, what is the Real Presence, then and now? How can we imagine a quickening of the dead zones of contemporary citizenship? The dramatist not only re-poses the Gospel question: Whom do you seek? He asks, too, who decides? To weep or not to weep, the living and the living dead?

[48] Kobialka, *This is My Body*, 157.

Chapter 6

Undeadness and the Tree of Life
Ecological Thought of Sovereignty

> . . . perpetual spirals of power and pleasure.
>
> Michel Foucault

Dead trees started to drift into gallery spaces in the late 1960s and they continue to wash up with tidal frequency on gallery shores today. Take, for example, the arresting tree-works of artists Robert Smithson (1969), Zoe Leonard (1997), and Anselm Kiefer (2006) (see Figures 1-2).[1] As I contemplated writ-

---

[1] For Zoe Leonard's *Tree* (1997), view the image at *ArtSEENsoHo* here: http://www.artseensoho.com/Art/COOPER/leonard97/leonard1. html. My reading of these dead trees is shaped by and also questions the boundary between creaturely life and animal life posed by Eric L. Santner in two books: *On Creaturely Life: Rilke, Benjamin, Sebald* (Chicago: University of Chicago Press, 2006) and *The Royal Remains: The People's Two Bodies and the Endgame of Sovereignty* (Chicago: University of Chicago Press, 2011). I am grateful to Randy

ing this essay on the medieval Tree of Life, I could not help but notice that dead trees began falling into galleries synchronous with the so-called revolution in molecular biology, one which redefined the molar (arboreal root and branch) to the molecular (the spiral and rhizome).[2] In the temporal shadow of sculptures of the DNA spiral, widely exhibited in the late 1950s, Michel Foucault, a seer of this shift from molar to molecular, from classical sovereign power ("to make die and let live") to modern biopower ("to make live and let die"), construed molecular biopolitics as a question of both power and pleasure: "perpetual spirals of power and pleasure."[3]

Schiff for reminding me of Agamben's beautiful meditation on vegetative life (Aristotle believed in a plant soul): Giorgio Agamben, *The Open: Man and Animal*, trans. Kevin Attell (Stanford: Stanford University Press, 2004), 12–19. For the work of Robert Smithson, see *Robert Smithson: The Collected Writings* (Berkeley: University of California Press, 1996); see Mark Godfrew on Zoe Leonard: "Mirror of Displacements: On the Art of Zoe Leonard," *Artforum International* 46 (March 2008): 292–302; and on Anselm Kiefer, see the review of *Palmsonntag* in *Whitehot Magazine*, April 2007, http:// whitehotmagazine.com/articles/white-cube-mason-s-yard/396. Smithson's installation was lovingly re-enacted in 1998 at the Pierogi Gallery, Brooklyn: Frances Richard, "A Tree dies in Brooklyn," *Art Forum*, 36 (Feb. 1998): 19–20. Likewise, Leonard's tree became part of the "After Nature" exhibition, New Museum of Contemporary Art, New York 2008.

[2] Bruno J. Strasser reflects on 50 years of DNA in "Who Cares About the Double Helix?" *Nature* 422 (April 24, 2003): 803–804. See also Suzanne Anker and Dorothy Nelkin, *The Molecular Gaze: Art in the Genetic Age* (New York: Cold Spring Harbor Laboratory Press, 2003).

[3] This essay addresses some of the intriguing points made by Tim Dean, "The Biopolitics of Pleasure," *South Atlantic Quarterly* 111 (Summer 2012): 477–495, although what is a vanishing act for Dean is a toggle for me. Dean draws attention to Foucault's molecular imagination of power and pleasure: Michel Foucault, *The History of Sexuality, Vol. 1: An Introduction*, trans. Robert Hurley (New York: Random House, 1978), 45 (cited in my epigraph here). Relevant to the subject of trees, molar and molecular, see Mark A. Ragan, "Trees

Figure 1. Robert Smithson, *Dead Tree* (1969). Photograph: Vaga Rights.

Figure 3. Anselm Kiefer, *Palmsonntag* (2006). Palm tree and 43 works on fiberboard with clay, paint, shellac, adhesive, metal, palm fronds, fabric and paper. Photograph: Gagosian Gallery. © Anselm Kiefer.

and Networks Before and After Darwin," *Biology Direct* 4:43 (2009), http://www.biology-direct.com/content/4/1/43.

Such spirals have become the instigation for important recent studies on vibrant matter and ecological thought by scholars such as Jane Bennett and Timothy Morton.[4] As Foucault envisioned his suggestive image, biotechnology laboratories had just figured out how to cut up spirals of DNA into molecular scraps to be spliced into engineered matter—think of such matter as souvenirs of the undeadness of the classical sovereign who can make die and let live. It is such undeadness, or what Eric Santner has called an archive of creaturely life, that animates, I argue, the undeadness of dead trees in gallery spaces, and, as I shall unfold, the undeadness of historical trees of life.[5]

This chapter therefore returns to the fearful symmetry proposed by Foucault—the classical sovereign who could make die and let live and the modern biopolitical sovereign who can make live and let die—in an effort to think the cut and the spiral together in an untimely way. This essay further asks whether it might be necessary to supplement the notion of *homo sacer* (the one who can be killed but who may not be sacrificed) with a diffracting notion of *res sacra* (the thing that can be cut, but may not be sacrificed).[6] Imagined another way: how to think of the undeadness of the tree of life?

[4] Jane Bennett, *Vibrant Matter: A Political Ecology of Things* (Durham: Duke University Press, 2010). Bennett's imagination of the *pluriverse* is one of vortices, spirals and eddies (110–122). Timothy Morton, *The Ecological Thought* (Cambridge: Harvard University Press, 2010). Ecological thought is a spiral for Morton (3). See also Jane Bennett, "Systems and Things: A Response to Graham Harman and Timothy Morton," *New Literary History* 43 (2012): 225–233.

[5] Santner, *On Creaturely Life*, xiii.

[6] For *homo sacer* as the sign of sovereignty, the one who decides on bare life, see Giorgio Agamben, *Homo Sacer: Sovereign Power and Bare Life*, trans. Daniel Heller-Roazen (Stanford: Stanford University Press, 1998).

BECOMING-TREE

> Since you cannot be my wife, you will be my tree.
> Ovid, *Metamorphoses*, Book 1, ll. 669–670[7]

Scholars of sovereignty have written much on the becoming-beast of the sovereign, but have little to say about the becoming-tree of sovereignty's objects, even though dendranthropy has fascinated fabulists such as Ovid.[8] Such muteness may be partially explained by the uncanny misfortunes of scholarly preservation: take, for example, the loss of Aristotle's book on plants, the companion piece to his well-studied book on animals; the forgetting of Wolfgang Goethe's amazing treatise on the *Metamorphosis of Plants* (with his exuberant imagining of the leaf as the evolutionary toggle). Likewise, Charles Darwin's prescient pedagogical immersion in botany is mostly marginalized in favor of his zoological dramas.[9] The animal turn of contemporary critique leaves plants on the verge. Yet, contemporary media rustles with trees, or what students of vibrant matter might call arboreal actants.[10] Take,

[7] "cui deus 'at, quoniam coniunx mea non potes esse, arbor eris certe' dixit": translation above from Ovid, *Metamorphoses*, trans. Charles Martin (New York: W.W. Norton, 2004).

[8] Jacques Derrida, *The Beast and the Sovereign, Vol. 1*, eds. Michel Lisse, Marie-Louise Mallet, and Ginette Michaud, trans. Geoffrey Bennington (Chicago: University of Chicago Press, 2009); Diego Rossello, "Hobbes and the Wolf-Man: Melancholy and Animality in Modern Sovereignty," *New Literary History* 43 (2012): 255–279.

[9] For an overview, see Mark A. Ragan, "Trees and Networks Before and After Darwin," *Biology Direct* 4.43 (2009): http://www.biology-direct.com/content/4/1/43 (doi:10.1186/1745-6150-4-43).

[10] Graham Harman has now become the arbiter of Bruno Latour's Actor Network Theory (ANT). See his *Prince of Networks: Bruno Latour and Metaphysics* (Melbourne: re.press, 2009). Harman on actants, also called objects (not things) by Harman: "No actor, however trivial, will be dismissed as mere noise in comparison with its essence, its context, its physical body, or its conditions of possibility. Everything will be absolutely concrete, all objects and all modes of dealing with objects will now be on the same footing" (13).

for example, the great tree-rhizome, the Home Tree, the star of James Cameron's recent film, *Avatar* (2009), whose proposed fate was to be bombed to splinters for the sake of colonial mineral extraction ("It is only a goddamn tree" as the sovereigns of the film exclaim). Or consider the mystical dance of Mrs. O'Brien (Jessica Chastaine), who levitates around the trunk of the tree of life in Terrence Malick's film of that same name (see Figure 3). Malick had uprooted this majestic oak (all 30 tons of it), whose trunk, branches, and leaves punctuate *The Tree of Life* (2011), and transported it eight miles to the movie set for transplanting. As I watched the YouTube video of the transport,[11] I understood that Malick wished to assure his viewer that this is the tree of life, not a life of a tree.

Figure 3. still image from Terrence Malick, dir., *Tree of Life* (2011)

These stories of arboreal uprooting trace the anxiety around the differences between life and "a life" closely observed by Jane Bennett: "A life thus names a restless activeness, a destructive-creative force-presence that does not coincide fully

A strong incarnational theology informs this vision. For a differing vision, see Bennett, "Systems and Things."

[11] "Tree of Life" [video], February 16, 2008, www.youtube.com/watch?v=sOfKsg7SH8c.

with any specific body."[12] It is this non-coincidence of a life, its spectral materialism, that I track in the following four splices.

SPLICE ONE // 2049 BCE, BRONZE CUTS WOOD:
SEAHENGE, NORTH-WEST COAST OF NORFOLK

It is springtime 2049 BCE on the northwest coast of Norfolk, England. The climate is warming; the sea is rising. The oak groves growing behind the shoreline are failing in the wet conditions. Enter a troupe of fifty or so bronze axe-wielding men and women with the aim to fell over 20 oak trees to build a palisade and, also, to uproot the massive trunk (measuring 5 feet across by 5-½ feet wide, with an estimated weight of two tons) of a huge century-old oak tree.[13] These armed folk were an elite entourage. Smiths were only just introducing into the Britain the sovereignty of metallurgy (smelting the metals of copper and tin).[14] Just like an iPhone today, bronze axes then were signs of the most avant-garde tool/weapon. In 2049 BCE, local Norfolk inhabitants would have been content with their elegantly knapped flint tools which were capable of murder, butchery, deforestation, and harvesting. Industrial-scale mining in nearby Grimes Grave, Norfolk, furnished an ample supply of flint. So why inaugu-

[12] Bennett, *Vibrant Matter*, 54.

[13] My reconstruction is based on the survey by Charlie Watson, *Seahenge: An Archaeological Conundrum* (Swindon: English Heritage, 2005). Della Hooke draws our attention to Seahenge in the opening of her *Trees in Anglo-Saxon England: Literature, Lore, and Landscape* (Suffolk: Boydell Press, 2010), 3.

[14] Here I am thinking of the reflections of Gilles Deleuze and Félix Guattari, *A Thousand Plateaus: Capitalism and Schizophrenia*, trans. Brian Massumi (Minneapolis: University of Minnesota, 1987), 404–423, on early metallurgy: how early smiths linked the metal with the weapon to constitute a new assemblage, a constellation that deducts from the flow, thus the notion of a sovereign cut. In their words, "Metal is neither a thing nor an organism, but a *body* without organs" (411).

rate an exceptional metal ritual of tree-cutting, one that excluded the use of contemporary flint tools (archaeologists have detected not one flint mark on the well-preserved timber from this excavation)?

Let us carry this question forward. Once tree-fellers finished their task, these metal people used honeysuckle ropes to drag the several tons of harvested wood along a timber pathway toward the coastal barrier, a distance of 80 or so feet. They had meticulously stripped the uprooted stump of its bark and relocated it *upside down* (roots facing upward) within the center of the henge-like palisade. They arranged the unstripped palisade posts with their bark side facing outward. An eight-inch gap in the palisade, barely an entranceway, was blocked by a post set before the gap. This metal community had thus created an uprooted stripped trunk set within a fabricated trunk-like structure of the palisade and for all intents and purposes sealed it off.

Fast forward to 1998 when the tidal currents exposed the submerged henge and it became the subject of archaeological investigation (see Figure 4). The palisade measured 24-½ feet in diameter and reached an estimated height of 13 feet. Druids and environmentalists protested what they saw as a desecrating excavation, but they lost their legal case. Eventually, earth-moving equipment lifted the central, inverted stump.

No evidence of Bronze Age burial or habitation was found within the wood henge. What to think, then, about this palisade designed by its makers to appear like a tree trunk enclosing the monumental inverted and stripped tree stump? The new life of metal ("we are walking, talking metals"[15]) collides in this wood henge with the vegetal world.

[15] My interpretation is inspired by Jane Bennett's discussion of a life of metal. Bennett quotes here Lynn Margulis and Dorion Sagan from their discussion of Soviet mineralogist Vladimir Ivanovich Vernadsky's notion of a "biosphere" in their book *What is Life?* (Berkeley: University of California Press, 2000), 49; see Bennett, *Vibrant Matter,* 52–61, Margulis and Sagan citation at 60.

Figure 4. Excavation at Seahenge, Norfolk England, 1998. Photograph: Newsprints, UK.

I like to think of this Seahenge as a chapter in the history of phenomenology before phenomenology. The bronze-axe wielders use the new life of metals to investigate the properties of arboreal life. With their understanding of the "polycrystalline structure of nonorganic matter,"[16] these metal people uprooted and stripped a life of a tree in order to produce an enclosure that captured it as the tree of life and punctuated the undead seam of the organic and the non-

[16] Bennett, *Vibrant Matter*, 60.

organic—a seam of violence and intensive labor. It is at such a seam that Franz Kafka wrote his short story of trees to remind us not to mistake a life of a tree for the tree of life. "For we are like tree trunks in the snow. In appearance they lie sleekly and a little push should be enough to set them rolling. No, it can't be done, for they are firmly wedded to the ground. But see, even that is only an appearance."[17]

SPLICE 2 // 8 CE, TOMIS ON THE BLACK SEA: "ALL THAT REMAINS OF HER IS A WARM GLOW"[18]

My second splice (8 CE) comes from Rome via the flat marshlands that border the Black Sea. There stood the Roman outpost of Tomis (now Constanta, Romania) to which the alleged traitor Ovid (43 BCE-17/18 CE) was exiled by the personal command of his patron and sovereign, Augustus Caesar. Tomis might seem far afield from Britain, yet Ovid nevertheless stood behind the writing desk of the leading British botanist of the late eighteenth century, Erasmus Darwin, just as he also guided Carl Linnaeus on his ethno-botanical tour of Lapland.[19] In the medieval school curriculum,

---

[17] The brief meditations on trees first appeared in 1912 in a collection called *Betrachtung*: see *Franz Kafka: The Complete Stories*, trans. Nahum Norbert Glatzer (New York: Schocken Books, 1995), 474.

[18] Ovid, *Metamorphoses*, trans. Martin, Book 1, l. 762.

[19] See, for example, Erasmus Darwin's proem to his "Loves of Plants," taken here from the second edition of his *Botanic Garden* (London: J. Nichols, 1790), available via Project Gutenberg (http://www.gutenberg.org/ebooks/10671):

Whereas P. OVIDIUS NASO, a great Necromancer in the famous Court of AUGUSTUS CAESAR, did by art poetic transmute Men, Women, and even Gods and Goddesses, into Trees and Flowers; I have undertaken by similar art to restore some of them to their original animality, after having remained prisoners so long in their respective vegetable mansions; and have here exhibited them before thee. Which thou may'st contemplate as diverse little pictures suspended over the chimney of a Lady's

the *Metamorphoses* powerfully shape-shifted medieval pedagogy and commentary and spawned a world of medieval talking trees.[20]

One strand of the contested publication history of the
Metamorphoses claims that Ovid put his finishing touches on
his work as he went into exile. Ovid, the rhetorical master of
becoming-animal and becoming-vegetal (whom, surprisingly, Deleuze and Guattari pass over silently), knew all too well
the state of exception, since the sovereign had decided on his
treason and exiled him. Bodies, understandably, are up for
grabs in the *Metamorphoses*. For the purposes of this splice, I
focus on the story of Apollo and Daphne, because it addresses a famous example of the becoming-tree of a human and
because her metamorphosis raised for Ovid the pain of the
radical exposure to sovereign *jouissance*. The poet rhetorically stages the sovereign cut in his description of Apollo's pursuit of Daphne. The closer the god gets to the fleeing nymph,
the more wolf-like he becomes. Ovid compares Apollo to a
Gallic hound, a large canine breed valued by Romans and

> dressing-room, connected only by a slight festoon of ribbons.
> And which, though thou may'st not be acquainted with the orig
> inals, may amuse thee by the beauty of their persons, their
> graceful attitudes, or the brilliancy of their dress.

Likewise, Linnaeus self-consciously fashioned his ethno-botany of
Lapland after Ovid: see Lisbet Koerner, *Linnaeus: Nature and Nation* (Cambridge: Harvard University Press, 1999).

[20] See the important reference essay by Alison Keith and Stephen
Rupp, "After Ovid: Classical, Medieval, and Early Modern Reception of the *Metamorphoses*," in *Metamorphosis: Changing Face of
Ovid in the Medieval, and Early Modern Periods*, eds. Alison Keith
and Stephen Rupp (Toronto: University of Toronto Press, 2007),
15–32, and also *Ovid in the Middle Ages*, eds. James G Blark, Frank
T. Coulson, and Kathryn L. McKinley (New York: Cambridge University Press, 2011). Dante relied on Ovid in his encounter with the
thorn-bush in the Wood of the Suicides (into which Pier delle Vigne
has metamorphosed): see Janis Vanacker, "'Why do you Break Me'?
Talking to a Human Tree in Dante's *Inferno*," *Neophilologus* 95
(2011): 431–445.

used for animal games in their amphitheaters: "he clings to her, is just about to spring, with his long muzzle straining at her heels, while she, not knowing whether she's been caught, in one swift burst, eludes those snapping jaws."[21] At the moment the sovereign Apollo rhetorically metamorphoses into a wolf-like creature, Daphne implores her father, Peneus, the river god, to transform her. She is arrested in mid-air as a thin layer of bark girdles her trunk and her feet turn into the roots of a laurel tree. Her head becomes a canopy: "all that remains of her is a warm glow."[22] Ovid suggests with "nitor" that her glow, her luster, her brightness is the elusive phenomenal intensity and excess of Daphne's shape-shifting. Walter Benjamin, a student of aura, helps us to understand how Daphne's aura belongs to a disjunctive temporality and medium of perception that glows with the biopolitical excitation of her radical exposure to Apollo's sovereign *jouissance*.[23] The becoming-tree of Daphne flickers with her sovereign abandonment. For Benjamin there was something human about objects, something vibrant, something noncoincidental with human labor. In a letter (May 7, 1940) written just a few months before his death, Benjamin attempted to explain aura to the skeptical Theodor W. Adorno: "The tree and the shrub vouchsafed to people are not made by them. Thus there must be something human about objects that is *not* bestowed by the work done."[24]

[21] *Metamorphoses*, I, 738–742.

[22] "Remanet nitor unus in illa": *Metamorphoses*, I, 761.

[23] The discussion that follows is inspired by the meticulous and radiant essay of Miriam Bratu Hansen, "Benjamin's Aura," *Critical Inquiry* 34 (2008): 336–375. Hansen questions the narrow understanding of Benjamin's notion of aura as articulated in many contemporary studies of the technology of aura. Her excavation of Benjamin's work offers a rich analysis of the disjunctive temporalities of aura that cannot be contained by any essentialist notion of technological media. See also, Beatrice Hanssen, *Walter Benjamin's Other History: Of Stones, Animals, Human Beings, and Angels* (Berkeley: University of California Press, 1998).

[24] Letter 238 in *The Correspondence of Walter Benjamin 1910-1940*, eds. Gershom Scholem and Theodor W. Adorno, trans. Manfred R.

SPLICE 3 // "RIPPED UP BY MY ROOTS . . . AFTER THE VOICE
DEPARTED UP"

The *Dream of the Rood*, an Anglo-Saxon poem about a talk-ing tree, opens with an interjection: Attention! The careful listener can hear the brutal sound of its uprooting at the hands of the enemy. It is then transported to Calvary where it will serve as the cross. Alone, it stands vigil by the corpse of Christ after the echoes of mourners have ceased to ring in the air. The poet plays with the Anglo-Saxon word *stefn*, a hom-ograph, which can mean "root" and also "voice."[25] This splice pays attention to that homographic toggle as it tacks back and forth between the poem and its neighbor, a famous sculptured talking tree, known as the Ruthwell Cross (see Figure 6, overleaf). These stone trees speak of radical expo-sure to the state of exception, the scene of the Crucifixion. They were re-excavated by exiled German-Jewish art histori-ans in the 1930s and 1940s (and beyond to Ernst Kantoro-wicz's belated intervention in the debate in 1960s).[26] This

Jacobson and Evelyn M. Jacobson (Chicago: University of Chicago Press, 1994), 629.

[25] "astyred of stefne minum" and "syððan [stefn] up gewat": l. 30 and l. 71 from *Dream of the Rood*, ed. Michael Swanton, in Elaine Traherne, ed., *Old and Middle English: An Anthology, c. 890-1400* (Oxford: Blackwell, 2004), 108–115.

[26] Ernst Kitzinger, "Anglo-Saxon Vine Scroll Ornament," *Antiquity* 10.37 (1936): 61–71; Fritz Saxl, "The Ruthwell Cross," *Journal of the Warburg and Courtauld Institutes* 6 (1943): 1–19; Meyer Schapiro, "The Religious Meaning of the Ruthwell Cross," *Art Bulletin* 26 (1944): 232–245; and Ernst H. Kantorowicz, "The Archer in the Ruthwell Cross," *Art Bulletin* 42 (1960): 57–59. On the emigration of German-Jewish art-historians in 1933, when the Nazis instituted their race laws in the university see, Karen Michels, "Art History, German-Jewish Immigrants, and the Emigration of Iconology," in *Jewish Identity in Modern Art History*, ed. Catherine M. Soussloff (Berkeley: University of California Press, 1999), 167–179, and Christopher S. Wood, "Art History's Normative Renaissance," in *The Italian Renaissance in the Twentieth Century* (Florence: Olschki, 2002), 65–92.

splice asks how these talking trees serve as aerials that transmit a trauma, such that it becomes transitive, or what Bracha Ettinger has called "transtraumatic."[27] Their transmission of the sovereign cut paradoxically opens up a linked border space between talking trees and scholars in exile.

Figure 6. Ruthwell Cross, South face, Dumfriesshire, Scotland. Photograph: Project Woruldhord, University of Oxford. © Trustees of the British Museum.

[27] Bracha L. Ettinger, *The Matrixial Borderspace*, ed. Brian Massumi (Minneapolis: University of Minnesota Press, 2006), 167. Her revisions of Lacanian psychoanalysis can productively open the boundaries between creaturely life and animal life defended by Santner (see footnote 1). In a post-, trans-traumatic era, the psychic (not the actual) trauma is no longer entirely personal and can only be partially scarred over, and only by borderlinking to others in further transsubjective and sub-subjective transcryption and cross-scription.

The Ruthwell Cross brings us again to the beach, this time to the west coast of Scotland. When, in the early 1790s, the pastor of the parish of Ruthwell, Dumfriesshire[28] prepared his returns for the *Statistical Account of Scotland*, he reported that once upon a time an ancient broken "obelisk" carved with runes and holy images stood at the seashore. According to "tradition," the obelisk was eventually uprooted and drawn by ox-cart to the churchyard where it stood until the Reformation.[29] The locals remembered well; archaeologists tell us that sea lapped the shores of early medieval Ruthwell, which lay much closer to the shoreline than the early modern parish.[30] In 1642, the cross was uprooted again and broken into pieces, one more casualty of sovereignty during the Civil War between King Charles I and his Parliament. In protest of the king's tyrannical and popish activities, the General Assembly of the Church of Scotland had ordered in July 1640 that idols, such as the Ruthwell Cross, be destroyed, and so it was (in July 1642). In 1887, the cross was reconstituted by sovereignty and dubbed an official "national monument."[31] Antiquarians and scholars have been putting together the fragments of these sovereign cuts ever since. It is a Humpty Dumpty network of pieces. Seeta Chaganti has already linked up part of the inscriptional network in her wonderful study of the stone, metal, and parchment at stake in the Ruthwell Cross and the *Dream of the Rood*.[32] My splice

[28] Map ref. 54.9933163,-3.4084523.

[29] John Sinclair, *Statistical Account of Scotland*, Vol. 10 (Edinburgh: William Creech, 1794), 226–227.

[30] Christopher Crowe, "Early Medieval Parish Formation in Dumfries and Galloway," in *The Cross Goes North: Processes of Conversion in Northern Europe AD 300-1300*, ed. Martin Carver (Suffolk: Boydell & Brewer, 2003), 195–206.

[31] Brendan Cassidy, "The Later Life of the Ruthwell Cross: From the Seventeenth Century to the Present," in *The Ruthwell Cross* (Princeton: Princeton University Press, 1992), 3–34.

[32] Seeta Chaganti, "Vestigial Signs: Inscription, Performance and *The Dream of The Rood*," *PMLA* 125 (2010): 48–72. I would add to her exemplary bibliography: Andy Orchard, "The Dream of the

seeks to link to her network other nodes: deathly fleas, ships, Jerusalem, Saracens and the Warburg Institute in exile, in order to get at the performance of enemy, speech and root that intertwine the Tree of Life incised on the Ruthwell Cross and the letters of the text of the *Dream of the Rood.*

The tale of death begins thirty miles to the east of Ruthwell at Bewcastle where,[33] to this day, a sculptured stone cross-shaft stands in the south churchyard. Scholars attribute the Bewcastle and Ruthwell sculptures to the same workshop and reckon them to be close in date. Éamonn Ó Carragáin emphatically dates the Ruthwell Cross between 730-760.[34] The Bewcastle sculptors ingeniously transformed a liturgical aid (known as a *liber vitae*) used for keeping track of the names of the dead to be commemorated during the celebration of the Mass into a solid stone cube sentiently bound on the East face of the shaft by the incised branches of the Tree of Life. The main west face of the Bewcastle shaft features a commemorative panel etched in runes, now faded, on which, it is conjectured, were inscribed the names of the dead. Blank panels on the south and north sides of the Bewcastle Cross await the inscription of more names. These blanks punctuate a network of actants that linked fleas and sputum, the bacillus, *yersina pestis,* brought by ship from the Mediterranean and overland routes to northern Britain. The infected fleabite and the cough devastated the densely occupied Northumbri-

Rood: Cross-References," in *New Readings in the Vercelli Book,* eds. Samantha Zacher and Andy Orchard (Toronto: University of Toronto Press, 2009), 225–253, and Crowe, "Early Medieval Parish Formation in Dumfries and Galloway," 195–206. I have found Kate Thomas's use of queer theory to imagine networks especially helpful: "Post Sex: On Being Too Slow, Too Stupid, Too Soon," in *After Sex? On Writing Since Queer Theory,* eds. Janet Halley and Andrew Parker (Durham: Duke University Press, 2011), 66–75.

[33] Map ref. 35.118979,-90.7234437.

[34] Éamonn Ó Carragáin, *Ritual and the Rood: Liturgical Images and the Old English Poems of the Dream of the Rood Tradition* (Toronto: University of Toronto Press, 2005), 213.

an monasteries in the late seventh century.[35] This epidemio-
logical catastrophe, archaeologists tell us, resulted in the reorganization of rural and monastic settlement, and I argue,
the commemoration of the dead. Fleas and sputum proliferated into a "forest" of sculptured stone crosses in the north of
Britain.[36]

The devastation of plague and the urgency of commemoration inspired a major project of sacred topography undertaken by Adomnán, abbot of Iona, who completed his treatise *De locis sanctis* in the plague ridden years of the 680s. He
presented his study to Aldfrith, King of Northumbia (685-
704), so that it could be more widely disseminated. The tales
of one shipwrecked, Arculf, who had visited the Holy Land
(679-682) and washed up at Iona, served as the alibi for
Adomnán's project on Christology and memorial topography.[37] Scholars have noted with great interest that Adomnán
had access to recent information about Jerusalem as he wrote
De locis sanctis. He mentions the Umayyad Caliph Mu'āwiya
and reports that the "Saracens" had built in Jerusalem "a rec-

---

[35] J.R. Maddicott, "Plague In Seventh-Century England," *Past and
Present* 156 (1997): 7–54.

[36] In 1927, W.G. Collingwood estimated that there were about 50
such carved crosses and the work of the *Corpus of Anglo-Saxon
Sculpture* continues to add to the total: *Northumbrian Crosses of the
Pre-Norman Age* (London: Faber, 1927). The University of Durham
has now posted online Volume 1 (Durham and Northumberland) of
the *Corpus of Anglo-Saxon Stone Sculpture* by Rosemary Cramp
(British Academy, 1977): http://www/as-corpus.ac.uk. See also
Richard N. Bailey, *England's Earliest Sculptors* (Toronto: Pontifical
Institute for Medieval Studies, 1996) and the important study,
*Fragments of History: Rethinking the Ruthwell and Bewcastle
Monuments*, eds. Fred Orton and Ian Wood, with Clare A. Lees
(Manchester: Manchester University Press, 2007).

[37] Thomas O'Loughlin, *Adomnán and the Holy Places: The Per-
ceptions of an Insular Monk on the Locations of the Biblical Drama*
(London: T&T Clark, 2007); Katharine Scarfe Beckett, *Anglo-Saxon
Perceptions of the Islamic World* (New York: Cambridge University
Press, 2003).

tangular house of prayer,"[38] perhaps the early stages of the construction of the Dome of the Rock, which was completed c. 692 CE. Likewise in Damascus, he observed that there existed a church of the non-believing Saracens. Bede abridged Adomnán's treatise, which further ensured its popularity. Thus we know that Bede was also apprised that Saracens were occupying the Holy Land. In his other writings, he tracked contemporary Muslim expansion in Europe. When he wrote his *Historia ecclesiastica*, he described Saracens as a *gravissima lues Sarracennorum* ("a terrible plague of Saracens").[39] In sum, an exegetical interest in sacred topography, especially tombs, refined by Adomnán during the plague years of the 680s, collided with new information about the expansions of a people of the desert (*deserta Sarracenorum*), whose inroad into Christian European space is likened to plague—the biological and the metaphorical here intertwine.

If we listen attentively to the Ruthwell talking tree, does it speak of the "terrible plague of Saracens" voiced by monastic contemporaries? To explore this question, I turn to the projects and publications of German-Jewish scholars and associates of the Warburg Institute, who in 1933 had fled from Nazi Germany to London, where the Warburg was relocated.[40]

---

[38] "quaedam etiam Sarracinorum ecclesia incredulorum": The Latin text of Admonán's *De Locis Sanctis* may be found in Paul Geyer, *Itinera Hiersolymitana saeculi iiii-viii*, Corpus Scriptorum Ecclesiasticorum Latinorum, Vol. 28 (1898), 296. Also available at: https://archive.org/details/itinerahierosol00geyegoog.

[39] See Scarfe Beckett, *Anglo-Saxon Perceptions of the Islamic World*, 123–124, for a summary of Bede's contemporary references.

[40] See *Common Knowledge* 18 (2012), a special issue on the Warburg Library, eds. Anthony Grafton and Jeffrey Hamburger, and also Katia Mazzucco, "1941: English Arts and the Mediterranean: A Photographic Exhibition by the Warburg Institute in London," *Journal of Art Historiography* 5 (2011): 1–28. Georges Didi-Huberman's arguments about the domestication of iconology and his concept of the "rend" of an image have influenced my reading: *Confronting Images: Questioning the Ends of a Certain History of Art*, trans. John Goodman (University Park: Pennsylvania State University Press, 2005).

Under pressure to earn its way in its new British home and to prove its Englishness, in 1941, the Warburg organized an exhibit of over 500 photos devoted to the topic "English Art and the Mediterranean." The exhibit proved to be a huge success and travelled to 18 British cities over a two-year period. Pride of place belonged to freshly taken photographs of the Ruthwell Cross. The re-exposure of the cross launched a spate of publications. But to backtrack for a moment: As early as 1936, Ernst Kitzinger, a German-Jewish art historian in exile at the British Museum, broached the scholarship of the Ruthwell Cross. He treated only the vine scrolls of the tree of life carved into two narrow sides of its shaft. His focus on ornament was exclusive. He ignored the incised runes that ran in a band around the vine scrolls; nor was he interested in the figural sculpture on the main faces of the cross. "Ornament" was what mattered. Through the careful comparison of photographs of different late Antique and Coptic sculptures, Kitzinger crafted an intricate argument that brought the Ruthwell tree of life into direct contact with the mosaic vine scrolls of the Dome of the Rock and the carved vine scrolls on the wooden roof-trusses of the Mosque at Damascus. What networks might have brought together Muslim Jerusalem and Ruthwell were not his concern.

Warburg scholars and associates radically shifted the study of the Ruthwell Cross in the 1940s.[41] Two scholars, Fritz Saxl and Meyer Schapiro, devoted themselves to interpreting the ensemble of figural images carved on the two main faces of the cross. Schapiro mentioned the runic inscriptions only in passing and ignored the tree of life vines on the narrow shafts of the cross. Saxl also took his distance from the tree of life. In his introduction, Saxl claimed to "fight shy" of former discussions of Ruthwell ornament (the tree of life carvings) in order to study the neglected figural program. The exclusions of the Ruthwell tree of life from both these essays had the effect of silencing the nodes of Ruthwell carvers and Muslim Jerusalem. But, as I shall show,

[41] Cassidy, "The Later Life of the Ruthwell Cross," 29–34.

things Islamic would come to haunt Ruthwell scholarship again in 1960.

In debate with the wartime articles of Saxl and Schapiro, Ernst Kantorowicz, the noted author of *The King's Two Bodies: A Study in Medieval Political Theology* (1957), and himself a German-Jewish exile at Berkeley and Princeton, belatedly turned his attention in 1960 to the figure known as the Ruthwell archer. Saxl had admitted that he was stumped by the figure: "but who is the archer beneath the cross-beam?"[42] Schapiro, in contrast, staunchly maintained that the archer was "the oldest medieval example of secular imagery."[43] Kantorowicz offered an uncharacteristic (for him) midrashic reading of the archer. Relying on the scholarship of Louis Ginzberg, a noted Talmudist and author of the multi-volume series, *Legends of the Jews*, Kantorowicz argued that the archer represented Ishmael, son of Hagar, around whom a midrash of a wilderness archer and wild man grew up. Kantorowicz, the scholar of premodern sovereignty extraordinaire, suggests here that the archer marks a sovereign cut on the Ruthwell Cross, meaning that the archer raises the question of the enemy. The talking tree of life, too, murmurs of this sovereign cut when it tell us through its runic inscription that it was "wounded with arrows." Scholars have wondered why the runes give the plural form of arrow, since in the singular, it might be possible to translate "spear," which would fit perfectly into the Gospel narrative. Here, I think, the rend of the Ruthwell image comes into play. The shipwrecked Arculf who had recited to Adomnán the stories of his stay in contemporary Muslim Jerusalem might have related how the skilled archers of the seventh-century Rashidun army, with their superior composite bows, struck fear into the hearts of their enemy. The archer of the Ruthwell cross, I argue, may be read as a toggle between a militant and sovereign Christian church and the sons of Hagar, noted and feared archers,

[42] Saxl, "The Ruthwell Cross," 6.
[43] Schapiro, "The Religious Meaning of the Ruthwell Cross," 38.

whom Christians would name as the "enemy."[44] In his article on the Ruthwell archer, published three years before his death, Kantorowicz finally revisited his own (suppressed) ancestral roots, first his genealogy as a grandson of a noted Poznan rabbi (since he uncharacteristically cited Jewish midrash), and, second, his work as a young military attaché in Istanbul during World War I, where he supervised the German work on the Orient Express and went on to write a dissertation on Muslim craft guilds. Kantorowicz was interested in the Tree of Life. It appears as an entry in index of *The King's Two Bodies*, "Tree, Inverted."[45]

SPLICE 4: "THE MEN OF YOUR CONFEDERACY HAVE DECEIVED YOU" (CLOISTERS CROSS)

The story of my fourth tree of life, the Cloisters Cross, a ceremonial cross carved out of walrus ivory, brings us on the beach one more time, now to the ice floes of the White Sea, where the Sami harvested walrus and paid tribute in ivory tusks to Norsemen, or so Ohthere, Norwegian chieftain and merchant, told King Alfred of Wessex (c. 890 CE) as he pre-

---

[44] See Biddick, "Dead Neighbor Archives: Jews, Muslims, and the Enemy's Two Bodies," in *Political Theology and Early Modernity*, eds. Graham Hammill and Julia Reinhard Lupton (Chicago: University of Chicago Press, 2012), 124–142 (and republished in this volume); on early Muslim archers and their large composite bows see, John W Jandora, "Archers of Islam: A Search for 'Lost' History," *Medieval History Journal* 13 (2010): 97–114 and David Nicolle, *The Great Islamic Conquests AD 637-750* (Oxford: Osprey Publishing, 2009). My interpretation pays attention to what Didi-Huberman calls the "rend" of an image and offers an alternative account of the archer to the one given by Éamonn Ó Carragáin, *Ritual and the Rood*, 141–143.

[45] Ernst H. Kantorowicz, The *King's Two Bodies: A Study in Medieval Political Theology* (Princeton: Princeton University Press, 1957), 565.

sented him with samples of this highly valued raw material. [46]

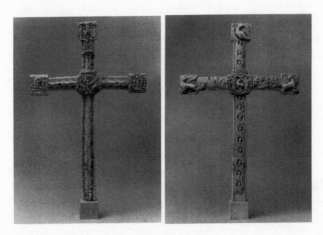

Figures 7-8. The Cloisters Cross (front and reverse). Photographs: Art Source.

Sometime during the plague years of the late seventh century, Sami hunters felled a walrus (radio carbon date 676-694 CE). Its tusks, an heirloom, would be carved, several centuries later, into a ceremonial cross standing 23 inches high with an arm span of 14-¼ inches (see Figures 7-8). [47]

---

[46] Else Roesdahl, "Walrus Ivory," in *Ohthere's Voyages: A Late 9th-Century Account of Voyages along the Coasts of Norway and Denmark in its Cultural Context,* eds. Janet Bately and Anton Englert (Roskilde: Viking Ship Museum, 2007), 92–93; Danielle Gaborit-Chopin, "Walrus Ivory in Western Europe," in *From Viking to Crusader: The Scandinavians and Europe 800-1200,* eds. Else Roesdahl and David M. Wilson (New York: Rizzoli, 1992), 204–205. Once Greenland was colonized, c. 985 CE, its icy waters also served as a source of walrus tusk which were traded along European trade routes: Marek E. Jasinski and Fredrik Søreide, "Norse Settlements in Greenland from a Maritime Perspective," in *Vinland Revisited: the Norse World at the Turn of the First Millennium,* ed. Shannon Lewis-Simpson (St. John's: Historic Sites Association of Newfoundland and Labrador, 2000), 123–132.

[47] For a comprehensive overview and bibliography of scholarly

Shady post-World War II art markets put the Cloisters Cross into modern circulation. Since its "unprovenanced" purchase in 1963 by the Metropolitan Museum of Art, debate over the cross has released an excess of historicism, as if historicism could resolve its enigma. Scholars disagree over the basics of geographical provenance—it could have been carved anywhere from England to Sicily and it could date anytime between 1050-1180 CE. I propose in this splice an untimely reading of this tree of life—not to decide its provenance or date—but instead to investigate how the Cloisters tree of life, another talking tree, transmits through its inscriptions a crisis of sovereignty and treason.[48]

debates about the cross to 2006, see Elizabeth C. Parker, "Editing the *Cloister's Cross," Gesta* 45 (2006): 147–160. For excellent photographs and details of the inscriptions, see Elizabeth C. Parker and Charles T. Little, *The Cloisters Cross: Its Art and Meaning* (New York: Metropolitan Museum of Art, 1994). The tree of life of the Cloisters Cross is not of the vine type of the Ruthwell Cross; instead, it is a carved "rough-hewn" cross whose trunk sections are rendered as the knots and stumps of the palm tree: Jennifer O'Reilly, "The Rough-Hewn Cross in Anglo-Saxon Art," in *Ireland and Insular Art A.D. 500-1200*, ed. Michael Ryan (Dublin: Royal Irish Academy, 1987), 153–158.

[48] My reading engages the work on the transtraumatic developed by Ettinger in *The Matrixial Borderspace* (see footnote 27). I read the cross as a borderlinking artifact. Judith Butler, in her generous foreward to Ettinger's book, emphasizes borderlinking: "We have to ask about historical losses, the ones that are transmitted to us without our knowing, at a level where we cannot hope to piece it together, where we are, at a psychic level, left in pieces, pieces that might be linked together in some way, but will not fully 'bind' the affect. This is the part of the work of borderlinking that Ettinger writes about, and it is, in her view, prior to identity, prior to any question of construction, a psychic landscape that gives itself as partial object, as grains and crumbs, as she puts it, as remnants that are, on the one hand, the result, the scattered effects of unknowable history of trauma, the trauma that others who precede us have lived through and, on the other hand, the very sites in which a new possibility for visual experience emerges, one that establishes a

The tree of life is carved on the front shaft of the Cloisters Cross. On its back carvers have arranged in niches the busts of thirteen Old Testament prophets, and the evangelist, Matthew. Each bears a scroll engraved with scriptural verses. The Cloisters Cross prophets draw upon and compound a performative tradition of liturgical drama of the *Ordo Prophetarum*, with its roots in the anti-Semitic Advent liturgy, as well as popular "quasi-liturgical" drama (*Jeu D'Adam*), sculptural programs embellishing the portals of Romanesque cathedrals, and the genealogies represented in stained-glass windows representing the Tree of Jesse.[49] The performative impulse of the Cloisters Cross with its noisy riot of inscription plunges the cross into complex dramaturgy with an Anti-Semitic genealogy.

The tree of life is carved on the front panel of the Cloisters cross. Running down both of its sides are two engraved Latin couplets that read: "The earth trembles, Death defeated groans with the buried one rising. / Life has been called, Synagogue has collapsed with great foolish effort."[50] On the nar-

---

temporality in which the past is not the past but is not present, in which the present emerges, but from the scattered and animated remains of a continuing, though not continuous, trauma" (in Ettinger, *The Matrixial Borderspace*, ix).

[49] The selection of prophets on the Cloisters Cross is most akin to the Rouen *Ordo Prophetarum*, which Edith Armstrong Wright thinks that Archbishop Hugues (1130-1164) introduced to Rouen from an earlier Laon version: *Dissemination of the Liturgical Drama in France* (Geneva: Slatkine Reprints, 1980), 56. For background on the Anti-Semitic aspects of this liturgical drama and the Laon tradition, see Regula Meyer Evitt, "Eschatology, Millenarian Apocalypticism, and the Liturgical Anti-Judaism of the Medieval Prophet Plays," in *The Apocalyptic Year 1000: Religious Expectation and Social Change, 950-1050*, eds. Richard Landes, Andrew Gow, and David C. Van Meter (Oxford: Oxford University Press, 2003), 205–229, and Robert C. Lagueux, "Sermons, Exegesis, and Performance: The Laon *Ordo Prophetarum* and the Meaning of Advent," *Comparative Drama* 43 (2009): 197–220.

[50] "Terra tremit mors victa gemit surgente sepulto / Vita cluit synagoga ruit molimine stult(o)."

row sides of the shaft two other couplet are inscribed: "Cham laughs when he sees the uncovered limbs of his parents/The Jews laughed at the pain of God suffering."[51] At the foot of the trunk of the tree of life, Adam and Eve hold on for dear life. The tree of life climbs up the shaft of the cross and passes through a medallion depicting Moses and the Brazen Serpent. Its trunk culminates in an innovative iconographical scene, which features the gospel story of Pilate and Caiaphas arguing over the wording of the titulus to be affixed to Christ's Cross. Pilate holds a scroll inscribed with the text of John 19:22: "What I have written, I have written" (*Quod Scripsi Scripsi*). The scroll held by Caiaphas features the text of John 19:21: "Write not the King of the Jews, but that he said: I am the King of the Jews."[52] The carved titulus above this scene features inscriptions in Latin, Greek and Hebrew; it is important to note that the titulus contradicts the theology of the scene below between Pilate and Caiaphas. Its mistranscriptions offer clues to the sovereign cut of this tree of life. The Hebrew inscription of the titulus is undecipherable (the carver invented an unreadable Hebrew Script); however, the Latin and Greek inscription are correct and contradict the Scripsi Scripsi scene; they inscribe their titulus to read: Jesus of Nazareth, King of the Confessors (Rex Confessorum) not King of the Jews (Rex Iudeorum).

The *Rex Confessorum* titulus concerns me here because its deliberate unscripting of *Scripsi Scripsi* links the cross to the fierce rhetorical and iconographic debate fomented by the sovereign crisis between King Henry II and his Archbishop of Canterbury, Thomas Becket. Their battle culminated in Becket's assassination in December 1170 (during the liturgi-

---

[51] "Cham ridet dum nuda videt pudibunda parentis / Iudeis risere dei penam mor(ientis)."

[52] Sabrina Langland, "Pilate Answered: What I have Written I have Written," *Metropolitan Museum of Art Bulletin* 26.19 (1968): 410–429. See also Colum Hourihane, *Pontius Pilate, Anti-Semitism, and the Passion in Medieval Art* (Princeton: Princeton University Press, 2009), 201–203.

cal season when the anti-Semitic treatises on the *Ordo Prophetarum* were read). By the time of his assassination, Becket was regarded by the royal party as a traitor; his own followers immediately dubbed him with the martyrial title of Confessor. Henry II had precipitated the crisis when he tried to bully his lay and ecclesiastical barons into accepting the Constitutions of Clarendon in 1164. Infamous among the articles was Article 15, which ruled as follows: "Pleas concerning debts, which are owed on the basis of an oath or in connection with which no oath has been taken, are in the king's justice."[53] With Article 15, the king was arrogating to himself sovereign control over oral promises (*nuda pacta*) in cases of debt. Article 15 announced that an oral faith-plight (otherwise known as a bare promise) in a debt transaction could *not* be the grounds for sending such disputes over moneylending to the church courts where such disputes were traditionally heard. Thus when it came to debt, both faith promise and documentary writing (an early notion of binding contract, *pactum vestitum*—a clothed or veiled pact— depended on written instruments) became the domain of the king's justice. Henry II thus declared oral promises to be the state of exception when it came to debt litigation and in so doing radically repositioned the sovereignty of written records and the nature of the archive itself.[54] Becket's resistance

[53] "Placita de debitis quae fide interposita debentur, vel absque interpositione fidei, sint in justicia regis": William Stubbs, *Selected Charters and other illustrations of English Constitutional History from early times to the reign of Edward the First* (Oxford: Clarendon Press, 1870), 167. See also Frederick Pollock and Frederic W. Maitland, *The History of English Law before the Time of Edward I*, Vol. 2 (Cambridge: Cambridge University Press, 1892), 195–202. For the long-term problematic of sovereign and liturgical conflict over debt claims, see Richard H. Helmholz, *Roman Canon Law in Reformation England* (Cambridge: Cambridge University Press, 1990), 25–33.

[54] This argument about the over-riding (overwriting) of what came to be known as the "nudum pactum," the naked pact made on faith between two legal persons, challenges us to rethink arguments about "memory to written record" as a crisis of sovereignty and faith and

to the Constitutions famously resulted in his trial for treason in October 1164. During this trial and after his precipitous flight from London court to exile in France, the Becket circle, a transnational clerical group with broadly based theological, juridical, and artistic connections, polemicized against Henry II by staging him as a Jew.[55] The Becket circle mapped Henry

not as some accretion of governmentality. See Michael Clanchy, *From Memory to Written Record: England 1066-1307*, 2nd edn. (Oxford: Blackwell, 1993).

[55] I think that Becket's Sicilian connections might be key for the provenance of the Cloisters Cross. On the transnational complexities of Becket's circle, see Anne Duggan, "Thomas Becket's Italian Network," in *Pope, Church and City: Essays in Honour of Brenda M. Bolton*, eds. Frances Andrews, Christoph Egger, and Constance M. Rousseau (Leiden: Brill, 2004), 177–204, and more generally her essay, "*De consultationibus*: The Role of Episcopal Consultation in the Shaping of Canon Law in the Twelfth Century," in *Bishops, Texts and the Use of Canon Law around 1100*, eds. Bruce C. Brasington and Kathleen G. Cushing (Burlington: Ashgate, 2008), 191–214. Becket as a patron of the arts is discussed by Ursula Nilgen, "Intellectuality and Splendour: Thomas Becket as a Patron of the Arts," in *Art and Patronage in the English Romanesque*, eds. Sarah Macready and F.H. Thompson (London: Society of Antiquaries, 1986), 145–158. For the relations of the Becket circle and the new professional illuminators of Paris see, Christopher F.R. De Hamel, *Glossed Books of the Bible and the Origins of the Paris Booktrade* (Suffolk: Boydell & Brewer, 1984), especially 55–63. More recently Patricia Stirnemann has linked these manuscripts associated with Becket to the Cistercian abbeys around Sens. "Indeed, the impetus behind the sudden emergence of this professional booktrade is not the schools, but the presence in Sens of three episcopal courts in the 1160s and 1170s: the papal court of Alexander III, the exiled archiepiscopal court of Thomas Becket, and the archiepiscopal court of Guillaume aux Blanches Mains, the brother of Henry the Liberal, who was elected to the bishopric of Chartres in 1164 and then simultaneously held the archbishopric of Sens as of 1168": Patricia Stirnemann, "The Study of French Twelfth-Century Manuscripts," in *Romanesque Art and Thought in the Twelfth Century*, ed. Colum Hourihane (Princeton: Princeton University Press, 2008), 87 [82–94].

II and his supporters as members of *synagoga*. They accused Henry and his baronial henchmen (lay and clerical) as behaving worse than the Jewish High Priests, Annas and Caiaphas, and the Roman procurator, Pontius Pilate, at the trial of Jesus. They compared the scandal of suffragan bishops judging Becket in the king's court (October 1164) to Ham (also called Cham), the son of Noah, who laughed at the "the uncovered parts of a father." By celebrating, on the morning of his trial, the mass of St. Stephen Proto-martyr, whose story of martyrdom had him dying at the hands of Jews, Becket further dramatized this judaization of sovereignty.[56] Although Becket did not directly compare himself to Moses and the Brazen Serpent (the central medallion on the front of the Cloisters Cross), there are iconographic overtones of that image when he, vested in his liturgical apparel, carried his own archiepiscopal cross (usually a cross-bearer carried the cross in front of the archbishop) into the royal trial-chamber. A fellow juror and royal partisan, the outraged Bishop of London (dubbed the *archisynagoga* in correspondence among Becket's friends), reprimanded Becket for coming to court "armed with a cross." After Becket's assassination, his circle intensified their judaization of the sovereignty at stake in his trial. They dubbed those clerics who allegedly betrayed Becket as Caiaphas and Pontius Pilate: "Indeed it is believed that his murder was arranged by the disciples who betrayed him, and planned by the chief priests: they outbid Annas and Caiaphas, Pilate and Herod in wickedness, in proportion as they took more pains to see that he was not brought before a judgment seat, was not summoned by accusers, did not appear before the face of a judge."[57]

---

[56] For a discussion of thirteenth-century depictions of Stephen, see Karen Ann Morrow, "Disputation in Stone: Jews Imagined on the St. Stephen Portal of Paris Cathedral," in *Beyond the Yellow Badge: Anti-Judaism and Antisemitism in Medieval and Early Modern Visual Culture*, ed. Michael B. Merback (Leiden: Brill, 2007), 64–86.

[57] Excerpted from Letter #305 in *Letters of John of Salisbury, Volume 2: The Later Letters (1163-1180)*, eds. W.J. Millor and C.N.L. Brooke (Oxford: Clarendon Press, 1979), 1171. John of Salisbury to John of

The Pilate and Caiaphas scene of the Cloisters Cross captures, I argue, the state of exception decided on by Henry II with the Constitutions of Clarendon and then uses iconography to judaize the sovereign decision. Sovereignty could be judaized and Jews could be biopoliticized in this traumatic juncture of sovereignty and biopolitics in the twelfth century.[58] All this could be pinned by sovereignty on the tree of life. The Cloisters Cross speaks of making die and making live, the cut and the spiral.

The undeadness of the Cloisters Cross lives on most notably in the recent and widely travelled installation by Anselm Kiefer entitled *Palmsonntag* (2006). Kiefer installed a massive palm tree, preserved in resin and fiberglass, on the gallery floor. Large glass-covered panels, displayed like the pages of an ancient text, show dead palm fronds, seedpods and dried roses beautifully arranged upon parched, cracked earth. The words *aperiatur terra et germinet salvatorem* are scrawled in handwriting against the dusty backdrop. They are the words of Isaiah 45:8: "You heavens above, rain down righteousness; let the clouds shower it down. Let the earth open wide, let salvation spring up, let righteousness grow with it; I, the Lord, have created it." When the artists of the Cloisters Cross invoked Isaiah on the central medallion depicting Moses and the Brazen Serpent, they chose a darker verse: "Why is thy apparel red and thy garments like theirs that tread in the winepress (Isaiah 63:2)"? These moments of arboreal undeadness link the untimeliness of the sovereign cut and biopolitical spiral in the borderspaces of spectral materialism.

Canterbury, Bishop of Poitiers: "Et quidem, ut creditur, necem ipsius traditores procuravere discipuli, sacerdotum principes formaverunt, tanto in malitia, Annam et Caipham, Pilatum et Herodem amplius praecedentes, quanto diligentius praecauerunt ne in iudicium traheretur, ne conveniretur ab accusatoribus, ne appareret ante faciem presidis."

[58] See Kathleen Biddick, "Arthur's Two Bodies and the Bare Life of the Archive," in *Cultural Diversity in the British Middle Ages: Archipelago, Island, England*, ed. Jeffrey Jerome Cohen (New York: Palgrave, 2008), 117–134 (and also included in this volume).

APPENDIX I

Judaizing the Becket Conflict (some selected references)

Accounts of the Trial, October 1164[59]

a. Cham ridet reference (p. 447):

However, he [Thomas Becket] complained much
more about his suffragan bishops than about the
judgment and the judging magnates, declaring that it
was an innovation and a new procedure to let an
archbishop be judges by his suffragans and a father by
his sons, adding that it would be a *lesser evil to laugh
at the uncovered parts of a father than to judge the person of the father himself.*

[Veruntamen multo magis quam de judicio seu pro-
ceribus judicantibus, de confratribus suis suffraganeis
coepiscopis querebatur, novam dicens formam hanc
et ordinem judiciorum novum, ut archipraesul a suis
suffraganeis, pater a filius, judicetur. Minus fore ma-
lum, adjiciens, verenda patris detecta derider, quam
patris ipsius personam judicare.]

b. Thomas and St. Stephen, protomartyr, who dies at
the hands of Jews (p. 434):

. . . and on the advice of wise men, he in the morning
before going to court, celebrated with great devotion
the mass of St. Stephen the proto-martyr, in whose office one reads the phrase: "Princes did sit and speak
against me (Ps. Cxix, 23), and he commended his
cause to the highest judge of matters, who is God.

---

[59] From *English Lawsuits from William I to Richard I,* ed. R.C. Van
Caenegem, Vol. 2: Henry II and Richard I (London: Selden Society,
1990), 433–457; each passage cited parenthetically by page number.

[. . . per consilium cujusdam sapientis, in crastino antequam ipse ad curiam pergeret, cum summa devotione celebravit missam de Sancto Stephano protomartyre, cujus officium tale est: "Etenim sederunt principles et adversum me loquebantur etc."; et causam suam summo judici, qui Deus ist, commendavit.]

c. Becket's archiepiscopal cross at the trial, with overtones of Moses and brazen serpent on the cross (p. 452):

As he entered the hall, the archbishop soon took the cross from the cross-bearer who walked in front of him and openly in the sight of everybody carried his cross himself, as the standard-bearer of the Lord carries the standard of the Lord in the battle of the Lord . . .

[Archipraesul vero, ut aulam ingreditur, a crucis bajulo ante ipsam crucem mox accipit et palam in omnium conspectu crucem ipsemet bajulavit, tanquam in praelio Domini signifier Domini vexilium Domini erigens . . .]

from *Letters of John of Salisbury*[60]

a. *Synagoga*:

about Gilbert Foliot (Bishop of London and opponent of Becket): *Archisynagaga*[61]

---

[60] Excerpted from *Letters of John of Salisbury*, Vol. 2 (1163-1180), ed. W.J. Millor and C.N.L. Brooke, eds. (Oxford, UK: Clarendon Press, 1979), hereafter cited by Letter #.

[61] Letter #174 (July 1166) to Bartholomew, Bishop of Exeter; Letter #187 (late 1166) to Baldwin, archdeacon of Totnes.

Doing Dead Time for the Sovereign
Archive, Abandonment, Performance

In his contribution to the major exhibition, "CTRL [SPACE]: Rhetorics of Surveillance from Bentham to Big Brother," held in 2001 at the ZKM (Center for Art and Media, Karlsruhe), critically acclaimed German film director, Harun Farocki (b. 1944), installed two videos with the intention of exploring the ontology of real-time computer imaging: "During real-time processes we cease to exist as historical beings and become caught up in the computer simulation even though we are living creatures."[1] He juxtaposed *Auge*, a video on real-time computer simulations (such as those guiding smart mis-

---

[1] Harun Farocki, "I believed to see prisoners; Eye," in *CTRL [SPACE]: Rhetorics of Surveillance from Bentham to Big Brother*, eds. Thomas Y. Levin, Ursula Frohne, and Peter Weibel (Cambridge: MIT Press, 2002), 423 [422–425]. This chapter originally appeared, in slightly different form, as Kathleen Biddick, "Doing dead time for the sovereign: Archive, abandonment, performance," *Rethinking History* 13.2 (June 2009): 137–151.

siles to their targets as they register the explosion of the war head) with another of his video projects, *Ich glaubte Gefangene zu sehen* (hereafter *Gefangene*).[2] In the latter, he critically sampled the celluloid archive of "prison" films from the silent-film era along with a contemporary archive of surveillance tapes recorded by cameras scanning the carceral space of a notorious high-security prison located in Corcoran, California. Through this juxtaposition, Farocki posed a question intrinsic to the discipline of history: what logic, what libido, what disciplinarity, prior to the so-called advent of real-time imaging processes, had ever guaranteed the notion of a historical event and the presence of historical subjects in such events?[3]

This essay uses *Gefangene* to think about the relations of event and archive through the concept of *dead time*. It first unfolds this notion of dead time as a critical concern of Farocki and then locates its historical constitution in Jeremy Bentham's panopticon. I shall trace how Bentham linked dead time intimately with sovereignty and archive. If historians and convicts are still doing dead time, as I propose they are, how can they reimagine event and archive? The final section of the essay explores performance as a way of thinking of a non-sovereign history. It recounts the story of my participation with the convicts of Mountjoy Prison, Dublin (a panoptical-style prison opened by the British in their Irish colony in 1851 and only recently closed by the Irish Government) in developing a public installation, held during the dead time of evening lockdown (in October 2003). At the outset, I ask my readers to indulge the structure of this essay. It is intentionally designed to echo the structure of *Gefangene*. As we shall see, Farocki uses the image plane of his video to mimic the control monitor typical of a surveillance terminal in a modern prison. Operators use this control display to manipulate digitally (rotation, zoom) surveillance

---

[2] Harun Farocki, "Controlling Observation," in *CTRL [SPACE]*, 102–107.

[3] Jacques Rancière, *The Future of the Image*, trans. Gregory Elliott (London: Verso, 2007).

feeds when they decide that a security camera is recording an incident (some infraction of the normative prison routine). Farocki deliberately marks this control process by dividing his video monitor into two screens on which he runs footage of separate events (in several instances, sampled from the archive of silent film and the archive of Corcoran surveillance video-tapes). By anomalously framing this material and allowing the interior corners of the two "windows" to run in overlap in the center of the screen, Farocki interrogates the panoptical desire of his viewers: which screen do you want to watch and how is your desire constituted and channeled by the narrative intercutting and its overlap? This essay features two separate but overlapping screens: theoretical and performative—their overlap is intrinsic to marking and rethinking the concept of dead time as it bears on concepts of sovereignty, event, history.

DEAD TIME

One of the many black and white placards screened in *Gefangene* (borrowed by Farocki from the protocol of silent films) reads: "What can be accelerated or increased in prison?" A similar question troubled early cinema. What to do with elapsing time that is perceived as "uneventful" in reference to the spectacle to be filmed? Take for example, the "live" filming of the electrocution of a rogue elephant undertaken in 1903 by Edison Films (*Electrocution of an Elephant*). What was the camera to make of the purportedly "uneventful" time involved in setting up the execution (protracted and clumsy procedures that included binding the animal to the electrical apparatus)? In her brilliant analysis of early film, Mary Ann Doane has shown how cinematographers developed different techniques to exclude or elide what she calls such "dead time."[4] She argues that dead time understood as that "in which nothing happens, time which is in some sense

---

[4] Mary Anne Doane, *The Emergence of Cinematic Time: Modernity, Contingency, the Archive* (Cambridge: Harvard University Press, 2002), 160.

'wasted,' expended without product,"[5] becomes the condition of possibility for the conceptualization of the event. The elision of dead time, either by stopping the camera on set and/or cutting out footage on the editing floor, fabricates an event as eventful.

Gefangene explores dead time in two ways. First, as I have already mentioned, Farocki juxtaposes two windows on which he runs different footage and has these windows overlap in their interior corners, thus creating what I call a pixilated scrap of quilt in which the temporal moments of the two different windows touch each other (for instance, the silent film footage and the Corcoran surveillance tape). Farocki thus produces a patch or remnant of temporal montage that opens up different temporalities and questions what counts as eventful and uneventful time. He further underscores the problem of uneventful time when in one of the windows of *Gefangene* he runs a clip taken from a Prison Corrections video in which an official analyzes the raw surveillance footage that recorded the death of convict William Martinez in a Corcoran prison yard on 7 April 1989. The expert describes how it took Corcoran guards a total of nine minutes and fifteen seconds to make their way into the yard to pacify and to aid the fatally wounded Martinez. The voiceover informs the viewer that the "process" has been condensed for the purposes of presentation and the surveillance footage is screened in fast forward to skip over dead time. Thus, the dead time of the prison yard is "accelerated" in order to get to the "event"—the intervention of prison guards in the yard and the removal of the dead body of Martinez. Farocki wants his viewers to see how the "cut"—whether it be a celluloid splice or a digital keyboard stroke[6]—produces the notion of the eventful and the uneventful. Such cutting is intrinsic to the *archive*. The Prison Correction video becomes the archive constructed out of and at the same time eliding the dead time of the raw surveillance footage recording the

---

[5] Doane, *The Emergence of Cinematic Time*, 160.
[6] Lev Manovich, *The Language of New Media* (Cambridge: MIT Press, 2002).

death of convict Martinez (all nine minutes and fifteen seconds of dying in dead time).

The archive, so cut, defends against the traumatic threat of time wasted, expended without a product, bodies that do not matter.[7] The archive constitutes itself out of dead time and paradoxically demands the ongoing production of dead time to guarantee the cut, the cut that constructs the status of the event as eventful. With the development of archives undertaken in the nineteenth century (especially the massive organization of national archives) and the contemporaneous dissemination of archivalizing media (photography, film, etc.), zones of abandonment (the space of dead time) have spread across the disciplinary landscape. By zones of abandonment, I mean those places where abandoned humans (the anthropologist, João Biehl has offered thoughtful arguments for terming such abandoned creatures as "ex-humans") wait with death and inhabit dead time.[8]

By this point in the argument, the historians are undoubtedly asking: is dead time simply a technological effect of media, especially cinematic media? *Gefangene* would suggest so and it thus shares a tendency toward technological essentialism typical of much contemporary media archaeology.[9] Such essentialism overlooks who or what makes the decision about what counts as dead time. More than two centuries ago, Jeremy Bentham, author of the famous treatise on the Panopticon and precursor of modern optical unconscious clearly answered this question: dead time is not a self-evident category, nor is it simply the effect of media technology.[10]

---

[7] Doane, *The Emergence of Cinematic Time*, 23; Jacques Derrida, *Archive Fever: A Freudian Impression*, trans. Eric Prenowitz (Chicago: University of Chicago Press, 1996).

[8] João Biehl, *Vita: Life in a Zone of Social Abandonment* (Berkeley: University of California Press, 2002); Jean-Luc Nancy, "Abandoned Being," in *The Birth of Presence*, trans. Brian Holmes (Stanford: Stanford University Press), 1992.

[9] Garrett Stewart, *Framed Time: Toward a Postfilmic Cinema* (Chicago: University of Chicago Press, 2007).

[10] *Jeremy Bentham: The Panopticon Writings*, ed. Miran Božovič

According to Bentham, it is the sovereign who decides dead time; the sovereign decides what counts as eventful.[11] Because scholarly study has tended to reduce the Panopticon to its architectural optics, it has neglected, indeed forgotten, panoptical temporality. In the next section, I excavate dead time in the Panopticon as a necessary step toward imagining what an unsovereign history might look like.

THE PANOPTICON'S TWO BODIES

Michel Foucault envisioned *Discipline and Punish* (1979), his great study of the Panopticon, as a lethal stroke decapitating what he viewed as the traditional study of sovereignty: "what we need, however, is a political philosophy that isn't erected around the problem of sovereignty, nor therefore around the problems of law and prohibition. We need to cut off the King's head: in political theory that has still to be done."[12] He forcefully argued that in the Panopticon, political anatomy superseded premodern sovereignty—the modern disciplinary body supersedes the twin body (political and theological) of the classical sovereign.[13] If we return to a reading of Bentham's treatise, we find the terms of panoptical embodiment to be more complicated than Foucault allowed. The inspector sees inmates without being seen by them and Bentham painstakingly designed the Panopticon to materialize this optics.[14]

(New York: Verso, 1995); Joan Copjec, *Read my Desire: Lacan Against the Historicists* (Cambridge: MIT Press, 1994); Jacques Alain Miller, "Jeremy Bentham's Panoptic Device," *October* 41 (1987): 3–20.

[11] Giorgio Agamben, *State of Exception*, trans. Kevin Attell (Chicago: University of Chicago Press, 2005); Eric L. Santner, *On Creaturely Life: Rilke, Benjamin, Sebald* (Chicago: University of Chicago Press, 2006), 72–73.

[12] Michel Foucault, *Power/Knowledge: Selected Interviews and Other Writings*, ed. Colin Gordon (New York: Pantheon Books, 1980), 121.

[13] Michel Foucault, *Discipline and Punish: The Birth of the Prison*, trans. Alan Sheridan (New York: Vintage Books, 1979), 28–30.

[14] Robin Evans, "Bentham's Panopticon: An Incident in the Social

What scholars (including Foucault) have failed to address adequately, however, are the crucial ways in which Bentham yoked a temporal archival machine to his panoptics—the inspector was not only the eye of the Panopticon but also its writing hand.

The inspector was to be the *inscriptor* who incessantly records the Panopticon.[15] Bentham went to great lengths to preserve this dual-office (archival and optical). For instance, he had to solve the problem of how the inspector could continue to write when darkness fell in the inspection lodge. Bentham imagined a contraption, a life-sized, hourglass-shaped lampshade, inside which the inspector would sit on a stool set close to a light source.[16] A series of small pinpricks in the shade, set at eye level, enabled the inspector to look out from the lodge at the galleries of convict cells at the same time as keeping his books by candlelight. He could be present or absent as long as the candle burned (like a camera running on a set) and produced a shadow observable by the prisoners. When he did enter the lodge for bookkeeping, he could decide on when he wished to scan activity in the cells and through which vantage among those serially provided by the spacing of the pinpricks. The pinpricks, cut into the fabric of the writing lantern, enabled the inspector to "sample" strategically the time of evening lockdown. The archive and dead time thus sutured themselves in this panoptical lantern of the inscriptor who, as its sovereign, could decide to be present and further, to decide on the eventful by choosing selected pinpricks as points of archival recording.

In so embodying the inspector/inscriptor, Bentham inhabited the Panopticon with a sovereign double body. In such twinning, the inspector/inscriptor bears uncanny resemblances to the double-body of the premodern sovereign incarnated by medieval and early-modern political theology as the king with two bodies—the first body political and mor-

History of Architecture," *Architectural Association Quarterly* 3.2 (1976): 21–37.

[15] Božovič, *Jeremy Bentham*, 52–53.
[16] Božovič, *Jeremy Bentham*, 105–106.

tal; the second body, theological and eternal.[17] As a good util-
itarian, Bentham eschewed such premodern political theology; nevertheless, it returned to haunt him in the guise of the
twin body he (in spite of himself) fabricated for his inspec-
tor/inscriptor. Foucault, like Bentham, also eschewed such an
afterlife of political theology in the Panopticon, but in this
case, he and Bentham missed their own ghosts: "[Foucault]
was far too quick to abandon the politicotheological dimen-
sion of the subject's inscription into power relations as a
premodern relic that merely occludes one's gaze on the conditions of possibilities of modernity."[18]

And if, as I have just shown (and others have argued),[19]
the politico-theological *coexists* in the Panopticon with so-
called modern sovereign biopolitics (the "political anatomy"
of Foucault's *History of Sexuality*),[20] then historians need to
ask what enables such persistence, such co-existence? One
such locus, I have proposed, is the archive, constituted by
inscriptor (the panoptical sovereign) as he samples prison
time through pinpricks cut in the lantern of the inspection
lodge. The sovereign inscriptor inscribes an eventful record
by sampling the cuts afforded by the pinprick into the long
hours (dead time) of the evening lockdown. Bentham's treatise thus imagined an eventful archive constituted by the
dead time of prison life. At the same time that Bentham was
conjuring dead time in his widely disseminated treatise, Parliamentary Commissions were investigating the feasibility of
founding a national archive. In the following section, I show
how notions of the national archive and Bentham's imagina-

[17] Ernst Kantorowicz, *The King's Two Bodies: A Study in Medieval Political Theology* (New Jersey: Princeton University Press, 1957).
[18] Santner, *On Creaturely Life*, 183–184.
[19] Hent de Vries and Lawrence E. Sullivan, *Political Theologies: Public Religions in a Post- Secular World* (New York: Fordham University Press, 2006); Santner, *On Creaturely Life*; Slavoj Žižek, Eric L. Santner, and Kenneth Reinhard, *The Neighbor: Three Inquiries in Political Theology* (Chicago: University of Chicago Press, 2005).
[20] Michel Foucault, *The History of Sexuality, Volume I: An Introduction*, trans. Robert Hurley (New York: Vintage, 1980).

tion of panoptical dead time are closely bound, the implications being that historians and convicts together are doing dead time for the sovereign (surely a process to be reimagined).

SPECTACLES OF ABANDONMENT

When Bentham enumerated the many applications for his inspection house (the list itemized prisons, houses of industry, workhouses, poor houses, manufactories, mad-houses, lazarettos, hospitals, schools), he left out the "archive-house." It should, however, have had pride of place on his comprehensive list. At the very moment that Bentham was cogitating on his Panopticon, early Victorian administrators began to conceive of a centralized space in which to confine archival records. Increasingly, such reformers were coming to perceive documents as scattered and unruly objects in need of national (panoptical) supervision. The pioneering measures taken to institutionalize a centralized, national archive in Britain, under the guise of the Public Record Office, ran in tandem with other panoptical initiatives undertaken by Parliament to establish a national penitentiary board and to legislate eventually a national penitentiary system.[21]

Just as British prison reformers searched out the dark and disordered recesses of eighteenth-century gaols and pressed for penal reform, so did the members of the first Royal Record Commission of 1800, constituted by Parliament, create its own panoptical survey of the scattered archives of the nation and pressed for archival reform.[22] By means of an ambi-

---

[21] Sean McConville, *A History of English Prison Administration, Volume 1: 1750–1877* (London: Routledge, 1981); John Cantwell, "The 1838 Public Record Office Act and its Aftermath: A New Perspective," *Journal of the Society of Archivists* 7 (1984): 277–286; Eric Ketelaar, "Archival Temples, Archival Prisons: Modes of Power and Protection," *Archival Science* 2 (2002): 221–238; Eric Stockdale, "The Rise of Joshua Jebb, 1837–1850," *British Journal of Criminology* 16 (1976): 164–170.

[22] Peter Walne, "The Record Commissions, 1800–1837," in *Prisca*

tious questionnaire, commissioners surveyed record depositories (300–400 of them dispersed across the country). Such archives ranged from those of the Royal Treasury and legal courts in London to parish chests stored in obscure rural churches. The commission discovered that (literally) tons of records (the national-archive-to-be) were chaotically scattered in dank buildings where they were stuffed into chests, presses, linen bags, bundles or simply heaped in unprotected piles of parchment and paper. In uncanny synchrony with parliamentary legislation (1835) to create a national inspectorate of British Prisons, Parliament passed in 1838 an act founding a national Public Record Office.[23] In his letter of 1839 endorsing a new centralized national archive, which was included in the *First Report of the Deputy Keeper of Public Records* (1840), Lord Langdale conceived of such an archive along the lines of an "inspection house": for the public service, it is necessary to provide a General Repository, consisting of a fire-proof building, sufficiently extensive, and in a central and convenient situation. With such a building, all the Records may be arranged in a regular and systematic order; the plan and management may be consistent and uniform, the number of officers required may be reduced to the lowest amount, the works to be performed may be carried on under the most effective inspection, and public convenience and economy would equally be consulted.[24]

The keepers of the Public Records estimated that a minimum space of just under 200,000 cubic feet would be re-

Monumenta: Studies in Archival and Administrative History, ed. Felicity Ranger (London: University of London Press, 1973), 9–18.

[23] Roger H. Ellis, "The Building of the Public Record Office," in *Essays in Memory of Sir Hilary Jenkinson*, ed. Albert E.J. Hollaender (Chichester: Moore and Tillyer, 1962), 9–30; Philippa Levine, "History in the Archives: The Public Record Office and its Staff, 1838–1886," *English Historical Review* 101 (1986): 21–41; R.B. Pugh, "Charles Abbot and the Public Records: The First Phase," *Bulletin of the Institute of Historical Research* 39 (1966): 69–85.

[24] *First Report of the Deputy Keeper of Public Records* (London: HMSO, 1840), 67.

quired to accommodate the newly centralized collection of records. They expected that each document transferred to the national depository (not unlike a new prisoner) would require cleaning, repairing, sorting, binding, stamping and numbering. Logistical disagreements arose over how the newly accessed records should then be stored. The first deputy keeper of the Public Records, Sir Francis Palgrave, directed that documents should be stored in presses with locked wire doors for security.[25] Even though this plan proved impracticable (prohibitively expensive and unmanageable as a security measure), it nevertheless shows how the panoptical imaginary had produced records as objects to be incarcerated in the archival inspection house. The architectural plan for the Public Record Office incorporated a reading room with features that ensured the exercise of maximum surveillance. Modeled on the Reading Room of the British Museum,[26] the circular, domed Literary Search Room featured an elevated desk at its center at which the archivist on duty could observe without obstruction readers handling the documents.

Given the closely intertwined histories of the Panopticon and the National Archive, the question of why Bentham did not list the Archive among his inspection houses becomes even more intriguing. At the same time that he incarnated a twin body in his inspection house, he disassociated the tactile scriptural acts of the inscriptor from the optical gaze of the inspector. By so cleaving sight and touch in the Panopticon (an oversized optical instrument), Bentham was establishing the conditions of possibility for dead time and its redefinition of the eventful as the event. Such a fundamental reorganization of vision (through the panoptical cut) would become, in the course of the nineteenth century, a fundamental reorganization of vision itself as a cognitive process:

The nineteenth-century optical devices I discuss, no less than the Panopticon, involved arrangements of bodies in

[25] Ellis, "The Building of the Public Record Office," 20.
[26] George Frederick Barwick, *The Reading Room of the British Museum* (London: Ernest Benn Limited, 1929).

space, regulations of activity, and the deployment of individual bodies, which codified and normalized the observer within rigidly defined systems of visual consumption.[27]

The Panopticon is thus not only about the construction of humans as *objects* under techniques of surveillance, as Foucault emphasized. It is just as much about the constitution of *subjects* of spectacles of abandonment through the cut of dead time, the normalization of vision, as elucidated by Crary,[28] the implications of which have been painfully unfolded by the anthropologist, João Biehl.[29] Traditionally, the timing of alignment of vision and spectacle is associated with the so-called advent of mass culture towards the end of the nineteenth century. I am arguing for a different time line, one that encompasses a neglected prehistory during which the Panopticon sundered tactility and sight and sutured that elision in the concept of dead time. My argument aligns this powerful cognitive knot of panoptical forms of overlapping sovereignties (political-theological and bio-political) on the notion of creaturely life luminously analyzed by Eric Santner: (creaturely life) is that "agitation introduced into human life" by the cuts that produce dead time.[30]

THE INSTALLATION *CELL*: MOVEMENT OF THOUGHT IN SPACE AND TIME

Upon its publication, Foucault's *Discipline and Punish* received immediate praise for making the architecture of sur-

---

[27] Jonathan Crary, *Techniques of the Observer: On Vision and Modernity in the Nineteenth Century* (Cambridge: MIT Press, 1990), 18.
[28] Jonathan Crary, *Suspension of Perception: Attention, Spectacle, and Modern Culture* (Cambridge: MIT Press, 1999); Crary, "Géricault, the Panorama, and Sites of Reality in the Early Nineteenth Century," *Grey Room* 9 (2002): 5–25.
[29] Biehl, *Vita*.
[30] Santner, "Miracles Happen: Benjamin, Rosenzweig, Freud, and the Matter of the Neighbor," in *The Neighbour*, 72.

veillance visible:[31]

> Your researches bear on things that are banal, or which
> have been made banal because they aren't seen. For in-
> stance I find it striking that prisons are in cities, and yet
> no one sees them. Or else, if one sees one, one wonders
> vaguely whether it's a prison, a school, a barracks or a
> hospital. Your book is an important event because it plac-
> es before our eyes something that no one was previously
> able to see.[32]

So far, I have argued that in rendering the Panopticon a major architecture of surveillance, Foucault created a consensus
of knowing that foreclosed a critical understanding of the
spectacle of abandonment *also* at stake in the panoptical project—not only for its objects of surveillance (inmates) but for
subjects (onlookers). By implication, I am contending that
we are not yet able to "see" prisons; they remain invisible in
crucial ways and thus continue to enable the ongoing normalization of the sovereign state of abandonment. Dead time
is by sovereign decision invisible time. In this final part of the
essay, I ask what practices might enable us to think of panoptical surveillance and the spectacle of sovereign abandonment together in order to engage in a disciplinary critique of
dead time.

I broached this methodological challenge in 2002-2003,
when I collaborated with inmates and staff at Mountjoy Prison in Dublin in a site-specific installation we entitled *Cell*.
Designed by Sir Joshua Jebb (Inspector General of the British
Penitentiary System) on the extreme "isolation" model (one
prisoner, one cell) of his Pentonville Prison (London, 1844),
Mountjoy Prison opened in 1850 as a part of English colonial
efforts (a system of national elementary schools being the
complementary architectural component) to discipline the
Irish.[33] During the spring of 2003 when I worked at Mount-

---

[31] Foucault, *Discipline and Punish.*
[32] Foucault, *Power/Knowledge*, 50.
[33] Tim Carey, *Mountjoy: The Story of a Prison* (Cork: Collins Press, 2000).

joy, extreme dilapidation had already resulted in the closure of one of its wings—the remaining three wings were inhabited to capacity by approximately 450 male prisoners. Mountjoy Prison is often considered for closure owing to its deteriorating fabric combined with the daunting difficulties (logistical and financial) of upgrading surveillance technologies in the Victorian structure.

The project *Cell* unfolded during my Fulbright Fellowship (2002–2003) at Media Lab Europe (MLE) in Dublin. Some background on MLE is useful for understanding the stakes of *Cell*. A partnership between Massachusetts Institute of Technology (MIT) and the Irish Government, MLE offered a European base for expansion of the 20-year-old Media Lab in Cambridge, U.S.A. This laboratory had been founded as a hybrid academic unit designed along the lines of a Renaissance "studio" composed of cross-disciplinary research clusters intended to "prototype" creative visions of digital futures. Questions about pedagogy, archive, and postcoloniality had attracted me to MLE as my Fulbright host institution in Ireland. Since I had had the opportunity in 1991-1992 to observe the early days of the Cambridge-based Media Lab as a "historian among the scientists and engineers" (with the generous support of the Lilly Foundation), I now wanted to revisit the media lab to learn about its unfolding globalizing strategies (at the time MLE opened in Dublin, MIT also opened a partnership in India).

As I made my way through Dublin, its colonial architecture left a strong disciplinary impression. I lived in an apartment complex recently furbished out of the monumental shell of an early nineteenth-century fever hospital built by the English. When I walked down the road to do my shopping, the hulk of Mountjoy Prison loomed forbiddingly over that end of the neighborhood. In the vicinity of MLE, young children still went to school in a fortress-like schoolhouse (Inchicore National School) constructed in 1853 according to the "model" architecture for national schools designed by the English. At the edge of the old Guinness Brewery Works where MLE was housed in a beautifully renovated hop-house, lay Fatima Mansions, a deeply impoverished housing project built in the interwar period and now scheduled for imminent demolition. Shortly after I arrived at MLE, the women's group of Fatima Mansions had invited me to collaborate with them on a history project devoted to documenting Fatima Mansions prior to its destruction. They were deeply curious about their new neighbor, MLE, and used to tease me by asking when the "Americans" would be launching their rocket ship. I soon came to realize that the children of Fatima Mansions attended Inchicore, the century-old national school, and that many young men from Fatima Mansions ended up in Mountjoy Prison on drug convictions.

My vivid exposure to this human circuit of abandonment in the course of my multi-media work at Fatima Mansions[34] seemed to be painfully sundered from my customary routine of archival research at the National Archive, where I pored over documents (architectural plans for Mountjoy Prison drawn up by Major Jebb; huge folio-size convict registers recording the first prisoners at Mountjoy Prison; substantial rulebooks written for the first prison officers and inmates at Mountjoy; and the endless parliamentary debates of the early nineteenth century over the appropriate physical form of confinement). The gap I encountered between archive and neighborhood recapitulated the discursive sundering of the visual and tactile staged by Bentham and Foucault. The time I spent in the archive and the time I spent in Fatima Mansions with the women's history group seemed to be profiling for me the epistemology of dead time as constituted in the event.

A pause overtook my work and I stepped back to ask how I might conceptualize a project that would somehow link together the tactile and the visual, the panoptical and aban-

---

[34] Mike Ananny, Kathleen Biddick, and Carol Strohecker, "Constructing Public Discourse with Ethno-SMS Texts," in *Human-Computer Interaction with Mobile Devices and Services*, ed. Luca Chittaro (Berlin: Springer-Verlag, 2003): 368–373, and "Shifting Scales on Common Ground: Developing Personal Expressions and Public Opinion," *International Journal of Continuing Engineering Education and Life Long Learning* 14.6 (2004): 484–505.

donment, surveillance and spectacle and would also draw the "eventful" archive into its shadow temporalities of dead time. I had no desire to "fix" or close these gaps, instead I wished to problematize them, so as to "change the coordinates of what is strategically possible within a historical constellation."[35] I began to explore the notion of a performative "installation" at Mountjoy Prison that would unfold in dead time and bring prisoners and public into temporal contact. I experimented with the following ideas: first, an installation would involve my collaboration with prisoners, prison-staff, my MLE colleagues, and the neighborhood, thus joining together groups designed to be separated by access and architecture and time (who, precisely, is doing dead time?) As Jane Jacobs would say, I wanted to work on changing the temporal borders of dead time into *seams*.[36] Conceptually, an installation performs the movement of thought through time and space and in so doing kinesthetically draws together those "bodies" whom confinement and surveillance would isolate into subject and object. Kinesthetics does not "cut" itself into dead time and event, rather, it interrupts the everyday cognitive habits of the visual and the tactile such that movement and temporality become modes of experience (and not "cuts" of representations). Because the work for any installation, especially a prison installation which involves so many layers of authorization and permission, is an emergent process (it can never be guaranteed in advance, especially in a prison), an installation demands simple fidelity to collaborative practice and to the time of that practice, however "uneventful" it might be. Such fidelity seemed to me a powerful counterpoint to spectacles of abandonment and to notions of the eventful.

With the permission of John Lonergan, Governor of Mountjoy Prison, I was able to work with a self-selecting team of inmates and staff over the spring of 2003. First, I would like to describe briefly how we developed materials for

[35] Slavoj Žižek, *Iraq: The Borrowed Kettle* (London: Verso, 2004), 81.
[36] Jane Jacobs, *The Death and Life of Great American Cities* (New York: Random House, 1961), 268.

the project and then to show how we mobilized them for a public multimedia installation, entitled *Cell*, held in October 2004. Our project began with the study of the first Mountjoy convict registers from the 1850s, pages of which I had digitized in the National Archive and then printed out for reading in our prison-staff working group. The "tabular" form of these registers, which incarcerated information on prisoners into rows and columns, viscerally struck the team and provided the subject of intense conversation. We spent time looking at how the tabular form of the register echoed the impulse of the panoptical prison to confine and isolate humans corporeally at the same time that it organized them archivally as eventful. We then asked, what would an archive drawn up by prisoners such as themselves look like? How can the paradox of the extreme exposure of the prisoner to dead time be archived: "The prisoner is exposed to the prison itself, a complex organism that consists of walls, gates, inmates, guards, and so forth."[37] In what ways did the historical convict register provide an uncanny platform for questioning the dead time of the prison through performance?

Based on these lively discussions, the team decided that they wanted to represent their own history of the prison— one that would somehow cross-cut the coordinates of the "table" of the convict register at the same time that it exposed uncanny continuities with contemporary inception of prisoners. Physically, their plan required that they construct a video during the dead time of the daily prison routine as they moved about in the dead spaces of the prison (yards, corridors, etc.). Such a proposal required very specific security permissions from the governor of Mountjoy Prison. Did his grant mean that dead time was no longer a constitutive concept in the modern prison life? Like Farocki, I do not think that the Governor of Mountjoy Prison had a solution for "dead time," but he certainly recognized the need for its radical deconstruction with and through prisoner guards and staff, with and through performative interventions that ques-

[37] Michael Hardt, "Prison Time," *Yale French Studies* 91 (1997): 68 [64–79].

tioned it not just as an internal issue but as a question of the neighborhood, the public. The governor allowed the use of a video camera (a gracious loan from MLE) in the prison. The team learned how to operate the camera and how to storyboard in order to produce their own video history of Mountjoy, then and now. Although always in the company of guards (whose cooperation was extraordinary), the prison team was able to range widely around the prison with the video camera. The one space closed to this camera were the small, single Victorian cells (part of the original design) in which they were locked down from 7:00 p.m.–7:00 a.m. The team sought permission to use the video camera to record this nocturnal time of isolation, when they most marked themselves marking time in their cells. They mounted the video camera on a tripod and proceeded to film themselves narrating what I call a "cellography," a kind of talking back to dead time. What the prisoners wanted to record was the "dead time" elided by Bentham's inscriptor and put on fast-forward in the Corcoran Prison Correction video of the death of convict Martinez. The team screened these cell tapes in the abandoned cells that served as the location for the public installation.

Once the prison team had recorded their library of films, we began to discuss how their archive could be brought in "touch" with the outside of the prison. We slowly hatched an idea for a public installation to be held in the abandoned wing of the prison. The public could only enter that wing during the dead time of evening lock-down hours. For security purposes, the prisoners, their invited families, prison-staff, and public visitors would all have to be locked together in the derelict wing. We then sought to conceptualize the installation so that surveillance and abandonment could be thought of together—just as the prisoners and prison staff had questioned issues of vision and tactility in creating their materials, so too would the public be invited to do so. The prison team received extraordinary permission from Governor Lonergan to be present with their invited families at the installation and we opened the installation, entitled *Cell*, to the public for two evenings in October 2003.

For security purposes, visitors to *Cell* were momentarily "imprisoned"; the installation deliberately constructed pauses to mark this momentary abandonment. Guests first passed through a security check-point at which time cell-phones were confiscated for the duration of the program. As a group, the public were then escorted by prison staff to the "eye" of the Panopticon, the inner circle, where they stood amidst the sounds, smells, sights, and touch of the locked-down prison. I had never entered a prison until I walked into Mountjoy Prison in spring 2003, but for thirty-years or so I had been haunted by what I heard and saw in 1971 when round-the-clock radio and television coverage witnessed the carnage of an uprising at Attica Prison in the state of New York. The composer Frederic Rzewski set to music the words of Sam Melville, a prisoner who died in that uprising. Those incantations came to my mind as I stood in the Mountjoy eye for the first time: "in the indifferent brutality, the incessant noise, the experimental chemistry of food, the ravings of lost hysterical men, I can act with clarity and meaning."[38]

In order to conjure the ghost of the classical sovereign incarnated in Bentham's inspector/inscriptor, we projected the archival image of Jebb's architectural ground-plan for Mountjoy (digitized in the National Archive) onto the floor of the "eye" in which the expectant visitors stood. As they milled in the eye, they literally walked through the incandescent glow of this digitized image. To mark the sense of hearing as a means of contemplating abandonment, we created an "audioscape" by stringing up a circle of speakers along the upper circumference of the "eye." Through them we piped the recordings we had made of the prison-team and the prison staff reading their respective section of rules from the original Victorian rulebook for Mountjoy Prison. We deliberately left the playback unsynchronized in order to heighten the irrational cacophony of the rules. The "chant" of the historical rules collided with the din of the prison evening (clang of doors, screams of prisoners): we wanted to ask what is the

[38] Frederic Rzewski, *Coming Together, Attica* (Hungaraton Records, 1972, reissued in 1993).

sound of dead time?

Guests stood in the "eye" for at least 15 minutes before the prison team and prison staff introduced the installation, explained security measures, and ushered the group to the abandoned wing where they were to be locked until it was time for the next "shift" of visitors to file in. In the depths of the abandoned cells, members of the prisoner team had arranged video monitors (gracious loan of MLE), on which their films looped. In order to view and discuss the work of the prison teams, the public had to crowd into these claustrophobic, decaying cells and experience how quickly a major architecture of surveillance becomes a minor architecture of abandonment and dead time. We thus wanted to ask the guests to think of a question posed by Elizabeth Grosz: "can architecture be thought, no longer as a whole, a complex unity, but as a set of and a site for becomings of all kinds?"[39]

Who were the guests? They were neighbors of the neighborhood of Mountjoy Prison: the invited families of the prison team; the newly arrived Irish Fulbright scholars shepherded by Carmel Coyle, Director of the Irish Fulbright Commission; a car-full of friends from Fatima Mansions; fellow colleagues from MLE and faculty from Dublin colleges and universities; the Edge from U2 who sat on the governing board of MLE; members of the Irish Prison Reform Commission; interested Dubliners who had heard the advertisement on the radio. It is through the encounter of the guests with prisoners and staff that the installation dissolved the cut between dead time and event.

The installation ran for two nights in two shifts. It was indeed only a "minor interruption" of the Panopticon, a refusal of the elision of dead time. We knew that after *Cell* each of us would return to marking our own dead time; but becoming "minor" is a powerful means by which the spectacle of abandonment can be momentarily suspended by problematizing it by threading thought through space and time along coordinates different from the optics and scriptures of politi-

[39] Elizabeth Grosz, *Space, Time, and Perversion: Essays on the Politics of Bodies* (New York: Routledge, 1995), 135.

cal theology. But for this essay, the copies of films made for the possession of the prison team and their families, the governor of Mountjoy Prison, and myself, there exists no official archive of this event. There is no expert that puts the performance of Mountjoy Prison into fast forward (as in the Corcoran surveillance tapes) or cuts them into a usable web page. The project was intended to unfold in-between the two inspection-houses (prison and National Archive) and the housing project and the prison. For a moment, *Cell* suspended the sovereign decision to cut the event from dead time and to incarnate in a major architecture (such as Mountjoy Prison) vision and touch as dichotomous. For a moment the panoptic trembled and the dead time of the historian and prisoner unfolded without a sovereign cut.

REFERENCES

ʒ

Abbas, Asma. "In Terror, In Love, Out of Time." In *At the Limits of Justice: Women of Color Theorize Terror,* eds. Sherene Razack and Suvendrini Pereira, 501–525. Toronto: University of Toronto Press, 2014.

Admonán of Iona. *De Locis Sanctis.* In *Itinera Hiersolymitana saeculi iiii-viii,* ed. Paul Geyer. Corpus Scriptorum Ecclesiasticorum Latinorum, Vol. 28 (1898), 296. Also available at: https://archive.org/details/itinerahierosol00geyegoog.

Aers, David. *Sanctifying Signs: Making Christian Tradition in Late Medieval England.* Notre Dame: University of Notre Dame Press, 2004.

Aers, David and Sarah Beckwith. "Eucharist." In *Cultural Reformations: Medieval and Renaissance in Literary History,* eds. Brian Cummings and James Simpson, 153–156. Oxford: Oxford University Press, 2010.

Agamben, Giorgio. *Homo Sacer: Sovereign Power and Bare Life,* trans. Daniel Heller-Roazen. Stanford: Stanford University Press, 1998.

---. "The Noon-day Demon." In Giorgio Agamben, *Stanzas: Word and Phantasm in Western Culture,* trans. Ronald L. Martinez, 3–10. Minneapolis: University of Minnesota Press, 1993.

---. *The Open: Man and Animal,* trans. Kevin Attell. Stanford: Stanford University Press, 2004.

---. *Remnants of Auschwitz: The Witness and the Archive,* trans. Daniel Heller-Roazen. New York: Zone Books, 1999.

---. *State of Exception,* trans. Kevin Attell. Chicago: University of Chicago Press, 2005.

---. *The Time that Remains: A Commentary on the Letter to the Romans,* trans. Patricia Dailey. Stanford: Stanford University Press, 2005.

Ambrose, Kirk. *The Nave Sculpture of Vézelay: The Art of Monastic Viewing.* Toronto: Pontifical Institute for Medieval Studies, 2006.

Ananny, Mike, Kathleen Biddick, and Carol Strohecker. "Constructing Public Discourse with Ethno-SMS Texts." In *Human-Computer Interaction with Mobile Devices and Services,* ed. Luca Chittaro (Berlin: Springer-Verlag, 2003): 368–373.

---. "Shifting Scales on Common Ground: Developing Personal Expressions and Public Opinion," *International Journal of Continuing Engineering Education and Life Long Learning* 14.6 (2004): 484–505.

Anker, Suzanne and Dorothy Nelkin. *The Molecular Gaze: Art in the Genetic Age.* New York: Cold Spring Harbor Laboratory Press, 2003.

Anidjar, Gil. *Blood: A Critique of Christianity.* New York: Columbia University Press, 2014.

---. *The Jew, The Arab: A History of the Enemy.* Stanford: Stanford University Press, 2003.

Badiou, Alain. *Saint Paul: The Foundation of Universalism,* trans. Ray Brassier. Stanford: Stanford University Press, 2003.

Bailey, Richard N. *England's Earliest Sculptors.* Toronto: Pontifical Institute for Medieval Studies, 1996.

Barad, Karen. *Meeting the Universe Halfway: Quantum Physics and the Entanglement of Matter and Meaning.* Durham: Duke University Press, 2007.

Barkan, Leonard. *The Gods Made Flesh: Metamorphoses and the Pursuit of Paganism.* New Haven: Yale University Press, 1986.

Barwick, George Frederick. *The Reading Room of the British Museum.* London: Ernest Benn Limited, 1929.

Bates, David. "Political Theology and the Nazi State: Carl Schmitt's Concept of the Institution." *Modern Intellectual History* 3 (2006): 415–422.

Beckett, Samuel. *Endgame: A Play in One Act.* London: Faber and Faber, 1958. Also available at: http://samuel-beckett.net/endgame.html.

Beckett, Katharine Scarfe. *Anglo-Saxon Perceptions of the Islamic World.* New York: Cambridge University Press, 2003.

Bedos-Rezak, Brigitte. "The Confrontation of Orality and Textuality: Jewish and Christian Literacy in the Eleventh and Twelfth Century in Northern France." In *Rashi 1049-1990*, ed. Gabrielle Sed-Rajna, 541–558. Paris: Les Editions du Cert, 1993.

———. "Medieval Identity: A Sign and a Concept." *American Historical Review* 105.5 (December 2000): 1489–1533.

Benjamin, Walter. *Correspondence of Walter Benjamin*, eds. Gershom Scholem and Theodor W. Adorno, trans. Manfred R. Jacobson and Evelyn M. Jacobson. Chicago: University of Chicago Press, 1994.

———. "Critique of Violence." In Walter Benjamin, *Reflections: Essays, Aphorisms, Writings*, trans. Edmund Jephcott, 277–300. New York: Schocken Books, 1978.

———. *The Origin of the German Tragic Drama*, trans. John Osborne. London: New Left Books, 1977.

———. "Theses on the Philosophy of History." In Walter Benjamin, *Illuminations: Essays and Reflections*, ed. Hannah Arendt, trans. Harry Zohn, 253–264. New York: Schocken Books, 1968.

———. "Two Poems by Friedrich Hölderlin." In *Walter Benjamin: Selected Writings, Volume 1: 1913-1926*, eds. Marcus Bullock and Michael William Jennings, trans. Edmund Jephcott, 18–36. Cambridge: Harvard University Press, 1996.

Bennett, Jane. "Systems and Things: A Response to Graham Harman and Timothy Morton." *New Literary History* 43 (2012): 225–233.

———. *Vibrant Matter: A Political Ecology of Things*. Durham: Duke University Press, 2010.

Bentham, Jeremy. *Jeremy Bentham: The Panopticon Writings*, ed. Miran Božovič. New York: Verso, 1995.

Biddick, Kathleen. "Arthur's Two Bodies and the Bare Life of the Archives." In *Cultural Diversity in the British Middle Ages: Archipelago, Island, England*, ed. Jeffrey Jerome Cohen 117–134. New York: Palgrave Macmillan, 2008.

———. "Dead Neighbor Archives: Jews, Muslims, and the Enemy's Two Bodies." In *Political Theology and Early Modernity*, eds. Graham Hammill and Julia Reinhard Lupton, 124–142. Chicago: University of Chicago Press, 2012.

———. "Doing Dead Time for the Sovereign: Archive, Abandonment, Performance." *Rethinking History* 13.2 (2009): 137–151.

———. "*The Legitimacy of the Middle Ages*, eds. Andrew Cole and D. Vance Smith [book review]." *The Medieval Review* 10.09.12 (2010): https://scholarworks.iu.edu/journals/index.php/tmr/article/view/17099/23217.

———. "People and Things: Power in Early English Development."

Comparative Studies in Society and History 32 (1990): 3–23.

———. "*Periodization and Sovereignty*, by Kathleen Davis [book review]." *The Medieval Review* 09.04.06 (2009): https://scholar works.iu.edu/journals/index.php/tmr/article/view/16784/22902.

———. "Tears of Reign: Big Sovereigns Do Cry." In *bodily fluids* [special issue], eds. Kamillea Aghtan, Michael O'Rourke and Karin Sellberg. *Inter/Alia: A Journal of Queer Studies* 9 (2014): 15–34.

———. "Trauma." In *Medievalism: Key Critical Terms*, eds. Elizabeth Emery and Richard Utz, 247–253. Cambridge: D.S. Brewer, 2014.

———. "Trans-medieval Mattering and the Untimeliness of the Real Presence." *postmedieval: a journal of medieval cultural studies* 4.2 (2013): 238–252.

———. *The Typological Imaginary: Circumcision, Technology, and History*. Philadelphia: University of Pennsylvania Press, 2003.

———. "Unbinding the Flesh in the Time that Remains: Crusader Martyrdom, Then and Now." *GLQ* 13.2–3 (2007): 197–225.

Biehl, João. *Vita: Life in a Zone of Social Abandonment*. Berkeley: University of California Press, 2002.

Blark, James G., Frank T. Coulson, and Kathryn L. McKinley, eds. *Ovid in the Middle Ages*. New York: Cambridge University Press, 2011.

Bojanić, Petar. "God the Revolutionist: On Radical Violence for the First Ultra-Leftist." *Filozofski vestnik* 29.2 (2008): 191–207.

Boureau, Alain. *Kantorowicz: Stories of a Historian*, trans. Stephen G. Nichols and Gabrielle M. Spiegel. Baltimore: Johns Hopkins University Press, 2001.

de Bracton, Henry. *On the Laws and Customs of England. De Legibus et Consuetudinibus Angliae,* ed. George E. Woodbine, trans. Samuel E. Thorne, 4 Vols. Cambridge: Harvard University Press, 1968-1977.

Brand, Paul. "The Age of Bracton." *Proceedings of the British Academy* 89 (1996): 65–89.

Brett, M. *The English Church under Henry I*. Oxford: Oxford University Press, 1975.

Brown, Judith. "Pretty Richard (in Three Parts)." In *Shakesqueer: A Queer Companion to the Complete Works of Shakespeare*, ed. Madhavi Menon, 286–301. Durham: Duke University Press, 2011.

Buber, Martin and Franz Rosenzweig. *Die Schrift*, 13 Vols. Berlin: Verlag Lambert Schneider, 1926-1938.

Burnett, Amy Nelson. "The Social History of Communion and the Reformation of the Eucharist." *Past and Present* 211 (2011): 77–

119.

Burnett, Charles. *Adelard of Bath: An English Scientist and Arabist of the Early Twelfth Century*. London: Warburg Institute Surveys and Texts, 1987.

Butler, Judith. *Parting Ways: Jewishness and the Critique of Zionism*. New York: Columbia University Press, 2012.

Bynum, Caroline Walker. *Wonderful Blood: Theology and Practice in Late Medieval Northern Germany and Beyond*. Philadelphia: University of Pennsylvania Press, 2007.

Campbell, Thomas P. and Clifford Davidson, eds. *The Fleury Playbook: Essays and Studies*. Kalamazoo: Medieval Institute Publications, 1985.

Cantor, Norman. *Church, Kingship and Lay Infrastructure in England*. Princeton: Princeton University Press, 1958.

Cantwell, John. "The 1838 Public Record Office Act and its Aftermath: A New Perspective." *Journal of the Society of Archivists* 7 (1984): 277–286.

Caputo, John D. *The Prayers and Tears of Jacques Derrida*. Bloomington: Indiana University Press, 1997.

Carey, Tim. *Mountjoy: The Story of a Prison*. Cork: Collins Press, 2000.

Carlson, Eric Gustav. "The Abbey Church of St.-Etienne at Caen in the Eleventh and Early Twelfth Centuries." Ph.D. diss., Yale University, 1968.

Carragáin, Éamonn Ó. *Ritual and the Rood: Liturgical Images and the Old English Poems of the Dream of the Rood Tradition*. Toronto: University of Toronto Press, 2005.

Casarino, Cesare. "Time Matters: Marx, Negri, Agamben, and the Corporeal." *Strategies* 16 (2003): 185–206.

Cassidy, Brendan. "The Later Life of the Ruthwell Cross: From the Seventeenth Century to the Present." In *The Ruthwell Cross: Papers from the Colloquium Sponsored by the Index of Christian Art, Princeton University, 8 December 1989*, ed. Brendan Cassidy, 3–34. Princeton: Princeton University Press, 1992.

Chaganti, Seeta. "Vestigial Signs: Inscription, Performance and *The Dream of The Rood*." *PMLA* 125 (2010): 48–72.

Christie, Deborah and Sara Juliet Laura, eds. *Better off Dead: The Evolution of the Zombie as Post-Human*. New York: Fordham University Press, 2011.

Clanchy, M.T. *From Memory to Written Record: England, 1066-1307*. Cambridge: Harvard University Press, 1979.

Cohen, Jeffrey Jerome. *Hybridity, Identity and Monstrosity in Medieval Britain: On Difficult Middles*. New York: Palgrave Macmillan, 2006.

Cole, Andrew and D. Vance Smith, eds. *The Legitimacy of the Middle Ages: On the Unwritten History of Theory.* Durham: Duke University Press, 2010.

Collingwood, W.G. *Northumbrian Crosses of the Pre-Norman Age.* London: Faber, 1927.

Copjec, Joan. *Read my Desire: Lacan Against the Historicists.* Cambridge: MIT Press, 1994.

Councils & Synods with Other Documents Relating to the English Church, Part II. 1066- 1204, ed. Frederick K. Maurice Powicke, text no. 134:750–754. Oxford: Clarendon University Press, 1981.

Cramp, Rosemary. *Corpus of Anglo-Saxon Stone* Sculpture, Vol. 1: County Durham and Northumberland. London: British Academy, 1984: http://www.britac.ac.uk/pubs/cat/casss.cfm.

Crary, Jonathan. "Géricault, the Panorama, and Sites of Reality in the Early Nineteenth Century." *Grey Room* 9 (2002): 5–25.

–––.*Suspension of Perception: Attention, Spectacle, and Modern Culture.* Cambridge: MIT Press, 1999.

–––. *Techniques of the Observer: On Vision and Modernity in the Nineteenth Century.* Cambridge: MIT Press, 1990.

Crowe, Christopher. "Early Medieval Parish Formation in Dumfries and Galloway." In *The Cross Goes North: Processes of Conversion in Northern Europe AD 300-1300,* ed. Martin Carver, 195–20. Suffolk: Boydell & Brewer, 2003.

Cvetkovich, Ann. *Depression: A Public Feeling.* Durham: Duke University Press, 2012.

Dante Alighieri. *Inferno, Purgatorio, Paradiso.* The Princeton Dante Project: http://www. princeton.edu/dante/.

Darwin, Erasmus. "Loves of Plants." In *Botanic Garden.* London: J. Nichols, 1790. Available via Project Gutenberg at: http://www.gutenberg.org/ebooks/10671.

Davis, Kathleen. *Periodization and Sovereignty: How Ideas of Feudalism and Secularization Govern the Politics of Time.* Philadelphia: University of Pennsylvania Press, 2008.

Dean, Tim. "The Biopolitics of Pleasure." *South Atlantic Quarterly,* 111 (Summer 2012): 477–495.

De Hamel, Christopher F.R. *Glossed Books of the Bible and the Origins of the Paris Booktrade.* Suffolk: Boydell & Brewer, 1984.

de Lubac, Henri. *Corpus Mysticum: The Eucharist and the Church in the Middle Ages: Historical Survey,* trans. Gemma Simmonds and Richard Price. Notre Dame: University of Notre Dame Press, 2006.

de Vries, Hent and Lawrence E. Sullivan, eds. *Political Theologies:*

Public Religions in a Post-Secular World. New York: Fordham University Press, 2006.

Denery II, Dallas G. *Seeing and Being Seen in the Later Medieval World: Optics, Theology and Religious Life.* New York: Cambridge University Press, 2005.

Deleuze, Gilles and Félix Guattari. *A Thousand Plateaus: Capitalism and Schizophrenia,* trans. Brian Massumi. Minneapolis: University of Minnesota, 1987.

Derrida, Jacques. *Archive Fever,* trans. Eric Prenowitz. Chicago: University of Chicago Press, 1996.

———. *The Beast and the Sovereign, Vol. 1,* trans. Geoffrey Bennington. Chicago: University of Chicago Press, 2009.

———. "Force of Law: The Mystical Foundations of Authority." *Cardozo Law Review* 11 (1989-90): 921–1045.

———. *Memoirs of the Blind: The Self-Portrait and Other Ruins,* trans. Pascale-Anne Brault and Michael Naas. Chicago: University of Chicago Press, 1993.

DeVries, Kelly. "Medieval Warfare and the Value of Human Life." In *Noble Ideals and Bloody Realities: Warfare in the Middle Ages,* eds. Niall Christie and Maya Yazigi, 27–56. Leiden: Brill 2000.

Didi-Huberman, Georges. *Confronting Images: Questioning the Ends of a Certain History of Art,* trans. John Goodman. University Park: The Pennsylvania State University Press, 2005.

Dinshaw, Carolyn. "Touching on the Past." In *The Boswell Thesis: Essays on Christianity, Social Tolerance, and Homosexuality,* ed. Mathew Kuefler, 57–73. Chicago: University of Chicago Press, 2006.

Doane, Mary Anne. *The Emergence of Cinematic Time: Modernity, Contingency, the Archive.* Cambridge: Harvard University Press, 2002.

Dolan, Diane. *Le drame liturgique de Pâques en Normandie et en Angleterre au moyen age.* Publications de L'Universite de Poitiers Lettres and Sciences Humaines. Vol. 16. Paris: Presses Universitaires de France, 1975.

Dream of the Rood, ed. Michael Swanton. In *Old and Middle English: An Anthology, c. 890-1400,* ed. Elaine Traherne, 108–115. Oxford: Blackwell, 2004.

Dressler, Rachel. "Deus *Hoc Vult:* Ideology, Identity, and Sculptural Rhetoric at the Time of the Crusades." *Medieval Encounters* 1 (1995): 188–218.

Duerfahrd, Lance. "Afterthoughts on Disability: Crying at William Wyler's *Best Years of Our Lives.*" In *On the Verge of Tears: Why the Movies, Television, Music, Art, Popular Culture, and the Real World Make us Cry,* eds. Michele Byers and David Lavery, 50–66. Newcastle-upon-Tyne: Cambridge Scholars Publishing, 2010.

Duggan, Anne. "*De consultationibus:* The Role of Episcopal Consultation in the Shaping of Canon Law in the Twelfth Century." In *Bishops, Texts and the Use of Canon Law around 1100,* eds. Bruce C. Brasington and Kathleen G. Cushing, 191–214. Burlington: Ashgate, 2008.

———. "Thomas Becket's Italian Network." In *Pope, Church and City: Essays in Honour of Brenda M. Bolton,* eds. Frances Andrews, Christoph Egger, and Constance M. Rousseau, 177–204. Leiden: Brill, 2004.

Dunne, Éamonn and Michael O'Rourke. "Miller's Idle Tears" (unpublished paper): https://www.academia.edu/6919392/Millers_ Idle_ Tears.

Eiland, Howard and Michael W. Jennings. *Walter Benjamin: A Critical Life.* Cambridge: Harvard University Press, 2014.

Ellis, Roger H. "The Building of the Public Record Office." In *Essays in Memory of Sir Hilary Jenkinson,* ed. Albert E.J. Hollaender, 9–30. Chichester: Moore and Tillyer, 1962.

Eng, David L. and David Kazanjian, eds. *Loss: The Politics of Mourning.* Berkeley: University of California Press, 2003.

Esposito, Roberto. *Bíos: Biopolitics and Philosophy,* trans. Timothy Campbell. Minneapolis: University of Minnesota Press, 2008.

———. "Flesh and Body in the Deconstruction of Christianity," trans. Janell Watson. *Minnesota Review* 75 (2010): 89–99.

Ettinger, Bracha L. *The Matrixial Boderspace,* ed. Brian Massumi. Minneapolis: University of Minnesota Press, 2006.

Evans, Robin. "Bentham's Panopticon: An Incident in the Social History of Architecture." *Architectural Association Quarterly* 3.2 (1976): 21–37.

Evitt, Regula Meyer. "Eschatology, Millenarian Apocalypticism, and the Liturgical Anti-Judaism of the Medieval Prophet Plays." In *The Apocalyptic Year 1000: Religious Expectation and Social Change, 950-1050,* eds. Richard Landes, Andrew Gow, and David C. Van Meter, 205– 229. Oxford: Oxford University Press, 2003.

Farocki, Harun. "Controlling Observation." In *CTRL [SPACE]: Rhetorics of Surveillance from Bentham to Big Brother,* eds. Thomas Y. Levin, Ursula Frohne, and Peter Weibel, 102–107. Boston: MIT Press, 2002.

———. "I believed to see prisoners; Eye." In *CTRL [SPACE]: Rhetorics of Surveillance from Bentham to Big Brother,* eds. Thomas Y. Levin, Ursula Frohne, and Peter Weibel, 422–425. Boston: MIT Press, 2002.

Federico, Sylvia. "Queer Times: Richard II in the Poems and Chronicles of Late Fourteenth-Century England." *Medium Aevum* 79 (2010): 25–46.

Fenves, Peter. "Renewed Question: Whether a Philosophy of History is Possible." *Modern Language Notes* 129.3 (2014): 514–524.

Ferber, Ilit. *Philosophy and Melancholy: Benjamin's Reflections on Theater and Language.* Stanford: Stanford University Press, 2013.

Finke, Laurie A. and Martin B. Shichtman. *King Arthur and the Myth of History.* Gainesville: University of Florida Press, 2004.

First Report of the Deputy Keeper of Public Records. London: HMSO, 1840.

Fitz Nigel, Richard. *Dialogus de Scaccario: The Course of the Exchequer,* ed. and trans. Charles Johnson with corrections by F.E.L. Carter and D.E. Greenway. Oxford: Clarendon Press, 1983.

Foucault, Michel. *Discipline and Punish: The Birth of the Prison,* trans. Allen Lane. New York: Penguin Books, 1977.

– – –. *The History of Sexuality, Vol. 1: An Introduction,* trans. Robert Hurley. New York: Random House, 1978.

– – –. *Power/Knowledge: Selected Interviews and other Writings (1972-77),* ed. Colin Gordon, trans. Colin Gordon, Leo Marshall, John Melham, and Kate Soper. New York: Pantheon Books, 1980.

– – –. *Society Must Be Defended: Lectures at the College de France, 1975-76,* eds. Mauro Bertani and Alessandro Fontana, trans. David Macey. New York: Palgrave, 2003.

Fradenburg, Louise and Carla Freccero. "Introduction: Caxton, Foucault, and the Pleasures of History." In *Premodern Sexualities,* eds. Louise Fradenburg and Carla Freccero, i–xxiv. New York: Routledge, 1996.

Freccero, Carla. *Queer/Early/Modern.* Durham: Duke University Press, 2006.

Freeman, Elizabeth. *Time Binds: Queer Temporalities, Queer Histories.* Durham: Duke University Press, 2010.

Fuchs, Barbara. *Mimesis and Empire: The New World, Islam, and European Identities.* Cambridge: Cambridge University Press, 2001.

Gaborit-Chopin, Danielle. "Walrus Ivory in Western Europe." In *From Viking to Crusader: The Scandinavians and Europe 800-*

1200, eds. Else Roesdahl and David M. Wilson, 204–205. New York: Rizzoli, 1992.

Geoffrey of Monmouth. *The Historia Regum Britanniae of Geoffrey of Monmouth: I. Bern, Burgerbibliothek, MS 568,* ed. Neil Wright. Cambridge: D.S. Brewer, 1984.

---. *History of the Kings of Britain,* trans. Lewis Thorpe. New York: Penguin, 1966.

Gertsman, Elina, ed. *Crying in the Middle Ages: Tears of History.* New York: Routledge, 2012.

Gillingham, John. "The Context and Purposes of Geoffrey of Monmouth's *History of the Kings of Britain.*" *Anglo-Norman Studies* 13 (1990-1991): 99–118.

Gilman, Ernest. *The Curious Perspective: Literary and Pictorial Wit in the Seventeenth Century.* New Haven: Yale University Press, 1978.

Glanville, Ranulf. *The Treatise on Laws and Customs of the Realm of England commonly called Glanvill,* ed. and trans. G.D.G. Hall, 2nd edn. Oxford: Oxford University Press, 1993.

Godfrew, Mark. "Review of Anselm Kiefer's *Palmsonntag.*" *Whitehot Magazine* (April 2007): http://whitehotmagazine.com/articles/white-cube-mason-s-yard/396.

---. "Mirror of Displacements: On the Art of Zoe Leonard." *Artforum International* 46 (March 2008): 292–302.

Golb, Norman. *The Jews in Medieval Normandy.* Cambridge: Cambridge University Press, 1998.

Gold, Joshua Robert. "The Dwarf in the Machine: A Theological Figure and its Sources." *Modern Language Notes* 121 (2006): 1220–1236.

Gourgouris, Stathis. *Does Literature Think? Literature as Theory for an Antimythical Era.* Stanford: Stanford University Press, 2003.

Green, Judith A. *English Sheriffs to 1154,* Public Record Office Handbooks 24. London: H.M. Stationery Office, 1970.

---. *The Government of England under Henry I.* Cambridge: Cambridge University Press, 1986.

Grafton, Anthony and Jeffrey Hamburger, eds. *The Warburg Institute: A Special Issue on The Library and Its Readers. Common Knowledge* 18.1 (2012).

Grivot, Denis and George Zarnecki. *Giselbertus: Sculptor of Autun.* New York: Orion Press, 1961.

Grosrichard, Alain. *The Sultan's Court: European Fantasies of the East,* trans. Liz Heron. New York: Verso, 1998.

Grosz, Elizabeth. *Space, Time, and Perversion: Essays on the Politics of Bodies.* New York: Routledge, 1995.

Grünewald, Eckhart. *Ernst Kantorowicz und Stefan George: Beiträge zur Bibliographie des Historikers bis zum Jahre 1938 und zu seinem Jugendwerk "Kaiser Friedrich der Zweite."* Frankfurter Historische Abhandlungen, Vol. 25. Wiesbaden: F. Steiner, 1982.

Hägglund, Martin. *Radical Atheism: Derrida and the Time of Life.* Stanford: Stanford University Press, 2008.

Hammill, Graham. *The Mosaic Constitution: Political Theology and Imagination from Machiavelli to Milton.* Chicago: University of Chicago Press, 2012.

Hansen, Miriam Bratu. "Benjamin's Aura." *Critical Inquiry* 34 (2008): 336–375.

Hanssen, Beatrice. *Walter Benjamin's Other History: Of Stones, Animals, Human Beings, and Angels.* Berkeley: University of California Press, 1998.

Hardt, Michael. "Prison Time." *Yale French Studies* 91 (1997): 64–79.

Harman, Graham. *Prince of Networks: Bruno Latour and Metaphysics.* Melbourne: re.press, 2009.

Harmon, A.G. "Shakespeare's Carved Saints." *Studies in English Literature* 45 (2005): 315–331.

Haskins, Charles Homer. *Studies in the History of Mediaeval Science.* Cambridge: Harvard University Press, 1924.

Healy, Patrick. "A Supposed Letter of Archbishop Lanfranc: Concepts of the Universal Church in the Investiture Contest." *English Historical Review* 121.494 (December 2006): 1385–1407.

Hebrew Chronicle of 1096. Hebraische Berichte über die Judenverfolgungen während der Kreuzzuge: Quellen zur Geschichten der Juden in Deutschland, trans. Seligman Baer, eds. Adolf Neubauer and Moritz Stern. Berlin: Leonhard Simion, 1892.

Helmholz, Richard H. *Roman Canon Law in Reformation England.* Cambridge: Cambridge University Press, 1990.

Hobbes, Thomas. *Leviathan*, eds. G.A.J. Rogers and Karl Schuhmann. Bristol: Thoemmes Continuum, 2003.

Hölderlin, Friedrich. *Friedrich Hölderlin: Selected Poems*, trans. Constantine, David. Newcastle-upon-Tyne: Bloodaxe Books, 1996.

Holsinger, Bruce. *The Premodern Condition: Medievalism and the Making of Theory.* Chicago: University of Chicago Press, 2005.

Hooke, Della. *Trees in Anglo-Saxon England: Literature, Lore, and Landscape.* Suffolk: Boydell Press, 2010.

Houliston, Victor. "Thomas Becket in the Propaganda of the English Reformation." *Renaissance Studies* 7 (1993): 43–70.

Hourihane, Colum. *Pontius Pilate, Anti-Semitism, and the Passion in Medieval Art.* Princeton: Princeton University Press, 2009.

Hoving, Thomas. *King of the Confessors.* New York: Simon and Schuster.

Hudson, John. "Anglo-Norman Land Law and the Origins of Property." In *Law and Government in Medieval England and Normandy: Essays in Honour of Sir James Holt,* eds. James Clarke Holt, George Garnett, and John Hudson, 198–223. Cambridge: Cambridge University Press, 1994.

Hyams, Paul R. "The Jews in Medieval England." In *England and Germany in the High Middle Ages,* eds. Alfred Haverkamp and Hanna Vollrath, 181–185. London: Oxford University Press, 1996.

Ingham, Patricia Clare. *Sovereign Fantasies: Arthurian Romance and the Making of Britain.* Philadelphia: University of Pennsylvania Press, 2001.

"Innerlich bleibt die Welt eine": Ausgewählte Texte von Franz Rosenzweig über den Islam, ed. Gesine Palmer. Bodenheim: Philo Verlag, 2002.

Iogna-Prat, Dominique. *Order and Exclusion: Cluny and Christendom face Heresy, Judaism, and Islam (1000-1150),* trans. Graham Robert Edwards. Ithaca: Cornell University Press, 2002.

Iser, Wolfgang. *Staging Politics: The Lasting Impact of Shakespeare's Histories,* trans. David Henry Wilson. New York: Columbia University Press, 1993.

Jacobs, Jane. *The Death and Life of Great American Cities.* New York: Random House, 1961.

Jandora, John W. "Archers of Islam: A Search for 'Lost' History." *Medieval History Journal* 13 (2010): 97–114.

Jasinski, Marek E. and Fredrik Søreide. "Norse Settlements in Greenland from a Maritime Perspective." In *Vinland Revisited: the Norse World at the Turn of the First Millennium,* ed. Shannon Lewis-Simpson, 123–132. St. John's: Historic Sites Association of Newfoundland and Labrador, 2000.

John of Salisbury. *Letters of John of Salisbury, Volume 2: The Later Letters (1163-1180),* eds. W.J. Millor and C.N.L. Brooke. Oxford: Clarendon Press, 1979.

Johns, Jeremy. *Arabic Administration in Norman Sicily.* Cambridge: Cambridge University Press, 2002.

Johnson, Hannah. *Blood Libel: The Ritual Murder Accusation at the Limit of Jewish History.* Ann Arbor: University of Michigan Press, 2012.

Jordan, William Chester. "Jews, Regalian Rights, and the Constitution in Medieval France." *AJS Review* 23 (1998): 1–16.

Kafka, Franz. *Franz Kafka: The Complete Stories,* trans. Nahum Norbert Glatzer. New York: Schocken Books, 1995.

Kantorowicz, Ernst H. "The Archer in the Ruthwell Cross." *Art Bulletin* 42 (1960): 57–59.

–––. *The King's Two Bodies: A Study in Medieval Political Theology.* Princeton: Princeton University Press, 1957.

Kaufman, Eleanor. "The Saturday of Messianic Times (Agamben and Badiou on the Apostle Paul)." *South Atlantic Quarterly* 107 (2008): 37–54.

Keith, Alison and Stephen Rupp, "After Ovid: Classical, Medieval, and Early Modern Reception of the *Metamorphoses.*" In *Metamorphosis: Changing Face of Ovid in the Medieval, and Early Modern Periods,* eds. Alison Keith and Stephen Rupp, 15–32. Toronto: University of Toronto Press, 2007.

Ketelaar, Eric. "Archival Temples, Archival Prisons: Modes of Power and Protection." *Archival Science* 2 (2002): 221–238.

Kinoshita, Sharon. "Re-viewing the Eastern Mediterranean." *postmedieval: a journal of medieval cultural studies* 2.3 (2011): 369–385.

Kitzinger, Ernst. "Anglo-Saxon Vine Scroll Ornament." *Antiquity* 10.37 (1936): 61–71.

Kleinberg-Levin, David Michael. *Sites of Vision: The Discursive Construction of Sight in the History of Philosophy.* Cambridge: MIT Press, 1997.

Kobialka, Michal. *This is My Body: Representational Practices in the Early Middle Ages.* Ann Arbor: University of Michigan Press, 1999.

Koerner, Lisbet. *Linnaeus: Nature and Nation.* Cambridge: Harvard University Press, 1999.

Koslofsky, Craig. "The Kiss of Peace in the German Reformation." In *The Kiss in History,* ed. Karen Harvey, 18–35. Manchester: Manchester University Press, 2005.

Kottman, Paul A. *A Politics of the Scene.* Stanford: Stanford University Press, 2008.

Kotsko, Adam. "On Agamben's use of Benjamin's 'Critique of Violence'." *Telos* 145 (Winter 2008): 119–129.

Krell, David Farrell. *Tragic Absolute: German Idealism and the Language of God.* Bloomington: Indiana University Press, 2005.

Kuchar, Gary. *Divine Subjection: The Rhetoric of Sacramental Devotion in Early Modern England.* Pittsburgh: Duquesne University Press, 2005.

–––. *The Poetry of Religious Sorrow in Early Modern England.* Cambridge: Cambridge University Press, 2008.

Lagueux, Robert C. "Sermons, Exegesis, and Performance: The Laon *Ordo Prophetarum* and the Meaning of Advent." *Comparative Drama* 43 (2009): 197–220.

Lanfranc of Canterbury, On the Body and Blood of the Lord & Guitmund of Aversa, On the Truth of the Body and Blood of Christ in the Eucharist, trans. M.G. Vaillancourt. The Fathers of the Church: Medieval Continuation, Vol. 10. Washington, DC: Catholic University of America Press, 2009.

Lanfranc of Bec. *Liber de corpora et sanguine Domini.* In *Patrologia Latina,* 161 Vols., ed. J-.P. Migne, 150:407–442. Paris, 1857-1866.

Lange, Marjory E. *Telling Tears in the English Renaissance.* New York: Brill, 1996.

Langmuir, Gavin. "The Jews and the Archives of Angevin England: Reflections on Medieval Anti-Semitism." *Traditio* 19 (1963): 183–244.

Langland, Sabrina. "Pilate Answered: What I have Written I have Written." *Metropolitan Museum of Art Bulletin* 26.19 (1968): 410– 429.

Lauro, Sarah Juliet and Karen Embry. "A Zombie Manifesto: The Non-Human Condition in the Era of Advanced Capitalism." *Boundary 2* 35 (2008): 85–108.

Le Thiec, Guy. "L'Empire ottoman, modèle de monarchie seigneuriale dans l'œuvre de Jean Bodin." In *L'Oeuvre de Jean Bodin: Actes du colloque tenu à Lyon à l'occasion du quatrième centenaire de sa mort,* eds. Gabriel-André Pérouse, Nicole Dockés-Lallement, and Jean-Michel Servet, 55–76. Paris: Honoré Champion Éditeur, 2004.

Lewis, Cynthia. "Soft Touch: On the Renaissance Staging and Meaning of the 'noli me tangere' Icon." *Comparative Drama* 36 (2002): 53–73.

Levine, Philippa. "History in the Archives: The Public Record Office and its Staff, 1838–1886." *English Historical Review* 101 (1986): 21–41.

Lezra, Jacques. *Wild Materialism: The Ethic of Terror and the Modern Republic.* New York: Fordham University Press, 2010.

Librett, Jeffrey S. "From the Sacrifice of the Letter to the Voice of Testimony: Giorgio Agamben's Fulfillment of Metaphysics." *Diacritics* 37 (2007): 11–33.

---. *The Rhetoric of Cultural Dialogue: Jews and Germans from Moses Mendelssohn to Richard Wagner and Beyond.* Stanford: Stanford University Press, 2000.

Lochrie, Karma. "Desiring Foucault." *Journal of Medieval and Early Modern Studies* 27.1 (1997): 3–16.

Lutz, Tom. *Crying: The Natural and Cultural History of Tears*. New York: Norton, 1999.

Maddicott, J.R. "Plague In Seventh-Century England." *Past and Present* 156 (1997): 7–54.

Maier, Charles S. "Targeting the City: Debates and Silence about the Aerial Bombing of World War II." *International Review of the Red Cross* 87.859 (2005): 429–444.

Malcolm, Noel. "The Title Page of *Leviathan*, seen in Curious Perspective." In Noel Malcolm, *Aspects of Hobbes*, 200–233. Oxford: Clarendon Press, 2002.

Manovich, Lev. *The Language of New Media*. Cambridge: MIT Press, 2002.

Margulis, Lynn and Dorion Sagan. *What is Life?* Berkeley: University of California Press, 2000.

Mastnak, Tomaž. *Crusading Peace: Christendom, the Muslim World, and Western Political Order*. Berkeley: University of California Press, 2002.

Matheson, Lister M. "English Chronicle Contexts for Shakespeare's Death of Richard II." In *From Page to Performance: Essays in Early English Drama*, ed. John A. Alford, 195–219. East Lansing: Michigan State University Press, 1995.

Mazzucco, Katia. "1941: English Arts and the Mediterranean: A Photographic Exhibition by the Warburg Institute in London." *Journal of Art Historiography* 5 (2011): 1–28.

McConville, Sean. *A History of English Prison Administration, Volume 1: 1750–1877*. London: Routledge, 1981.

McEntire, Sandra J. *The Doctrine of Compunction in Medieval England: Holy Tears*. Lewiston: Mellen Press, 1990.

McKay, Carolyn. "Murder Ob/scene: The Seen, the Unseen, and Ob/scene in Murder Trials." *Law, Text, Culture* 14.1 (2010): 79–93.

McNulty, Tracy. "The Commandment Against the Law: Writing and Divine Justice in Walter Benjamin's 'Critique of Violence'." *Diacritics* 37 (2007): 34–60.

Marchand, Suzanne. "Nazism, 'Orientalism,' and Humanism." In *Nazi Germany and the Humanities,* eds. Wolfgang Bialas and Anson Rabinbach, 267–305. Oxford: Oneworld Publications, 2007.

Medieval Drama, ed. David Bevington. Boston: Houghton Mifflin, 1975.

Michels, Karen. "Art History, German-Jewish Immigrants, and the

Emigration of Iconology." In *Jewish Identity in Modern Art History*, ed. Catherine M. Soussloff, 167–179. Berkeley: University of California Press, 1999.

Miller, Jacques Alain. "Jeremy Bentham's Panoptic Device." *October* 41 (1987): 3–20.

Miller, Steven. *War After Death: On Violence and Its Limits*. New York: Fordham University Press, 2014.

Montclos, Jean de. *Lanfranc et Bérenger: La controverse eucharistique du XIe siecle*. Louvain: Spicilegium Sacrum Lovaniense, 1971.

–––. "Lanfranc et Bérenger: les origines de la doctrine de la Transsubstantiation." In *Lanfranco de Pavia e l'Europa del secolo XI*, ed. G. D'Onofrio, 297–326. Italia Sacra: Studie Documenti di Storia Ecclesiastica, Vol. 51. Rome: Herder Editrice e Libreria, 1993.

Moore, R.I. *The Formation of a Persecuting Society: Power and Deviance in Western Europe, 950–1250*, 2nd edn. New York: Blackwell, 2007.

Morrow, Karen Ann. "Disputation in Stone: Jews Imagined on the St. Stephen Portal of Paris Cathedral." In *Beyond the Yellow Badge: Anti-Judaism and Antisemitism in Medieval and Early Modern Visual Culture*, ed. Michael B. Merback, 64–86. Leiden: Brill, 2007.

Morton, Timothy. *The Ecological Thought*. Cambridge: Harvard University Press, 2010.

Murphy, Kevin D. *Memory and Modernity: Viollet-le-Duc at Vézelay*. University Park: Pennsylvania State University Press, 2000.

Nancy, Jean-Luc. "Abandoned Being." In *The Birth of Presence*, trans. Brian Holmes. Stanford: Stanford University Press, 1992.

–––. *Corpus*, trans. Richard A. Rand. New York: Fordham University Press, 2008.

–––. *Dis-Enclosure: The Deconstruction of Christianity*, trans. Bettina Bergo, Gabriel Malenfant, and Michael B. Smith. New York: Fordham University Press, 2008.

Nicolle, David. *The Great Islamic Conquests, AD 637-750*. Oxford: Osprey Publishing, 2009.

Nilgen, Ursula. "Intellectuality and Splendour: Thomas Becket as a Patron of the Arts." In *Art and Patronage in the English Romanesque*, eds. Sarah Macready and F.H. Thompson, 145–158. London: Society of Antiquaries, 1986.

Norton, Anne. "Call me Ishmael." In *Derrida and the Time of the Political*, eds. Pheng Cheah and Suzanne Guerlac, 158–176. Durham: Duke University Press, 2009.

Norton, Robert E. *Secret Germany: Stefan George and His Circle.* Ithaca: Cornell University Press, 2002.

O'Brien, Bruce R. *God's Peace and King's Peace: The Laws of Edward the Confessor.* Philadelphia: University of Pennsylvania Press, 1999.

O'Donovan, Oliver and Joan Lockwood O'Donovan. *From Irenaeus to Grotius: A Source-book in Christian Political Thought.* Cambridge: William B. Eerdmans, 1999.

O'Loughlin, Thomas. *Adomnán and the Holy Places: The Perceptions of an Insular Monk on the Locations of the Biblical Drama.* London: T&T Clark, 2007.

O'Reilly, Jennifer. "The Rough-Hewn Cross in Anglo-Saxon Art." In *Ireland and Insular Art A.D. 500-1200,* ed. Michael Ryan, 153–158. Dublin: Royal Irish Academy, 1987.

Olszowy-Schlanger, Judith. "The Knowledge and Practice of Hebrew Grammar among Christian Scholars in Pre-Expulsion England: The Evidence of 'Bi-lingual' Hebrew-Latin Manuscripts." In *Hebrew Scholarship and the Medieval World,* ed. Nicholas De Lange, 107–130. Cambridge: Cambridge University Press, 2001.

Orchard, Andy. "The Dream of the Rood: Cross-References." In *New Readings in the Vercelli Book,* eds. Samantha Zacher and Andy Orchard, 225–253. Toronto: University of Toronto Press, 2009.

Orton, Fred and Ian Wood (with Clare A. Lees). *Fragments of History: Rethinking the Ruthwell and Bewcastle Monuments.* Manchester: Manchester University Press, 2007.

Ostovich, Helen. "'Here in this garden': The Iconography of the Virgin Queen in Shakespeare's *Richard II.*" In *Marian Moments in Early Modern British Drama,* eds. Regina Buccola and Lisa Hopkins, 21–34. Burlington: Ashgate, 2007.

Ovid. *Metamorphoses,* trans. Rolfe Humphries. Bloomington: Indiana University Press, 1983.

Panofsky, Erwin. *Abbot Suger on the Abbey Church of St.-Denis and its Art Treasures.* Princeton: Princeton University Press, 1946.

Parker, Elizabeth C. "Editing the *Cloister's Cross.*" *Gesta* 45 (2006): 147–160.

Parker, Elizabeth C. and Charles T. Little. *The Cloisters Cross: Its Art and Meaning.* New York: Harry N. Abrams, 1994.

Patton, Kimberley Christine and John Stratton Hawley. *Holy Tears: Weeping in the Religious Imagination.* Princeton: Princeton University Press, 2005.

Peter of Poitiers. *Epistola,* ed. Reinhold Glei. In *Petrus Venerabilis*

Schriften zum Islam, Corpus Islamico-Christianum, Series Latina, 1:228. Altenberg, 1985.

Peter the Venerable. *Adversus Iudeorum inveteratam duritiem,* ed. Yvonne Friedmann, Corpus Christianorum, Continuatio Medievalis, Vol. 58. Turnhout: Brepols, 1985.

———. *Contra sectam Sarracenorum,* ed. James Kritzeck, 212–214. In James A. Kritzeck, *Peter the Venerable and Islam.* Princeton: Princeton University Press, 1964.

The Pipe Roll of 31 Henry I. Michaelmas 1130. London: H.M. Stationery Office, 1929.

Phillips, Heather. "John Wyclif and the Optics of the Eucharist." In *From Ockham to Wyclif,* eds. Anne Hudson and Michael Wilks, 245–258. Studies in Church History, Subsidia 5. Oxford: Basil Blackwell, 1987.

Poe, Edgar Allan. "Maelzel's Chess Player." *Saturday Literary Messenger* (April 1836): 318–326. Also available at: http://www.eapoe.org/works/essays/maelzel.htm.

Pollock, Frederick and Frederic W. Maitland. *The History of English Law before the Time of Edward I,* Vol. 2. Cambridge: Cambridge University Press, 1892.

Poole, Reginald L. *The Exchequer in the Twelfth Century.* Oxford: Clarendon, 1912.

Pugh, R.B. "Charles Abbot and the Public Records: The First Phase." *Bulletin of the Institute of Historical Research* 39 (1966): 69–85.

Pye, Christopher. "The Betrayal of the Gaze: *Richard II.*" In *The Regal Phantasm: Shakespeare and the Politics of the Spectacle,* 82–105. New York: Routledge, 1990.

Rabinow, Paul and Nikolas Rose. "Biopower Today." *Biosciences* 1 (2006): 195–217.

Radding, Charles M. and Francis Newton. *Theology, Rhetoric, and Politics in the Eucharistic Controversy, 1078–1079: Alberic of Monte Cassino against Berengar of Tours.* New York: Columbia University Press, 2003.

Ragan, Mark A. "Trees and Networks Before and After Darwin." *Biology Direct* 4:43 (2009): http://www.biology-direct.com/content/4/1/43.

Rancière, Jacques. *The Future of the Image,* trans. Gregory Elliott. London: Verso, 2007.

Reinhard, Kenneth, Eric L. Santner, and Slavoj Žižek. *The Neighbor: Three Inquiries in Political Theology.* Chicago: University of Chicago Press, 2005.

Resnick, Irven M. *Marks of Distinction: Christian Perception of Jews in the High Middle Ages.* Washington, DC: Catholic University of America Press, 2012.

Richard, Frances. "A Tree Dies in Brooklyn." *Art Forum* 36 (Feb. 1998): 19–20.

Roesdahl, Else. "Walrus Ivory." In *Ohthere's Voyages: A Late 9th-Century Account of Voyages along the Coasts of Norway and Denmark in its Cultural Context,* eds. Janet Bately and Anton Englert, 92–93. Roskilde: Viking Ship Museum, 2007.

Rosenwein, Barbara H. *Negotiating Space: Power, Restraint and Privileges of Immunity in Early Medieval Europe.* Ithaca: Cornell University Press, 1999.

Rosenzweig, Franz. *The Star of Redemption,* trans. Barbara E. Galli. Madison: University of Wisconsin Press, 2005.

Rossello, Diego. "Hobbes and the Wolf-Man: Melancholy and Animality in Modern Sovereignty." *New Literary History* 43 (2012): 255–279.

Ruehl, Martin A. "'Imperium Transcendat Hominem': Reich and Rulership in Ernst Kantorowicz's *Kaiser Friedrich der Zweite.*" In *A Poet's Reich: Politics and Culture in the Georg Circle,* eds. Melissa Slane and Martin Ruehl, 204–248. Rochester: Boydell and Brewer, 2011.

Rzewski, Frederic. *Coming Together, Attica.* Hungaraton Records, 1972 (reissued in 1993).

Salter, H.E. "Geoffrey of Monmouth and Oxford." *English Historical Review* 34 (July 1919): 382–385.

Santner, Eric L. *On Creaturely Life.* Chicago: University of Chicago Press, 2006.

–––. *On the Psychotheology of Everyday Life: Reflections on Freud and Rosenzweig.* Chicago: University of Chicago Press, 2001.

–––. *The Royal Remains: The People's Two Bodies and the Endgames of Sovereignty.* Chicago: University of Chicago Press, 2011.

Saxl, Fritz. "The Ruthwell Cross." *Journal of the Warburg and Courtauld Institutes* 6 (1943): 1–19.

Scammell, Jean. "The Rural Chapter in England from the Eleventh to the Fourteenth Century." *English Historical Review* 86 (1971): 1–21.

Scarfe, Norman. "The Walrus-Ivory Cross in the Metropolitan Museum of Art: the Masterpiece of Master Hugo of Bury?" In Norman Scarfe, *Suffolk in the Middle Ages,* 81–98. Woodbridge: Boydell Press, 1986.

Schapiro, Meyer. "The Religious Meaning of the Ruthwell Cross." *Art Bulletin* 26 (1944): 232–245.

Schmitt, Carl. *The Concept of the Political*, trans. George Schwab. Chicago: University of Chicago Press, 1996.

———. *The Nomos of the Earth in the International Law of the Jus Publicum Europaeum*, trans. G. L. Ulmen. New York: Telos Press, 2003.

———. *Political Theology: Four Chapters on the Concept of Sovereignty*, trans. George Schwab. Chicago: University of Chicago Press, 1985.

———. *Theorie des Partisanen*. Berlin: Dunckat and Humblot, 1963.

———. *Theory of the Partisan*, trans. G.L. Ulmen. New York: Telos Press, 2007.

Schuler, Robert M. "Magic Mirrors in *Richard II*." *Comparative Drama* 38 (2004): 151–172.

Schwartz, Regina Mara. *Sacramental Poetics at the Dawn of Secularism*. Stanford: Stanford University Press, 2008.

Schwenger, Peter. *The Tears of Things: Melancholy and Physical Objects*. Minneapolis: University of Minnesota Press, 2006.

Scott, John A. "Treachery in Dante." In *Studies the Italian Essays in Memory of Arnolfo B. Ferruolo*, eds. Gian Paolo Biasin, Albert N. Mancini, and Nicolas J. Perella, 27–39. Naples: Società Editrice Napoletana, 1985.

Scully, Robert E. "The Unmaking of a Saint: Thomas Becket and the English Reformation." *Catholic Historical Review* 86 (October 2000): 579–602.

Sedgwick, Eve Kosofsky. *The Epistemology of the Closet*. Berkeley: University of California Press, 1990.

Seidel, Linda. *Legends in Limestone: Lazarus, Gislebertus and the Cathedral at Autun*. Chicago: University of Chicago Press, 1999.

Seidman, Naomi. *Faithful Renderings: Jewish-Christian Difference and the Politics of Translation*. Chicago: University of Chicago Press, 2006.

Setton, Kenneth M. "Western Hostility to Islam and Prophecies of Turkish Doom." *Memoirs of the American Philosophical Society*, Vol. 201. Philadelphia: American Philosophical Society, 1992.

Shickman, Allan. "The 'Perspective Glass' in Shakespeare's *Richard II*." *Studies in English Literature* 18 (Spring 1978): 217–228.

———. "'Turning Pictures' in Shakespeare's England." *The Art Bulletin* 59 (March 1977): 67–70.

Sinclair, John. *Statistical Account of Scotland*, Vol. 10. Edinburgh: William Creech, 1794.

Sinnerbrink, Robert. "Violence, Destruction and Sovereignty: Derrida, Agamben on Benjamin's Critique of Violence." In *Walter Benjamin and the Architecture of Modernity*, eds. Andrew Benjamin and Charles Rice, 77–91. Melbourne: re.press, 2009.

Skinner, Patricia, ed. *The Jews of Medieval Britain: Historical, Literary and Archaeological Perspectives.* Woodbridge: Boydell & Brewer, 2003.

Smithson, Robert. *Robert Smithson: The Collected Writings.* Berkeley: University of California Press, 1996.

Soussloff, Catherine M., ed. *Jewish Identity in Modern Art History.* Berkeley: University of California Press, 1999

Spitzer, Anais N. "Soliciting Philosophy's Tears." In *Derrida, Myth and the Impossibility of Philosophy,* 24–45. New York: Continuum, 2011.

Standage, Tom. *The Turk: The Life and Times of the Famous Eighteenth-Century Chess-Playing Machine.* New York: Walker and Company, 2002.

Starn, Randolph. *Contrary Commonwealth: The Theme of Exile in Medieval and Renaissance Italy.* Berkeley: University of California Press, 1982.

Stewart, Garrett. *Framed Time: Toward a Postfilmic Cinema.* Chicago: University of Chicago Press, 2007.

Stirnemann, Patricia. "The Study of French Twelfth-Century Manuscripts." In *Romanesque Art and Thought in the Twelfth Century,* ed. Colum Hourihane, 82–94. Princeton: Princeton University Press, 2008.

Stock, Brian. *The Implications of Literacy: Written Language and Models of Interpretation in the Eleventh and Twelfth Centuries.* Princeton: Princeton University Press, 1983.

Stockdale, Eric. "The Rise of Joshua Jebb, 1837–1850." *British Journal of Criminology* 16 (1976): 164–170.

Strasser, Bruno J. "Who Cares About the Double Helix?" *Nature* 422 (24 April 2003): 803–804; doi:10.1038/422803a.

Streit, Kevin T. "The Expansion of the English Jewish Community in the Reign of King Stephen." *Albion* 15 (1993): 177–192.

Stroll, Mary. *The Jewish Pope: Ideology and Politics in the Papal Schism 1130.* Leiden: Brill, 1987.

Stubbs, William. *Selected Charters and other illustrations of English Constitutional History from early times to the reign of Edward the First.* Oxford: Clarendon Press, 1870.

Tambling, Jeffrey. "Dreaming the Siren: Dante and Melancholy." *Forum for Modern Language Studies* 40 (2004): 56–69.

Tasso, Torquato. *Jerusalem Delivered,* trans. Anthony M. Esolin. Baltimore: Johns Hopkins University Press, 2000.

Taubes, Jacob. *The Political Theology of Paul,* trans. Dana Hollander. Stanford: Stanford University Press, 2004.

Thiem, Annika. "Adorno's Tears: Textures of Philosophical Emotionality." *Modern Language Notes* 124 (2009): 592–613.

Thomas, Hugh M. *The English and the Normans: Ethnic Hostility, Assimilation, and Identity 1066-c.1220.* Oxford: Oxford University Press, 2003.

Thomas, Kate. "Post Sex: On Being Too Slow, Too Stupid, Too Soon." In *After Sex? On Writing Since Queer Theory,* eds. Janet Halley and Andrew Parker, 66–75. Durham: Duke University Press, 2011.

Thorne, Alison. *Vision and Rhetoric in Shakespeare: Looking Through Language.* New York: St. Martin's Press, 2000.

Tinkle, Theresa. "Jews in the Fleury Playbook." *Comparative Drama* 38.1 (2004): 1–38.

Tolan, John V. *Saracens: Islam in the Medieval European Imagination.* New York: Columbia University Press, 2002.

Tomasch, Sylvia. "Judecca, Dante's Satan and the Displaced Jew." In *Text and Territory: The Geographical Imaginary in the European Middle Ages,* eds. Sylvia Tomasch and Sealy Gilles, 247–267. Philadelphia: University of Pennsylvania Press, 1998.

Trodd, Tama. "Drawing in the Archive: Paul Klee's Oil Transfers." *Oxford Art Journal* 31.1 (2008): 75–95.

Truitt, Ellie. "Trei poete, sages dotors, qui mout sorent di nigromance: Knowledge and Automata in Twelfth-Century French Literature." *Configurations* 12 (2004): 167–193.

Uebel, Michael. "Opening Time: Psychoanalysis and Medieval Culture." In *Cultural Studies of the Modern Middle Ages,* eds. Eileen A. Joy, Myra J. Seaman, Kimberley K. Bell and Mary K. Ramsey, 269–274. New York: Palgrave, 2007.

Ullmann, Walter. "On the Influence of Geoffrey of Monmouth on Legal History." *Speculum Historiale: Geschichte im Spiegel von Geschichtsschreibung und Geschichtsdeutung,* eds. C. Bauer, L. Bohn, and M. Muller, 258–276. Freiburg: Verlag Karl Alber, 1965.

Valensi, Lucette. *The Birth of the Despot: Venice and the Sublime Port,* trans. Arthur Denner. Ithaca: Cornell University Press, 1993.

Van Caenegem, R.C., ed. *English Lawsuits from William I to Richard I,* Vol. 2: Henry II and Richard I (London: Selden Society, 1990).

Vanacker, Janis. "'Why do you Break Me'? Talking to a Human Tree in Dante's Inferno." *Neophilologus* 95 (2011): 431–445.

Walne, Peter. "The Record Commissions, 1800–1837." In *Prisca Monumenta: Studies in Archival and Administrative History,* ed. Felicity Ranger, 9–18. London: University of London Press,

1973.

Warren, Michelle R. *History on the Edge: Excalibur and the Borders of Britain, 1100-1300.* Minneapolis: University of Minnesota Press, 2000.

Watson, Charlie. *Seahenge: An Archaeological Conundrum.* Swindon: English Heritage, 2005.

Weber, Samuel. "Taking Exception to Decision: Theatrical-Theological Politics: Walter Benjamin and Carl Schmitt." In *Walter Benjamin, 1892-1940,* ed. Uwe Steiner, 123–138. New York: Peter Lang, 1992.

Weigel, Sigrid. *Walter Benjamin: Images, the Creaturely, and the Holy,* trans. Chadwick Truscott Smith. Stanford: Stanford University Press, 2013.

Wenzel, Siegfried. *The Sin of Sloth: Acedia in Medieval Thought and Literature.* Chapel Hill: University of North Carolina Press, 1967.

Williams, George H. *The Norman Anonymous of 1100 A.D.: Towards the Identification and Evaluation of the So-called Anonymous of York.* Harvard Theological Studies, Vol. 18. Cambridge: Harvard University Press, 1951.

Womersley, David. *Divinity and State.* Oxford: Oxford University Press, 2010.

Wood, Christopher S. "Art History's Normative Renaissance." In *The Italian Renaissance in the Twentieth Century,* eds. Allen J. Grieco, Michael Rocke, and Fiorella Giofreddi Superbi, 65–92. Florence: Olschki, 2002.

Wormald, Patrick. *The Making of English Law: King Alfred to the Twelfth Century,* 2 Vols. Oxford: Blackwell, 1999.

Wright, Edith Armstrong. *Dissemination of the Liturgical Drama in France.* Geneva: Slatkine Reprints, 1980.

Yuval, Israel Jacob. *Two Nations in Your Womb: Perceptions of Jews and Christians in Late Antiquity and the Middle Ages.* Berkeley: University of California Press, 2006.

Ziolkowski, Theodore. *Ovid and the Moderns.* Ithaca: Cornell University Press, 2004.

Žižek, Slavoj. *The Fright of Real Tears: Krzysztof Kieslowski Between Theory and Post-Theory.* London: British Film Institute, 2001.

–––. *Iraq: The Borrowed Kettle.* London: Verso, 2004.

INDEX